THE
RUSSIAN
MANAGEMENT
REVOLUTION

THE
RUSSIAN
MANAGEMENT
REVOLUTION

Preparing Managers for the Market Economy

Edited by Sheila M. Puffer, College of
Business Administration, Northeastern University

With a foreword by Lawrence McKibbin,
School of Business, Washburn University of Topeka

M.E. Sharpe
Armonk, New York
London, England

Library of Congress Cataloging-in-Publication Data

The Russian management revolution: preparing managers for the market economy /
edited by Sheila M. Puffer
Pp.   cm.
Includes index.
ISBN 1-56324-042-4—ISBN 1-56324-043-2 (pbk.)
1. Management—Study and teaching—Soviet Union.
2. Executives—Training of—Soviet Union.
3. Exchange of persons programs, Soviet—United States
I. Puffer, Sheila M.
HD30.12.S65R87   1992
658.4′071243′0947—dc20
92-9034
CIP

Printed in the United States of America

The paper used in this publication meets the minimum requirements of
American National Standard for Information Sciences—
Permanence of Paper for Printed Library Materials,
ANSI Z39.48–1984.

BM (c)   10   9   8   7   6   5   4   3   2   1
BM (p)   10   9   8   7   6   5   4   3   2   1

To Bohdan Plaskacz,
an inspiring Russian teacher

Contents

About the Contributors

Sheila M. Puffer is an assistant professor at the College of Business Administration, Northeastern University and a fellow at the Russian Research Center, Harvard University. She earned her Ph.D. in management at the University of California, Berkeley and is also a graduate of the executive management program at the Plekhanov Institute of the National Economy in Moscow. She has conducted extensive research on management issues in the former USSR including managerial decision making and rewards and disciplinary action. Professor Puffer is a co-author of the book *Behind the Factory Walls: Decision Making in Soviet and U.S. Enterprises* (Boston: Harvard Business School Press, 1990) and is currently studying the emergence of entrepreneurship in Russia.

A. Orlov, at the time the chapter was written, was deputy chairman of the USSR Council of Ministers' State Commission for Economic Reform.

Iu. Tkachenko, at the time the chapter was written, was a chief specialist at the USSR Council of Ministers' Commission for Economic Reform.

Anatolii V. Zhuplev, Candidate of Science in Economics, was a visiting professor at the College of Business Administration, Northeastern University in 1989–90, and at the College of Business Administration,

Loyola Marymount University in 1990–91. He has held several positions in Soviet universities and research institutes and rejoined Loyola Marymount University in 1992.

Viacheslav V. Kruglov, Doctor of Science, is vice-rector of the Voznesenskii Institute of Finance and Economics in St. Petersburg.

Oleg S. Vikhanskii, Doctor of Science, is the director of the School of Management at Moscow State University. He was a visiting professor at the College of Business Administration, Northeastern University in 1991 and 1992.

Nikolai A. Kaniskin is the chief executive officer of the company, Sibelektrotiazmash, in Novosibirsk.

Evgenii I. Komarov is a Russian management specialist.

Valentin S. Rapoport is a Russian management consultant.

Arkadii I. Prigozhin is a doctor of philosophical sciences and a leading research associate in the Scientific Research Institute of Systems Research, Russian Academy of Sciences.

Vladimir K. Tarasov, Candidate of Science, is the founder and director of the Tallinn School of Managers, a management training school based in Estonia. It has twelve branches in cities throughout the former Soviet republics.

Iurii Iu. Ekaterinoslavskii, Doctor of Science in Economics, is professor and department head at the Central Training Institute for Civil Engineering in Moscow. He is also a senior research fellow at the Institute of Systems Research at the Academy of Sciences, a member of the board of directors of a U.S.-Russian joint venture in construction management, and a founding member of the Russian Academy of Entrepreneurship.

Irina V. Zhezhko, Candidate of Science, is an organizational consultant and an active member of the open-game movement. She has led ten games herself and has taken part in ten other games as a member of the game team. Her primary field of expertise is organizational development and design.

Stanislav V. Shekshnia graduated from the MBA program at the College of Business Administration, Northeastern University, and is a graduate student in economics at Moscow State University. He is one of the first students to participate in the exchange program between the two universities. He has founded his own business in Russia and has worked in Moscow in the Polaroid joint venture. He is currently doing research on Russian entrepreneurs.

Daniel J. McCarthy, Ph.D., is professor of strategic management at the College of Business Administration, Northeastern University. His research, publishing, and consulting are in the areas of strategic management and R&D in high technology organizations, as well as managerial decision making and strategy in Russia. He is currently studying the emergence of entrepreneurship in Russia.

Donna L. Wiley, Ph.D., is an associate professor in the department of management and finance at California State University at Hayward.

Shyam J. Kamath, Ph.D., is an associate professor in the department of economics at California State University at Hayward.

Bruce MacNab, Ph.D., is an associate professor in the department of marketing, and the director of the Institute of Research and Business Development at California State University at Hayward.

Gordon Lankton is president of Nypro, Inc., Clinton, Massachusetts.

Jack Medzorian is the former vice-president and general manager of Baird Corporation, Bedford, Massachusetts.

Peter Hemingway spent more than two years (1989–1991) in Moscow as country manager for the USSR, Polaroid Corporation, Cambridge, Massachusetts.

Glen Steeves is the operations supervisor of McDonald's Restaurants in Moscow.

Foreword

Lawrence E. McKibbin

The transition of the former Soviet Union from centrally controlled to diverse market economies—a course which appears irrevocable—presents exciting opportunities for educators and students eager to help shape the emerging economic and social orders. For the Western business community, the prospect of vast new markets extending from Europe eastward to the northern Pacific has to be alluring, in the face of ever-increasing competition and sluggish economies at home. But the quality and effectiveness of educational products and the success of business ventures will depend in large measure on the knowledge of the potential clients' cultures possessed by those who would be players in these markets. A resource book providing insight into the managerial systems and practices in those countries formerly comprising the Soviet Union could hardly be more timely.

While dramatic political and economic changes—a managerial revolution—have suddenly opened doors to Western providers of management education and development, both corporate and collegiate, those who charge into this virtual klondike of opportunity should be forewarned that the successful identification and exploitation of entrepreneurial mother lodes will require a great deal of hard spadework and artful adaptation of western models. It may be all too tempting for many to assume that what works in America and Western Europe will be as effective in Russia and other republics. However, simple transplants or implants of that with which we are comfortable may be inappropriate or counterproductive in an environment where generations have been conditioned to look to central authority and planning for direction.

For Western schools of business, the opportunity for institution building seems especially propitious. For decades, many of us in the professoriat have exhorted colleagues to internationalize curricula and to establish links abroad. Lyman Porter and I, in our study of management education and development in the United States in the mid-1980s, found most business schools to have limited vision of their potential roles in international development. Business school deans were complacent, on the whole. They saw little need for dramatic change; ironically, in the light of recent developments, they were concerned more with curtailing demand than with the creation and recognition of new markets. That circumstance has abruptly changed, with many schools now facing declining enrollments.

Of over-arching importance for business schools and perhaps the most compelling argument for getting involved in the development process abroad is the impact such participation can have on the schools themselves. Russian and other managers are looking to Westerners for new paradigms; we are looking for new paradigms for ourselves. Perhaps in the quest for the right answers for a different world than we are accustomed to we will revitalize ourselves and become, not the patrons, but the reapers of the greatest ultimate rewards from our efforts.

Professor Puffer has presented a broad-ranging set of writings from Soviet and American authors. She has artfully organized papers from both consumers and producers of management education. Those who wish to learn about, or better still, play a role in reshaping what is arguably the most sweeping economic development project in history would be well advised to include in their preparation a reading of this important work.

School of Business
Washburn University of Topeka
Topeka, Kansas

Preface

A revolution is now under way in the realm of management and management training in all the countries of the former Soviet Union. Beginning in the mid-1980s, with the inception of *perestroika*, the idea began to take hold that the Soviet system of centrally controlled economic planning must give way to a market system. With the disintegration of the Soviet state and the demise of the Communist Party in 1991, the transition of the Soviet successor states to market economies became a virtual certainty. Today, a massive effort is required to train millions of people at all managerial levels in the knowledge and skills that will enable them to function in new conditions.

The training of managers able to operate effectively in a market economy is being championed both in the newly independent former Soviet republics and in the West. Proponents of liberal economic reform have begun to create Western-style business schools at home and to send high-potential managers abroad for training in market-based business methods. At the same time, accelerating economic reforms in the Soviet successor states have sparked the interest of Western educators and business people. A growing number of American universities are conducting management development programs for managers from the former USSR, and many hopeful Western business people have begun to plant seeds for business development there.

A resource handbook for educators and managers

This book has been designed to meet the needs of two Western audiences—the academic community of business educators and students, and the business community of practitioners interested in doing business in the former Soviet Union. Both groups will already be aware that there is a dearth of information available in English about managerial education and practices in the former USSR. This volume is intended as a resource handbook for these audiences.

The information gathered here will help readers to understand the distinctive managerial style and culture of the former Soviet Union and how it is being transformed today. It will be of particular value to educators, whether they are designing training programs for managers from the former USSR or teaching courses on international business more generally. Specifically, the book will provide educators with background on current management education practices in the former USSR and will explore, in the chapters on U.S.-Soviet joint ventures, the issues that must be resolved to facilitate effective cross-cultural business relationships. Business practitioners will benefit from the pioneering experiences of the Westerners interviewed in the volume and their insights into the way management thought and practice can affect collaboration. Western managers who have some familiarity with management education in the former USSR will be better equipped to understand their counterparts' professional attitudes and behavior.

Organization of the volume

The volume is divided into four parts. The first two were written by Russians and the last two feature Westerners, so that the book offers a balance of perspectives on the way to bring "post-Soviet" managers into the market economy. In an era of increasing globalization and international cooperation, it is not only fitting, but essential, that this task be accomplished by combining the intellectual and material resources of East and West. This massive historic undertaking will affect millions of people worldwide by setting the pattern of international economic and trade relationships in the coming decades.

In Part I, which is devoted to the status of management education in the former USSR, the contributors give an overview of the types of programs and curricula that have been developed there, and the challenges that lie ahead. Part II focuses on the instructional methodologies, such as business games and cases, that have been developed by management educators in the former USSR. Of the twelve articles included in the first two parts, half were prepared especially for this volume and half were selected from works recently published in Russian. These chapters bring English-language readers into contact with the leading scholars who today are actively engaged in developing curricula, teaching in newly created programs, and collaborating in management-training efforts with Western partners.

In Parts III and IV we hear from Westerners who have had considerable contact with Soviet managers. Part III features a variety of management training programs established at American universities for senior executives from different regions of the former Soviet Union. In Part IV Western executives of companies involved in joint ventures discuss the challenges of learning how to work with their Soviet partners and finding the most effective ways to train, motivate, and reward them.[*]

Translation issues

A few words about my approach to the translation of chapters originally written in Russian. In editing the fine translation by Kim Braithwaite, I have made every effort to use terminology that is common to the management field in the English-speaking world in preference to a literal translation from Russian. I believe this gives readers a better sense of the intended meaning while at the same time making the material more accessible. For example, I have translated the Russian word *direktor* as senior executive or chief executive officer rather than as "director" (which might be misinterpreted to mean a member of a board of directors). Similarly, I decided to translate *programmy povysheniia kvalifikatsii* simply as training programs or management development programs rather than the literal rendition, "programs of upgrading of qualifications." It is important to keep in mind, however, that the use of familiar management terminology does not guarantee a complete equivalence of meaning. The interested reader would be advised to explore these subtleties with Russian-speaking management experts.

---

[*]A broadcast-quality video of Sheila M. Puffer's interviews in Part IV is available from the editor. Please call (617) 437-5249 or fax (617) 437-2056.

Another translation issue involves gender. In the twelve chapters originally written in Russian, without exception, managers are referred to with male pronouns. I resisted the temptation to edit the translation for gender neutrality. Although managers in the former USSR come in both genders, it is also a reality that management is considered a male preserve and that discrimination against women in management is widespread.

Finally, a note on how to read these chapters in light of the cataclysmic events of 1991—the failure of the anti-Gorbachev coup, the demise of the Communist Party, and ultimately the dissolution of the Soviet state. No longer can we legitimately use the term "Soviet management" in the present or future tense, of course, yet no convenient substitute has gained currency. More to the point, these epochal changes shift some of the topics discussed in this volume—for example, the dominant role of the party in enterprise management and the election of managers by workers, mentioned in chapters 5 and 11—into the historical background; yet the authors' basic arguments and ideas remain relevant. Most important, the accelerated pace of change has created an ever more urgent need for the revolution in management education advocated by the authors of these chapters.

The task ahead

The chapters in this volume sparkle with the freshness and excitement of individuals dedicated to helping the republics of the former Soviet Union become full participants in the international economy. The greatest challenge, of course, is not designing curricula and developing materials; it involves the human factor. A massive campaign of attitude change is imperative.[1] As the authors of our first chapter put it: "The support of every worker for the program of stabilization and transition to a market economy will largely determine our progress. It is very important now to bring large numbers of working people out of their state of indifference, out of their lack of confidence in tomorrow." To accomplish this herculean feat of attitude change, management educators must not be satisfied with simply lecturing their students on management in a market economy. They will need to create opportunities for students and managers actually to apply this knowledge in their training programs, and then give them feedback about their attitudes and behavior. Only by using tested theories and practices—such as

methods of attitude change, empowerment, and organizational transformation—can educators expect to make a significant impact on managerial attitudes and abilities and, ultimately, managerial style. A good
place to initiate such changes is in joint ventures such as those described in Part IV of this volume. These organizations not only have
access to the latest management techniques, they also attract highly
competent and motivated local personnel who are likely to adapt to
such programs successfully.

It is my hope that the Western management educators and business
professionals who read this book will not only gain an understanding
of the revolution in management education under way in the former
USSR but will find ways to lend their expertise to this historic educational effort.

Acknowledgments

I am grateful to Anthony Jones, my colleague at Northeastern University and the Russian Research Center of Harvard University, who gave
me the opportunity that led to the publication of this volume. Professor
Jones invited me to serve as guest editor of two special issues on
management education in the journal *Soviet Education*.[2] M.E. Sharpe
executive editor Patricia Kolb then invited me to develop the project
into a book, and graciously indulged my whims as the book expanded.
I would also like to express my appreciation to the editorial and administrative staff at M.E. Sharpe, especially Leslie English, Ana Erlic,
Elizabeth Granda, Nancy Walsh, and Aud Thiessen. This book is also
made possible by the McNeice Applied Research Fund at the College
of Business Administration of Northeastern University. Finally, thanks
are due to my academic colleagues in the former USSR and my academic and business colleagues in the United States who so willingly
accepted my invitation to participate in this volume.

Notes

1. On this topic see Aleksandr Tsipko, "Man Cannot Change His Nature,"
Soviet Education, vol. 32, no. 3 (March 1990), pp. 7–30, and V. Pechenev,
"Change So As to Preserve Oneself and One's Nature," *ibid.*, pp. 31–43.

2. See *Soviet Education*, vol. 33, nos. 11 and 12 (November and December
1991). The journal is now published under the title *Russian Education and Society*.

Part I

MANAGEMENT EDUCATION IN TRANSITION

Introduction

Over the past several years the status of management education in the former USSR has come under the scrutiny of people in virtually every sphere of society. First, the general public blames its low standard of living largely on the mismanagement of the economy. Second, managers themselves realize that their training and skills are outmoded and inadequate for transforming their enterprises into viable competitors in the market economy. Third, government officials want to find ways of ensuring that their economic policies can be effectively implemented at the operational level in enterprises.

The onus of reforming and redesigning management education falls squarely on the shoulders of management educators. In Part I of this volume several experts in management education present their assessment of the status of the field and describe their efforts to design new programs to meet the market-driven needs of contemporary managers.

Overview

In the first chapter in Part I, "How to Teach about the Market Economy," Orlov and Tkachenko set the stage by describing the monumental task of training managers to function in a market economy.[1] They outline the types of courses that are needed as well as the instructional methodologies required to ensure a successful transfer of knowledge. They also provide practical information on published materials cur-

1

rently available for use in training programs. When this article was first published in Russian in 1990, Orlov and Tkachenko were affiliated with the USSR Council of Ministers' State Commission for Economic Reform, a body that no longer exists. Today the responsibility for management education has been dispersed among the independent republics. Thus the article serves as a benchmark against which the "post-Soviet" educational policies being formulated by each republic can be compared.

In chapter 2, "Management Education in a Time of Change," Anatolii V. Zhuplev takes a sweeping look at the evolution of management education in the USSR from the founding of the Soviet state in 1917 to its dissolution in 1991. The role of the West in assisting in this training effort is discussed and recommendations for the future are proposed.

As Orlov and Tkachenko point out in chapter 1, the Academy of the National Economy and the State Committee for Public Education[2] took the lead in designing sample curricula and syllabi, but decisions about the specific forms of training, their duration, and methods for evaluating their effectiveness were left to individual management institutes at the local level. Chapter 3, "Recent Developments in Management Education in the Former USSR," by V.V. Kruglov, and chapter 4, "Let's Train Managers for the Market Economy," by O.S. Vikhanskii, provide two examples. These chapters describe how two prestigious institutions, the Voznesenskii Institute of Finance and Economics in St. Petersburg and the School of Management at Moscow State University, have developed a variety of programs to meet the needs of different clienteles.

The last two chapters in Part I focus on the recipients of these new forms of management education—the managers themselves. Nikolai Kaniskin, for example, is the chief executive officer of a large enterprise in Novosibirsk. In chapter 5, "The Western Executive and the Soviet Executive," Kaniskin describes his experience as one of the first Soviet managers to be sent to West Germany for training in 1989. His assessment of the experience will be useful for Western management educators who are designing programs for former Soviet managers. Chapter 6 describes a frequently ignored group of managers—women. Author Evgenii I. Komarov shows that women managers, though significant in number, have little influence and often suffer from negative stereotyping and discrimination.

Three themes

Three broad themes developed in the chapters in Part I are (1) *the revolution in management education in the former USSR;* (2) *collaboration with the West in management education;* and (3) *managerial style.* I believe it is important to take these themes into account in formulating and implementing policies and practices for training managers in the former USSR.

First, the revolution in management education has been as fast-paced and varied as the revolution in politics, the economy, and society as a whole. The need for people skilled in market-based management outstrips the supply of quality programs that currently offer training in these subjects. It is ironic, but hardly surprising, that individuals attracted by the opportunity to "make a quick ruble" have skimmed the market by offering seminars that do not in fact provide in-depth and practical information to course participants. Zhuplev, Vikhanskii, and Kruglov all refer to these courses and provide countervailing examples of how high-quality programs are structured.

The prevalence of inadequate training gives rise to two questions. First, has a "quick-and-dirty" approach to management training created disillusionment and frustration among people who truly want to develop their managerial skills? And second, what is the most effective way to train the greatest number of managers as quickly as possible and at the same time avoid these abuses? Up to this point, I doubt that poor-quality management programs have done much good, but neither have they done much harm. Many managers may have attended out of curiosity and a need to appear *au courant*, rather than with the express intention of changing the way they manage. There is still too much confusion about what managers' responsibilities are and how much authority they have, not to mention the problem of stifled personal initiative and accountability that is the legacy of the old administrative-command system.

Many options are available for training large numbers of managers. Zhuplev, Kruglov, and Vikhanskii describe programs that include short seminars, full-time and evening programs for practicing managers, and full-time two-year degree programs similar to Western MBA (Master of Business Administration) programs. These approaches to management training are useful for conveying information but they suffer from several drawbacks: they take time; not everyone can be sent for training, given work commitments and funding constraints; and there is no guarantee that newly acquired knowledge will be implemented. To make up for these deficiencies, other approaches should be added to the educational repertoire. For example, a televised series of management courses and sets of videotapes could be developed to spread the message to a wider audience. In fact, there is a prototype of this approach currently offered in Moscow. Another alternative is to conduct long-term educational and organizational change programs that involve all the employees in an organization. Although difficult to implement, this approach improves the odds that new ideas will be adopted and that new attitudes and behaviors will take hold. An enterprise-wide training effort supplants the approach of simply sending a few people for training. The latter is a "quick fix" that is unlikely to succeed, since the converted few stand little chance of making a difference in an unchanged organization. To facilitate these change efforts, groups of the most talented and motivated employees from all organizational levels should be given comprehensive training. They can then serve as change agents throughout the organization and help employees develop self-managing work groups. This method, while painful and time-consuming, has the potential for addressing the root of the problem—an underdeveloped sense of personal initiative and accountability in the workplace.

The pressing need for massive doses of management education suggests a role for Western experts—the second theme of these chapters. Zhuplev, Kruglov, and Vikhanskii all advocate Western involvement, but with reservations. As they point out, many managers are eager to study abroad, but they may be ill-equipped to absorb the training fully and then implement it at home. Sending business faculty to the West for training is more efficient than sending managers, because of the multiplier effect: each management educator will be able to train large numbers of managers. Management educators must take the best that Western business schools have to offer and adapt it to their own conditions.

This "train the trainer" concept is one of the most promising avenues for Western involvement. Other useful approaches include training managers through internships in Western companies, promoting academic exchanges of students and faculty, and holding competitions on the model of the first international students' olympiad in economics.[3] Western management educators would be well advised to heed Kaniskin's words and find creative ways to impart new knowledge without underestimating the intellectual ability and managerial experience of their trainees. The viewpoints of these experienced managers and educators familiar with Western management training programs for Soviets should be kept in mind when reading the articles in Part III, Training Programs for Soviet Managers in the United States.

The third theme running through these chapters is managerial style. This theme is treated explicitly in the chapters by Kaniskin and Komarov and implicitly in the other chapters. Kaniskin describes some of the differences in Russian and Western managerial styles that he became aware of while studying in Germany. Like most Soviet managers, Kaniskin had a technical education; his exposure to the humanities component of management programs in Germany gave him an appreciation of its value in managerial work. Kaniskin came to recognize the importance of attitudes (for example, not being rude or arrogant), and the difference between incentives and motivation: "We have incentives, they have motivation. An incentive, as is well known, is a stick with a pointed end." Kaniskin is also critical of the docility that has been bred in managers in the former USSR: "Don't make waves—this principle remains dominant in our lives." He admires the ability of top managers in Germany to delegate many decisions and responsibilities to lower levels. On the positive side, Kaniskin gives his compatriots credit for their hard work and dedication. They work long hours; in fact, as my colleagues and I have found in our research, managers in the former Soviet Union joke that they work an eight-hour day—from 8 A.M. to 8 P.M.[4] As Kaniskin points out, although many managers have high responsibility and low pay, they carry on out of sheer enthusiasm and a sense of responsibility (in addition, one presumes, to the opportunities to exercise influence in important decisions as well as to receive material perquisites).

From Kaniskin's assessment we can anticipate some of the difficulties that managers may encounter in adapting their style to new conditions. They may feel threatened about relinquishing control to subordinates and fear a diminution of their authority if subordinates are empowered to make decisions. They may also find it unnatural to use motivational techniques such as positive reinforcement that are crucial to winning employees' confidence and respect. Mastery of these techniques requires patience and practice and a conscious effort to resist punitive measures. Finally, managers will naturally fear change because it requires them to make decisions in areas unfamiliar to them.

In light of the new demands on managers to transform organizations and the people working in them, it is imperative that management development programs provide opportunities for managers to understand their managerial style and modify it as necessary. Managers need to be convinced that only when their style is change-oriented and employee-centered can they expect change to be implemented in their organizations.

The managerial style of women is discussed in the chapter by Komarov. There are so many negative stereotypes of women managers that Komarov classified them into several categories. These stereotypes persist in spite of the fact that women comprise a large proportion of managers, are well educated, and are generally acknowledged to have good work habits. It is important to keep in mind that Komarov is presenting perceptions and stereotypes; this portrayal needs to be counterbalanced by an examination of the actual performance and attitudes of women managers themselves. In my view, the implications of Komarov's chapter for management education are twofold. First, women represent a grossly underutilized group in managerial work who should be given access to management education and other resources to pursue managerial careers. Second, the issue of stereotypes and discrimination against women in managerial positions needs to be addressed openly in management development programs in order to eliminate its negative impact on women's effectiveness and career advancement.

Notes

1. For a description of the financing of higher education before the dissolution of the USSR see A.P. Lukoshkin and E.V. Min'ko, "The Cost-Accounting Mechanism in Higher Educational Institutions," *Soviet Education*, vol. 32, no. 3 (March 1990), pp. 85–91.

2. The State Committee for Public Education was an all-union organization which officially ceased to exist once the USSR was dissolved. The Academy of the National Economy continues to function.

3. See B.B. Burn, *Raising the Curtain: A Report with Recommendations on Academic Exchanges with East Central Europe and the USSR* (New York: Institute of International Education, 1991); Columbia Business School, *Business Education's Response to Eastern Europe: Background Papers* (New York: Columbia University, 1 May 1991); and C. Danielsson, *The European Technical Consultations on the Problems of Formal and Non-Formal Education: The First International Students' Olympiad in Economics* (Linkoping, Sweden: Linkoping Institute of Technology, Department of Management and Economics, 29 August 1991).

4. S. Puffer and V. Ozira. "Hiring and Firing Managers," chapter 7 in P.R. Lawrence et al., *Behind the Factory Walls: Decision Making in Soviet and U.S. Enterprises* (Boston: Harvard Business School Press, 1990), pp. 151–82.

How to Teach About the Market Economy

A. Orlov and Iu. Tkachenko

It is clear that our lack of preparedness will be a most serious obstacle on the way to a market economy. After all, we will have to make the transition from managing an economy with low labor productivity, low wages, abnormal prices, and universally scarce goods (and accordingly a complete lack of producer and consumer freedom), on the one hand, to a totally different system of management, on the other. It involves free choice of one's business and active fostering of entrepreneurship, especially small-scale entrepreneurship. It involves a high level of labor effort and, consequently, substantially rising wages and new market prices. A change of this sort is something that most of our managers, including those of the highest rank, are not ready for. What, then, can we require of workers, peasants, and employees?

It is also essential to dispel fear of the market. This fear can be overcome only by informing people honestly and making them aware of what transition to a market economy entails. It is vitally important to do this without hypocrisy or unnecessary promises.

Here is an example that confirms the foregoing. The Vorgashorskaia Mine is well known to many, and not just because of the strikes in Vorkuta. The employees decided to convert it into a stock company in

Russian text © 1990 by "Ekonomika i zhizn'." "Kak uchit' rynku," *Ekonomika i zhizn'*, no. 40, October 1990, p. 7. A publication of the Central Committee of the CPSU.

order to improve managerial effectiveness, increase miners' wages, and improve conditions. But in practical terms, how is the process of destatization or privatization to be accomplished? What is the difference between these processes? For example, answers are needed to questions such as: how do stocks differ from bonds? What is the nature of dividends? How are commodity stock exchanges to be formed? People want to know what, why, and what for—but frequently they can't figure it out. They are aware that every worker who becomes a coproprietor, an owner of part of the mine's property, is at the same time also taking upon himself the burden of responsibility for the results of his production activity. . . .

What conclusion is to be drawn? *Training managers, specialists, and especially workers and peasants to work under conditions of stabilization and a market economy is an extremely urgent problem and needs to be solved immediately.*

In order to make a rapid change in the existing situation it is advisable to issue a presidential decree calling for urgent measures to train people to work in a socially oriented market economy. The authority of the president of the USSR is very important in matters where the all-union state strategy is decisive. The support of every worker for the program of stabilization and transition to a market economy will largely determine our progress. It is very important now to bring large numbers of working people out of their state of indifference, out of their lack of confidence in tomorrow. This has to be done very vigorously, through totally honest and open discussion.

A presidential decree would set forth the most important requirements on the organization of the mass training of workers, training of the most capable young specialists in a state internship program, and the selection, goal-oriented training, and assignment of managers to go abroad.

The system of production and management training of workers is spinning its wheels, and in a number of republics it is actually close to collapse. The former training system has outlived its usefulness, while a new one has yet to be developed. After all, the apportionment of targets for training from the central government has ceased to function. There are, in addition, the problems of what to teach and who the instructors are. Also needed are fundamentally new criteria of training effectiveness. Any resurrection of the previous kind of education and excessive organization would be not only unpromising but even harmful. A new approach is needed, one centered on motivating the worker, the entrepreneur, and the manager to work. It must meet their real needs and interests.

It is essential this academic year to organize production and management training around the principles of the social-market economy, and legislative and normative acts reflecting the legal and economic basis of such an economy. *Immediate answers are needed to the question of what a market economy is and what its pluses and minuses are.* What is needed is clarification of the characteristic features of a market economy, the characteristics of the various forms of ownership within the system of market relations, social guarantees, planning and finance and credit, administration under market conditions, and ways to make the transition to a market economy.

The specific forms, the time and total length of the training, the composition and number of trainees, and procedures for determining the results of studies and evaluating workers' economic knowledge, are to be determined locally. It is advisable to select forms of training that are lively and creative, like a dialogue, offering studies that require the trainee to spend part or all of his time away from the job, in the form of short-term courses covering thirty to forty class hours. The new content of the training must be backed up by improved teaching and methodology.

The Academy of the National Economy (which reports to the USSR Council of Ministers) and the USSR State Committee for Public Education have jointly drawn up sample syllabi and curricula for a course in the principles of the market economy. The USSR State Committee for Public Education has prepared for publication a collection of sample curricula and programs for training managers and specialists in foreign economic relations. A collection of standard curricula is being revised for various categories of workers.

New study aids are being prepared for the curricula. The Ekonomika Publishing House has published a booklet titled *The Difficult Transition to a Market Economy*,[1] which continues and develops the materials of the National Academic and Practitioner Conference on Radical Economic Reform, which was held in Moscow in November 1989 (materials from which were published this year by Politizdat in the collection *Economic Reform: The Search for Solutions*).[2] Publication of the booklet is to continue. In the fourth quarter of this year, the following study aids will be published: *Leasing and Leasing Relationships in the USSR*,[3] *Principles of Socioeconomic Analysis in Enterprises*,[4] *One Hundred Questions and Answers about the Market Economy*,[5] *Active Instructional Methods*,[6] *A Collection of Business Games, Cases, and Practical Exercises*,[7] *The Organization and Meth-*

odology of Production and Management Training,[8] and others.

Considering the strong influence of the mass media, in particular the newspapers *Ekonomika i zhizn'* [Economics and Life], *Pravda,* and *Trud* [Labor], they should play a decisive role during the new academic year. Articles dealing with questions and problems of the transition to a market economy can be utilized as up-to-date materials in training programs.

A crucial problem is that of instructors. We need radical changes in work with them and new approaches to their selection, training, and certification. People to be recruited to serve as instructors should be those academics, managers, and entrepreneurs who, through their own production experience, have a feel for a market economy, in particular people who have spent time abroad.

In training cadres, it is necessary to proceed on the basis of current needs—to help every worker gain new knowledge and master the skills and abilities necessary for normal work under the new conditions. Most important, it is necessary to demonstrate the advantages of a market economy compared with the administrative-command system, the pluses of converting to a socially oriented market economy, and the possibility of ensuring that people are vitally interested in the results of their own labor.

Notes

1. *Trudnyi povorot k rynku.*
2. *Ekonomicheskaia reforma: poisk reshenii.*
3. *Arenda i arendnye otnosheniia v SSSR.*
4. *Osnovy sotsial'no-ekonomicheskogo analiza na predpriiatii.*
5. *Sto voprosov i otvetov o rynke.*
6. *Metody aktivnogo obucheniia.*
7. *Sbornik delovykh igr, konkretnykh situatsii, i prakticheskikh zadach.*
8. *Organizatsiia i metodika proizvodstvenno-ekonomicheskoi ucheby.*

2

Management Education
in a Time of Change

Anatolii V. Zhuplev

Introduction

The former Soviet Union has entered a period of decisive changes. The problems that exist today have been created by people and will have to be solved by people. Professional management education will have to play a major role in assuring the success of the transition to a market economy. Whereas the radical changes taking place in former Soviet political and economic management are comparatively well known to a great many American readers, the changes that are taking place in the structure and content of management education are not so well known, even to a narrow range of specialists.

Section 1 of the present article contains a brief description and analysis of the Soviet system of management education and key tendencies in its current development. Through the evolution of the Soviet economic system, the article characterizes changes in the caliber of education of Soviet managers and draws the conclusion that if the economic changes are to be successful in the foreseeable future a great deal will have to be done both to increase the quantitative level of education of Soviet managers at all levels and to achieve a substantial

Russian text © 1991 by Anatolii V. Zhuplev. The original title and introduction of this unpublished manuscript were given in English. It is printed here with the permission of the author.

11

qualitative improvement and structural changes in that system, geared to a market-oriented rather than to a bureaucratic, centralized management.

Section 2 describes the organization of managerial training as it existed in the USSR in the middle of the 1980s (when Gorbachev's reforms were started). It presents a compact overview of the key points in the reform in the sphere of Soviet management education at the end of the 1980s.

Section 3 argues that it will be impossible to achieve success in the former USSR's transition to a market economy or in effective changes in the system of management education unless there is intensive cooperation with Western countries, in particular the United States. This section summarizes factors that speak in favor of such cooperation on the part of the former USSR. It presents examples of cooperation between Soviet and American centers of management training. The concluding section of the article describes key characteristics of various types of Soviet management training centers, which in the initial stages can serve to foster the initiation and development of contacts between American and Soviet management training centers.

1. From revolution to revolution

Today's difficulties in the economy and administration of the former USSR are to some extent reflections and direct consequences of numerous "revolutionary" experiments and socioeconomic upheavals that the country has gone through under seventy-three years of communism.[1]

The forcible demolition of the economic and managerial structures that resulted from the 1917 Revolution in Russia from the very outset led to the expulsion and emigration of large numbers of qualified executives, specialists, and businessmen. A great many new people entered management from the workers' ranks, people who had no professional education. A survey conducted in the USSR in 1922 among managers and boards of trustees of 159 enterprises showed that 64 percent had only a minimum education (a few grades of primary education). A survey of 646 executives in 1930 revealed that more than half of them had a minimal or "home-grown" education. In 1927, on the eve of Stalin's industrialization campaign, there were only 65 engineers and 68 technicians for every 10,000 workers employed in industry in the USSR—a figure several times smaller than in Germany and the United States.[2] More than 30 percent were practitioners who did not have either a higher education or the appropriate specialized secondary edu-

Table 1

Educational Level of Workers Holding Managerial Posts, by Particular Position, as of November 15, 1985[3]

Groups of Managers	Thousands of persons	Distribution by education, %		
		Higher	Secondary specialized	No higher or secondary specialized education
Managers and deputy managers of enterprises, institutions, and organizations	1,355	69	23	8
Managers of service and other facilities, enterprises, institutions, and organizations	76	39	46	15
Managers of departments, sections, bureaus, sectors, and groups	1,350	70	25	5
Chief specialists of all specialties (except for head bookkeepers)	477	69	27	4
Head bookkeepers	453	23	58	19
Chiefs of shops, shifts, sections; heads of departments, farm sections, etc.	1,381	28	46	26
Foremen	2,202	24	57	19
Work superintendents	226	38	52	10

cation. By the beginning of Gorbachev's economic-managerial transformations, which essentially turned into yet another revolution, remarkable quantitative progress had been achieved in upgrading the educational level of specialists and executives (Table 1).

At the same time, as these data show, the proportion of managers of different levels not holding degrees in higher education (an institute or a university with a five-year term of instruction), as of the mid-1980s, added up to a substantial percentage:

• managers and deputies of enterprises and institutes—31 percent;
• managers of functional services (departments, sections, bureaus, sectors, and groups)—30 percent;
• low-level line managers of shops, sections, farm sections, and so on in industry and agriculture—72 percent;

• foremen of all categories—76 percent.

In the context of the current economic changes, therefore, the professional educational level of economic managers of almost all levels needs to be substantially increased quantitatively, quite aside from the need for improvement in its structure and content.

By way of illustrating the technocratic tendencies that exist in Soviet management we may cite the fact that at the end of 1980s the proportion of managers of associations, enterprises, and organizations throughout the national economy with basic technical education amounted to between 80 and 85 percent.[4] The majority of them never studied marketing, leadership, business communications, personnel management, and other subjects that constitute the basis of managerial training in most developed countries. Of all the top leaders in USSR history, only V. I. Lenin and M. S. Gorbachev had a higher education, both in law. The top managers of soviet, state, party, or sectorial management organs in the pre-Gorbachev era with a management education were about as rare as snow in Los Angeles.

2. The organization of management training in the USSR

The state system

According to various estimates, as of the middle of the 1980s the total population of the USSR amounted to 285 million persons; the number of those employed in the national economy came to 131 million, and the number of those employed in management totaled 18.6 million, including 9.3 million management personnel of various categories.[5]

In accordance with the constitutional, administrative-legal, and political-economic structures that were in place in the USSR in the mid-1980s (prior to the start of the radical changes initiated by Gorbachev), the system of professional management training was organized along three lines.

1. Party–state management. The educational institutions providing training for professional party cadres:

• A basic professional party education (four or five years of college) did not exist. People initially came to work professionally in the sphere of party management having an ordinary higher education.

• A basic education for organs of legislative, executive, or judicial authority was provided in the law faculties of universities and in the higher juridical educational institutions operating with programs requiring five or six years.

• The Academy of Social Sciences under the CPSU Central Committee in Moscow was the leading institution providing training of officials for professional work in the top levels of the party and state hierarchy, offering programs of varying length (from several days to two years). The CPSU Central Committee Academy of Social Sciences also conducted scientific research and methodological supervision over a network of educational institutions.

• Higher party schools and their affiliates, specialized faculties, and courses conducted regional programs of instruction for middle- and low-level party cadres. The most famous of the higher party schools operated in Moscow and Leningrad.

• Permanently operating and one-time training seminars and various programs for training party workers under republic-level, regional, city, and district party organs, as well as directly within enterprises and in primary-level organizations.

2. *Trade unions and Komsomol work.* As in the case of party management, no basic training was provided for cadres for professional work in trade unions, the Komsomol, and other social organizations.

• The training of cadres for the top hierarchy of the trade unions and the Komsomol was provided, respectively, by the Higher School of the Trade Union Movement (in Moscow, subordinate to the All-Union Central Council of Trade Unions), and the Higher Komsomol School (in Moscow, subordinate to the Central Komsomol Committee).

• In addition to the Higher School of the Trade Union Movement and the Higher Komsomol School in Moscow, similar educational functions were carried out by trade union and Komsomol training centers that were in constant operation, or by occasional training programs, in every union republic, and on the regional, city, and district levels. Enterprises and primary-level organizations also carried out various forms of permanent or occasional training.

At the present time, in connection with the self-dissolution of the central trade unions and substantial changes in the functions and structure of the Komsomol in the USSR, the fate of these training centers will have to be decided in a new context that is not yet clarified.

3. *Enterprise management.* The organization and functioning of education for managers in the former USSR took place in a system of dual

subordination. On the one hand, the financing and general administration (planning, organization, coordination, and monitoring) of the various management institutions were handled by the USSR State Committee for Public Education and through the corresponding committees for public education and their offices in the union republics, territories, and regions. On the other hand, some higher educational institutions involved in training managers were financed and administratively controlled by the sectorial ministries and directly by major companies. In the latter case, within the framework of the principle of dual subordination, the USSR State Committee for Public Education provided methodological control and coordination on a nationwide scale, for institutions and management programs that functioned within the system of sectorial ministries and major companies.

The consolidated organizational structure of the system of management training in the former USSR is presented in the chart on the following page.

In 1988, within the framework of the general reform of the Soviet educational system, the system of management training also underwent changes. For the umpteenth time in the history of Soviet administration this reform was adopted centrally, using the method of "planned revolution" that came from above.

The following were listed as the main goals in reforming Soviet management education in 1988:

• Enhancing the professionalism of managers and specialists;

• Overcoming technocratism and developing socioeconomic-humanitarian aspects in the practice of management;

• Perfecting management education itself (its organizational structure, financing, and also interaction with academic research on management and the needs of practitioners).

The reform of 1988 introduced the following gradation of types of training in the sequence of going through professional *retraining of management personnel*:

• Systematic independent training of the worker (self-education) according to an individual plan approved and monitored by his immediate supervisor;

• Participation at least once every month in permanent seminars having to do with production and managerial problems, both in the workplace and in other enterprises and organizations;

• Short-term (as needed, but not less than once every year) training in the workplace or in educational institutions (subunits);

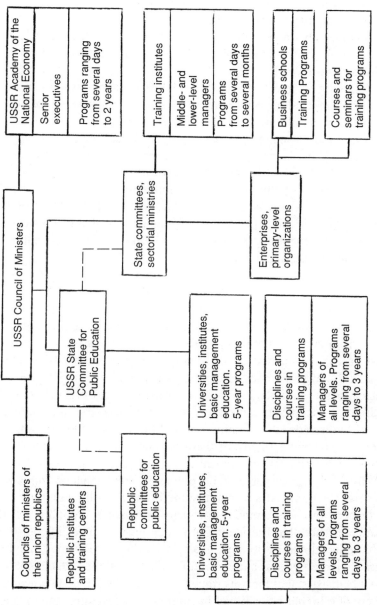

Organization of Management Training in the USSR (mid-1980s)

• Lengthy periodic training (not less than once every six years) in educational institutions (subunits) of the system of retraining and upgrading of qualifications of cadres;
• On-the-job training in leading enterprises and leading scientific organizations as well as higher educational institutions, which may include going abroad;
• Training in a special-purpose graduate studies program or doctoral program dealing with themes that are of interest to the particular organization or enterprise;
• Retraining—acquiring a new specialty in academies, training institutes, in specialized faculties of higher educational institutions and in departments of secondary specialized educational institutions.[6]

The adoption of this reform was motivationally backed up by the introduction of a new and more rigorous statewide procedure of systematic professional certification, and mechanisms that make workers' career advancement and salaries more closely tied to participation in continuous management education.

Starting in 1988, procedures for financing the training of specialists in the higher educational institutions of the USSR were changed, in particular the training of managers (a basic five-year education). Instead of paying the expenses of training college students from state or republic-level budgets, these costs are now, in most cases, reimbursed by the enterprises and organizations themselves. This was intended to shift the financial burden from the state budget to the shoulders of Soviet enterprises and organizations. In addition, it was designed to improve facilities and the financial position of higher education institutions and training institutes by making them self-financing (many of them are located in dilapidated buildings and have obsolete equipment).

While helping to solve some problems, this financial innovation gave rise to others. At a recent meeting in the Kremlin with top political leaders, the representatives of many universities from all over the country insisted that President Gorbachev provide financial aid to the higher educational institutions in step with the USSR's movement toward a market system and decentralization of higher education. The students insisted that the government continue the previous practice of subsidizing higher educational institutions in substantial amounts and rescind the intention to make higher educational institutions themselves, and students, responsible for seeking sources to finance higher education. At this meeting, Soviet Prime Minister Ryzhkov acknowledged that students are the least-protected segment of Soviet society.[7]

With respect to management training programs (as shown in Chart 1, the system included the USSR Academy of the National Economy, training institutes in sectorial ministries, business schools, and training programs affiliated with higher educational institutions and enterprises), the reform gave many of them considerable organizational and financial flexibility and independence in their relationships with clients and ministries.

3. Foreign partnership

There are those who are of the conviction—which is widespread on both sides of the ocean and is shared by me—that the former USSR is not going to be able to make the transition to a dynamic market system without the active participation of the West. Help and cooperation in management education with the developed countries of the West, in particular the United States, is exceptionally important and attractive at present to the former Soviet Union, for the following reasons.

1. The presence in the West of a variety of practical experience in managing in a market economy

2. Well-developed theoretical models and experience in their application

3. A well-developed network of educational, research, and consulting institutes and methodologies and—most important—highly qualified personnel employed in these institutions

4. Management education programs can serve as more than merely means of professional training for Soviet managers, to acquaint them with the culture and educational traditions of the West. These programs, as experience has shown, can serve as an effective channel for developing business contacts in industrial, financial, and governmental circles.*

5. For a number of reasons, management programs could play the role of catalyst to intensify the international migration of labor power, which is increasing in tempo in connection with global re-

---

*In 1989–90 I took part in organizing management programs for Soviet executives at Northeastern University in Boston, Massachusetts (fourteen weeks) and Loyola Marymount University in Los Angeles, California (four weeks). These programs were successful for more than academic reasons. They helped establish promising Soviet-American business ties, on the enterprise level, that are continuing to develop.

structuring and the strengthening of the competitive position of EEC–92, the countries of the Asian-Pacific region, and what used to be Eastern Europe.*

In light of the tendency to step up international competition, participation in such managerial education programs could be mutually beneficial as well for American universities and, over the long term, for American business.

At the present time there are several types of Soviet organizations that are cooperating, or have shown interest in establishing cooperation, with the United States in management training.

Higher educational institutions

Of the 898 higher educational institutions in the former USSR,[9] only a very few have five-year management programs. Of these, the most active in establishing contacts with business schools in Europe and the United States are the Moscow Institute of Management, the Plekhanov Institute of the National Economy,[10] and Moscow State University.[11]

As potential partners of American business schools, Soviet higher educational institutions have the following characteristics.

1. A contingent of students and instructors that is substantial in terms of quantity (for example, the daytime and evening departments of the Moscow Management Institute have a total enrollment of around 10,000 students in the various management specialties, and the faculty of professors and instructors totals 800).

2. Extensive facilities (lecture halls, offices, dormitories, laboratories, audiovisual aids, and so on). In many cases, however, the buildings and equipment are quite old and are in need of major renovation.

3. The human factor. Probably around 95 percent of the students of Soviet business schools would love to go through an American course of management training.** But only 5 percent are objectively prepared

*The State Committee for Education as well as Soviet emigration authorities have projected that 1.5 million of the most qualified of the former USSR's 15 million scientists and technical specialists could leave over the next decade under the new emigration regulations promulgated in late 1990.[8]

**Up to 1,200 applicants participated in the entrance exam for a privileged sixty-two slots in the recently created evening business school at Moscow State University under the Russian-American University umbrella.[12]

for it (for the majority, the obstacles are the language barrier, differences in cultural, cognitive, and behavioral styles, and the traditional Russian homesickness when abroad for very long).

For the same reasons, at the present time only a few professors of Soviet higher educational institutions are able to work as visiting professors in American business schools, teaching subjects relating either to Soviet or American management. In addition to the above-mentioned barriers that await students, a Soviet professor working in an American university experiences additional pressure for the following reasons.

• The principles and organization of instruction in an American college are radically different from those in a Soviet higher educational institution. Initial cultural and professional adaptation takes at least three or four months, which is not generally stipulated in the work contract and gives rise to stress.

• The professor's work and relations with students in class and colleagues and the administration in an American college are structured on the basis of individualism, equality, privacy, and meticulous quantitative commensurability of inputs (research, teaching, and community service) and outputs (rewards, career growth, and tenure benefits). In a Soviet higher educational institution, meanwhile, it is structured to a greater extent on the principle of seniority. For this reason, a rapid transition from one system to the other may lead to organizational and psychological stress.

• Both in the academic world and in the life of students themselves in American business schools, a major role in career success is played by quantitative evaluations of the work done. In a Soviet higher educational institution, on the other hand, quantitative assessments play a less important role in practice, both for the professor and for the students. In reality, therefore, relations between the students, the professor, and the administration in a Soviet higher educational institution are much less regulated by the system, less competitive, and more rarely subject to conflicts than in the American situation.

• Both in Soviet and in American higher educational institutions it is expected that professors take active part in research. My own experience—eleven years working in a Soviet higher educational institution and two years as a visiting professor in American business schools—leads me to the conclusion that in the American system, professors devote considerably more attention and time to research than do their Soviet colleagues.*

Another important difference is that in a Soviet higher educational institution the syllabi, curriculum, and even, to a certain extent, the instructional methods are standardized on the department level or even in the higher educational institution as a whole. This means that every professor devotes less time and attention to developing and updating these documents for every new course, and, consequently, psychologically he bears less individual responsibility for the strategic organization and development of the course. In an American business school, on the other hand, the syllabus and methods of instruction are matters of individual preference, of individual expertise, and, in the final analysis, the professor's individual professional responsibility to the students, his colleagues, and himself for the success of the course. The professor is supposed to be a "boss" in his class.

Having dealings with a Soviet higher educational institution and proceeding on the basis of the specifics of the current financial situation in which the USSR finds itself, an American business school can most probably either count on what is known as noncurrency exchange,** or can find additional sources of its own to finance training programs for Soviet students in hard currency (i.e., dollars).***

----

*We would do well, however, to listen to Richard R. West, dean of New York University's Graduate School of Business, who says: "If I weren't a dean of this school I'd be writing a book on the bankruptcy of American management education. The critics say that professors are spending far too much time on fuzzy academic theories in narrowly defined disciplines at a time when American business is beset with a host of competitive problems. And some B-school deans surveyed recently by *Business Week* go so far as to say that well over half the resources devoted to research are squandered. As much as 80 percent of management research may be irrelevant."[13]

**For example, Northeastern University recently signed an agreement with Moscow State University to establish quantitative parity, which involves an equivalent exchange of students. On this basis, in 1992, two Soviet students graduated from the MBA program at Northeastern University's College of Business Administration (see chapter 12, "The American MBA Program: A Russian Student's View").

***The subsidizing of training programs for Soviet students is not generally characteristic of American business schools. During the initial stages of Gorbachev's reforms this route was used to a greater extent by Western European training centers, with active financial and political cooperation on the part of the governments of the countries in question, for example, Germany. Among American business schools mention can be made of the Fuqua School of Business, Duke University, which recently committed four million dollars to develop a program to educate Soviet managers (see chapter 16, "The Fuqua School of Business Program for Soviet Executives").

These restrictions stem from the fact that, as a rule, Soviet higher educational institutions do not have their own hard currency, and most of them will not have any chance to earn it in the immediate future. In addition, higher education in the former USSR is financed from the state budget, as a result of which the Soviet higher educational institution may also have extremely limited opportunities for paying the costs of international managerial training programs for students, even in rubles.

Management development centers

The Academy of the National Economy and several senior-level schools that specialize in international business (they are not shown in Chart 1) already have fairly well-developed international ties with business schools and other training centers in the United States and Western Europe. These training centers, although they do suffer from certain currency and organizational limitations in regard to cooperation with the West in management training, research, and consulting, nevertheless do have the basic conditions needed to develop such cooperation successfully.*

At the present time, the sectorial ministries' management development institutes, with few exceptions, do not have sufficient resources to organize programs jointly with Western partners, for the following reasons:

• the lack of their own hard currency funds and, in many cases, sufficient ruble funds as well;

• poor facilities (absent or unsatisfactory classroom facilities, dormitories, cafeterias, audiovisual services, transportation, etc.);

• the overwhelming majority of professors and instructors are not proficient in foreign languages and are unfamiliar with Western

---

*For example, at Moscow's Advanced Management School, which teaches management in the market economy, most students complete two- to three-month courses at Soviet institutes. They then spend three to four weeks studying marketing, financial markets, supply logistics, banking, and business administration in other countries. Next, they often do brief stints at companies that sponsor academic work. Soviet sponsors pay only the students' travel costs. The balance can range from about $5,000 for a three-week program run by the London Business School to $15,000 for a one-year work-study program in Hessen, a West German state.[14]

business practices and methods of instruction in business schools;

• bureaucratic control of organizational and financial decisions by sectorial ministries makes it very difficult and unpredictable for sectorial training institutes to take part in joint international management programs.

Joint ventures and nongovernmental training centers for management training

In accordance with new laws and governmental decrees, the former USSR began to encourage joint ventures, including those in management training and consulting. The most energetic activity in management training is being done by joint ventures such as Manager Service (USSR–Denmark),[15] Mirbis (USSR–Italy),[16] Sinergia (USSR–Italy), and a number of Soviet–Finnish,[17] Soviet–British, and other firms.

The advantage of joint ventures is that the Soviet side is made up of the most enterprising, energetic, and qualified managers and professionals who are experienced in contacts with Westerners. In many cases they have their own hard currency funds and have the necessary contacts in central and local governmental, scientific and academic, and industrial circles; they have their own up-to-date communications, office equipment, and cars.

It is interesting to note that state higher educational institutions are beginning to combine their efforts with joint venture companies and are providing management education and consulting services. For example, Moscow's Plekhanov Institute has under its umbrella two joint venture firms—Mirbis[18] and Sinergia.[19] This alliance makes it possible to combine the benefits of both types of management institution in a way that is mutually advantageous.

Rapid growth characterizes a market for management consulting services and short-term training programs, services that are provided by a variety of cooperatives and professional associations. Currently, there are more than 100 such centers and their affiliates within the former USSR. The most well-known among them are operating in Moscow, Leningrad, and Kiev, as well as a few of the major cities in Siberia.

As a rule, centers of this type have very small full-time staffs. For the most part, they recruit the most well-known professors and scientists from the state higher educational institutions and other institutions to serve as instructors and consultants on a short-term basis. Remuneration in such cases tends to be ten to twenty times greater than their earnings in their main job, depending on the instructor's qualifications, the teaching load, the subject being taught, and the rating given by the participants in the training programs.

* * *

The economy, the practice and theory of management, and management education are now in a state of radical transition to market concepts. Along with new opportunities this brings new practical and theoretical problems, the solution to which would be greatly benefited by the organizational, practical, and theoretical experience of the United States in the field of management. The involvement of American business schools and other management training centers to exploit the new opportunities in Eastern Europe and the former USSR would also be consistent with the new interests of the United States in the face of global *perestroika*.

Notes

1. For a brief survey of the development of Soviet economic institutes see *Behind the Factory Walls. Decision Making in Soviet and U.S. Enterprises*, eds. P. R. Lawrence and C. A. Vlachoutsicos (Boston: Harvard Business School Press, 1990), pp. 37–55.

2. *Literaturnaia gazeta*, 1975, no. 45, p. 11; R. A. Belousov, *Istoricheskii opyt planovogo upravleniia ekonomikoi SSSR* [Historical Experience of the Planned Administration of the Economy of the USSR] (Moscow: Mysl', 1983), p. 143.

3. *Sbornik statisticheskikh materialov* [Collection of Statistical Materials] (Moscow: Finansy i statistika, 1987), p. 50.

4. A. V. Zhuplev, *Rukovoditel' i kollektiv. Prakticheskoe posobie* [The Manager and the Collective. A Practical Handbook] (Stavropol': Stavropol'skoe knizhnoe izdatel'stvo, 1989), p. 9.

5. A. V. Zhuplev, *Effekt gorizonta. Rukovoditel' i kadry* [The Horizon Effect. Managers and Employees] (Moscow: Moskovskii rabochii, 1989), p. 27.

6. Ibid., p. 39.

7. "Soviet Students Urge Government Not to Reduce Aid to Their Institutions during Economic Transition," *The Chronicle of Higher Education*, 14 November 1990, p. A43.

8. "Tidal Wave of Emigration Carries Off Soviet 'Brains,' " *The Los Angeles Times*, 8 October 1990, p. A1.

9. *Narodnoe khoziaistvo SSSR v 1987 g.* [The National Economy of the USSR in 1987] (Moscow: Finansy i statistika, 1988), 500 pp.

10. *The Chronicle of Higher Education*, 26 September 1990, p. A49.

11. *The New York Times*, 7 November 1990, p. A4.

12. Ibid.

13. "Is Research in Ivory Tower, Fuzzy, Irrelevant, Pretentious?" *Business Week*, 29 October 1990, p. 62.

14. "Crash Course in Capitalism for Ivan the Globe-Trotter," *Business Week*, 28 May 1990, p. 42.

15. A. L. Katkov, *Sovmestnye predpriiatiia. Ekonomicheskie, organizatsionnye i upravlencheskie aspekty* [Joint Ventures. Economic, Organizational, and Management Aspects] (Leningrad: Mashinostroenie. Leningradskoe otdelenie, 1990), p. 168.

16. *Business Week*, 28 May 1990, p. 44.

17. "Capitalism Up Close," *The Los Angeles Times*, 26 July 1990, pp. D1, D2.

18. D. Brown, "Welcome, Comrades, to Marketing 101," *Management Review*, March 1990, p. 32.

19. "Capitalism Up Close."

3

Recent Developments in Management Education

Viacheslav V. Kruglov

Since 1988, the process of *perestroika* in the USSR has spread intensively to the economic sphere. The reform of our national economy, whose ultimate purpose is to convert to market principles and mechanisms, has revealed the wide discrepancy between the principles of market economics and the inability of the traditional economic structures and the system of economic knowledge to grasp these principles and implement them under conditions of economic activity that are totally new to us. The overwhelming majority of managers and workers do not have a clear understanding of how to work under market conditions, unfettered by numerous bureaucratic prescriptions. Traditional economic education consisted of training the specialist who had a knowledge of economic concepts and categories necessary to understand the numerous instructions, commands, and directives issued by numerous central and sectorial economic departments and apply them in his work.

Conversion to the market economy will require substantial changes in the structure of economic institutions—in particular, the abolition of the old structures on the all-union, republic, and regional levels, and the creation of new institutions. Thus, for example, the market economy makes sectorial ministries superfluous and entails a considerable

Russian text © 1991 by Viacheslav V. Kruglov. "Novoe v ekonomicheskom obrazovanii v SSSR (biznes i obrazovanie)." This unpublished manuscript is translated here with the permission of the author.

cutting back of the unwieldy apparatus along with fundamental changes in Gosplan [State Committee for Planning], the State Committee for Prices, the State Committee for Standards, and so on. On the other hand, an increased role will be assigned to banking institutions; stock, commodity, and labor exchanges will have to be created. Also due for substantial restructuring are information and production services.

Economic education has also been confronted by the fact that enterprises, economic and trade organizations, and production cooperatives have been given the right to go into foreign markets on their own and to create joint enterprises with foreign partners. Up to 1988, all foreign economic ties were conducted through central, all-union organizations. They required a relatively small number of specialists, whose training was provided by the Academy of the Ministry of Foreign Trade and the Moscow State Institute for International Relations. The new conditions of conducting foreign economic relations have given rise to an urgent need for specialists who are able to do this work in Soviet enterprises.

The transition to a variety of forms of property ownership (cooperative, private, stock-company, collective, and mixed forms have come into being along with state ownership) has revealed a vacuum of economic and legal knowledge in this sphere.

This constitutes a very brief and incomplete list of all the problems and trends that our economic science will have to "assimilate" so that they can also be "assimilated" in the practice of running the national economy.

All the urgent problems of the country's transition to a mechanism of economic relations and ties that are totally new to us have confronted economic education with many new tasks. In particular, we will have to make fundamental changes in the curricula for most of the training programs and develop new courses (management, marketing, principles of the market economy, international economic relations, new forms of entrepreneurship, and so on). A number of schools have inaugurated training in new specialties, of which the greatest interest is enjoyed by "international economic relations." Training in this specialty has been launched, for example, in our institute. In contrast to other specialties, it incorporates a large array of disciplines relating to the world market, international and regional financial and banking organizations, and different branches of law (including Russian economic law, international private law, and characteristics of the national economic legislation of a number of countries). Considerable attention is focused on the study of foreign languages. For example, our students must master two foreign languages (English being mandatory). We are attempting to provide these students with the opportunity to spend part of their training in Western colleges and universities. In our opinion, the curriculum that we have developed for specialists in international economic relations ought to serve as an initial model for the training of economists for other economic specialties, because it takes greater account of the specific nature of economic work in a market economy.

At the same time, the training of a new generation of specialists is a lengthy process. As a rule, students in economics attend school for five years. After graduating from the institute, in addition, they must spend a number of years developing into first-class specialists who are capable of taking charge of economic programs.

Hence, the "normal" structures of higher educational institutions take several (three to five) years to provide the country's national economy with the kind of specialists needed under the new conditions. Meanwhile, there is an acute need for such professionals already. But what can these training programs offer the economy now? Who is going to fill that vacuum that has come into being in the course of economic transformations in our country? As is well known, nature abhors a vacuum, which becomes immediately filled. Who is to fill this vacuum, and by what means?

An extremely superficial analysis of tendencies and processes that are being observed in education has enabled us to delineate the following typical forms:

1. The first response to the national economy's emergent need for new managerial personnel and knowledge was the organization of various short-term seminars, courses, and scientific-practical conferences to deal with relevant themes. As a rule, these courses and seminars are organized on a paying basis in amounts that exceed by several times the compensation paid to instructors and scientific workers as stipulated in state directives. For taking part in such seminars and courses, specialists and academics were getting 10 to 100 times more than for working in the state educational institutions. Yet even in cases where the fee for taking part in such seminars was relatively high, recruiting participants was never a problem. Given the dearth of information relating to new problems of economic life, organizations willingly paid for participation in such seminars.

Because market conditions were favorable for such training-information courses, it was primarily the dynamic structures that undertook to organize them—various academic, informational, and consulting cooperatives and centers, created in accordance with the Law on Cooperation and Individual Labor Activity. The state educational institutions, fettered by various restrictions and prohibitions, remained out of this endeavor at first.

An acute demand for new economic and legal information came into being. Especially in demand were prominent economists from Moscow and other cities where well-known educational and scientific centers are concentrated. Riding the wave of this acute demand, many academic economists became popular and successfully became part of legislative bodies on the national and republic levels and in the major cities. It is sufficient, in this connection, to mention G. Kh. Popov, N. P. Shmelev, A. A. Sobchak, T. I. Zaslavskaia, V. S. Advadze, and V. S. Kabakov, for example.

The intense demand for information started first in the major cities and then spread "in waves" to the periphery.

Short-term seminars have already passed their peak of popularity. This form of obtaining economic knowledge, although it does continue to be practiced, can no longer satisfy the need to acquire new knowledge. In addition, such seminars were frequently organized by incompetent people who were striving to get rich quickly.

2. Short-term seminars featuring foreign experts enjoyed high popularity, and continue to do so. The lengthy isolation of Soviet society as a whole, and the formerly rigid centralization of international contacts, have resulted in heightened euphoria with regard to making use of the achievements of Western economic thought and economic practice.

This form of replenishing and updating economic knowledge is being used by all institutions having anything to do with economic education. In my institute alone, for example, the services of foreign experts are being sought by the institute itself, four scientific-consulting cooperatives, the state-training organization affiliated with the institute, and a branch of the Razvitie [Development] Stock Company of Moscow. Also holding such seminars are consulting firms, the Chamber of Commerce and Industry, and major industrial firms.

The craving for foreign experience is enormous, and the trainees in such seminars, as a rule, are willing to pay higher prices to participate.

Among the foreign experts—academics and practitioners—who

speak at the seminars, there is a predominance of opportunists who are taking advantage of the chance to get acquainted with the former Soviet Union during this dramatic period in its history.

3. In addition to short-term, one-time seminars, permanent educational institutions are also being set up, including those with foreign participation. Thus, for example, the St. Petersburg Polytechnical University has a business school functioning jointly with the University of Stuttgart (Germany) with the financial support of the State of Baden-Wurttemberg. St. Petersburg State University has set up the St. Petersburg International Management Institute jointly with the University of Bacconi (Italy). Joint enterprises are being set up that have the task, among others, of training managers. This is the task, in particular, of a joint enterprise that involves the St. Petersburg Institute of Finance and Economics, two St. Petersburg banks, and a French consulting firm.

4. The retraining of specialists in new economic knowledge is now being undertaken on a fee basis by a number of new organizations. Very indicative in this regard is the activity of Moscow's Razvitie Stock Company. The network of affiliates that it has created is designed to train members of cooperatives and small and medium-sized enterprises, including private ones. As a rule, it involves courses of intensive training in specialties such as "bookkeeping," "cooperative theory and history," "the financial and banking system," "principles of foreign economic activity," and others. Razvitie publishes a newspaper, *Menedzher* (issued twice every month), in press runs of 120,000 copies. The newspaper offers up-to-date economic information, advertising, consulting, and the opinions of well-known experts regarding the most urgent problems of our economic life.

Under pressure from the new educational organizations, which are operating dynamically and aggressively and attracting new, qualified academics and practitioners, the state educational institutions are also beginning to transform themselves. They include, in particular, various organizations that provide training programs for professionals. One advantage these organizations have is their material resources. They own buildings with classrooms and dormitories for the trainees and they are given budget appropriations. The new organizations, on the other hand, have to lease facilities and frequently do not have permanent facilities for offices. At the same time, they are not bound by various prescriptions and directives or financial prohibitions; they can regulate instructors' pay in a flexible manner and select the most highly qualified faculty; they are not bound by numerous restrictions of labor legislation that are mandatory for state educational institutions.

At present, preparations are under way for a new state reform of the system of higher education, because the 1986 reform demonstrated the glaring inadequacy of the measures that were envisioned to modernize the system. The first step along the path to this reform was the declaration of the autonomy of higher educational institutions, expanding their independence in many matters, including the field of international ties.

One of the most urgent problems at the present time is that of educational literature. The enormous stocks of educational literature that were accumulated during the years of domination of the administrative-command system have in many ways become useless under the new conditions. There are still far too few textbooks, and they are generally sold out almost immediately. Translated textbooks by foreign authors are enjoying enormous success. Thus, for example, the marketing textbook written by Professor Kotler (United States), with a publication run of 40,000 copies, was selling on the black market at a price ten times higher than face value—that is, the official state price. A number of cooperative and private publishing houses have been set up for the purpose of printing textbooks and republishing the works of Russian academics from the turn of the century. Naturally, we would like very much to translate and publish well-known Western textbooks, but the acute shortage of hard currency presents serious obstacles in carrying out this idea.

There are more than enough problems facing contemporary economic education in the USSR (as in every other sphere of our life). But I should like in this connection to quote two Russian sayings: "The eyes are afraid, but the hands do the work," and "The dream is frightful, but God is merciful."

4

Let's Train Managers for the Market Economy

Oleg S. Vikhanskii

Not many services are keeping pace with rapidly rising demand. Almost everything that might be of the slightest value to the consumer is in short supply. Against this background of mass shortages, however, certain types of activity contrive to expand so rapidly that there is actually no shortage of them at all. Among those types of activity, apparently, we can list the training of managers. The number of all kinds of business schools is increasing at a very rapid pace. The situation has reached a point, in fact, where many of these schools go looking for clients, despite the fact that the transition to a market economy is pushing all kinds of new enthusiasts—or hostages of the old system—into college classrooms in order to get the chance to succeed (which is what many dream of) or to survive (which is what others hope for) as business people.

From the point of view of a normal society, the headlong increase in the number of business schools ought to be viewed as completely abnormal. There are developed countries, such as the United States, where there is a large number of management training centers. There is also the example of Japan, where the number of business schools in the direct sense can be counted on a few fingers. There are world-famous

Russian text © 1991 by Oleg S. Vikhanskii. "Gotovim menedzherov dlia rynichnoi ekonomiki." This unpublished manuscript is translated here with the permission of the author.

business schools such as, for example, IMD [the International Institute for Management Development] in Lausanne or INSEAD [l'Institut européen d'administration des affaires] near Paris. And there are small ones of the sort that we might call business schools of local significance. However, for all the diversity of these schools, the different orientations of their activities, the varying lengths of their curricula, and so on, it is possible to discern one feature in common—all of these schools represent a significant social phenomenon, and the appearance of each of them is an important event.

In our country, business schools are almost as easy to set up now as shish kebab stands at busy intersections—and this in a country where the very concept of business, to say nothing of the activities involved, used to be considered extremely negative. Indeed, management as it is presently interpreted was lacking, and the corresponding theories of the modern classics of management were examined only from the angle of critically unmasking their bourgeois essence. It must be pointed out, at the same time, that literally only a handful of people in the entire country have a fairly adequate grasp of modern business and management, and only a few are able not only to discuss it but also to teach it, using the necessary methodological techniques of instruction and exercises. And yet in this situation we have hundreds and perhaps thousands of business schools, and their number is multiplying constantly. Isn't this a paradox? Beyond all doubt. Any normal person would find it absurd if engineers were to undertake to train physicians or artists. Yet everybody is undertaking to create business schools and train managers, not only without regard to the profile of their education but without any education at all. What could be easier: Put a group of people in a classroom (it's nice if it's really a classroom—sometimes there's not even a blackboard) and bring in a well-known economist (it's very easy to get one, because you can pay him very well). He'll talk two or three hours about the grievous problems our economy faces today, and there you are—you've trained business people and managers. This is not a spoof. It is something I have personally witnessed a number of times.

How can this be possible? Evidently we need to point out a number of factors here. First of all, the customer is totally ignorant of the commodity he is about to buy. He wants to become a businessman, a manager, but doesn't know how. And so they foist God knows what on him and assure him that it's just what he needs.

However regretfully, nevertheless, the customer has to swallow this uninteresting and useless swill. The money, after all, has already been paid. And who knows? Maybe he'll get something out of it.

Second, the unshackling of the creative activity of the masses brought about thousands of energetic young entrepreneurs appearing on the scene; they know how to lease a facility, make a deal with a hotel, and get airline tickets—but that's all. And on the basis of just these abilities and skills they set up schools that are supposed to train businessmen and managers. In doing so, they are not at all concerned with the main consideration—the educational process. The organizers of business schools are businessmen; what they care about is money. As long as the money comes in, they will keep doing this activity. I am not condemning them, they're just doing business. If there are no customers to buy their product, they will stop doing it and find something else to earn a profit. In my opinion, however, moral responsibility for a product of no value is borne by the venerable scientists and professors who have so easily lent their names—for substantial compensation—to covering up real consumer fraud. And even if they do conduct their own classes brilliantly and successfully, the overall absence of a developed curriculum and the necessary instructional methodology make it impossible to achieve the kind of results that would correspond to the tasks of a business school.

Third, a major problem is that there is practically no training of instructors for business schools. Literally just a few individuals have had the chance to attend management training centers abroad. As for the rest, most are self-taught and approach everything by the trial-and-error method. Of course, it is primarily the trainees who will end up paying for the errors. What happens is that the teacher is himself learning as he teaches others, and the future manager is the one who suffers and loses. At present, however, it is impossible to organize the proper training of instructors for business schools in this country, primarily because nobody really wants to train people who will compete against him.

In connection with this issue of training instructors for business schools in training centers abroad, I should like to focus attention on one important factor that relates to the former Soviet Union's increasing contacts with the developed countries—placing orders for management training.

I venture to claim that the situation that has now become established is not yielding effective results to develop managers in the USSR. Lately, numerous not-very-substantial (to put it mildly) educational institutions involved in management training have discovered a gold mine for themselves. This gold mine consists of the opportunity to send Soviet managers to developed countries, in particular the United States, for training.

Judging by the examples I have seen, these schools are the big winners—and, evidently, their Western partners are getting something out of it too. As far as the managers who went abroad for training are concerned, because of their inadequate preparation (for the training abroad), lack of real interest in training, usually poor knowledge of a foreign language, and so on, they are actually learning very little that will help improve their professional level. A great many people desire to go abroad to study, in various forms—from ocean cruises to on-the-job training in enterprises. And there are opportunities to do so, because many enterprises and organizations have hard currency now. In my opinion, however, the main thing that interests the managers on these junkets is the opportunity to visit the United States or other countries, to do a little personal shopping, have a good time, and so on.

The problem of training our managers in the developed countries of the West is a rather serious and complex one, because it might lead to a negative reaction on the part of the public with regard to the actual idea of training managers abroad. It seems to me, therefore, that what we need is a more serious and careful approach to the selection of the Soviet partner.

With regard to training Soviet managers with the help of the developed countries of the West, I should like to suggest that at the present time, it would be much more productive to have instructors for Soviet business schools undergo training in the West. After that, Western schools could collaborate with them to design and deliver courses for Soviet managers.

The idea of setting up a school of management at Moscow State University came into being several years ago, when the opinion became relatively widespread that the country's leading university ought to make its own contribution to management training, as is customary in most of the leading countries. At the time, there were already a few business schools in existence; in particular, the Plekhanov Institute of the National Economy's School of Managers had become widely known.

We obviously wanted to open this school as soon as possible. However, a sense of professional responsibility held out over impatience, and it was decided to start training managers only when we would be able to offer a genuinely quality program.

In preparing to open the School of Management we focused our main attention on the following issues. First, the preparation of properly equipped classrooms. For this we attempted to acquire the necessary furniture, white blackboards, equipment for showing slides and films, and so on. There was nothing of this kind—and there still isn't—in the majority of training centers. Despite all the resource problems, however, we did not start the training process until we had properly equipped the classrooms. This was necessary not just because we wanted to have attractive, up-to-date, well-equipped classrooms, but also chiefly because this was required by the instructional methods that we had decided to use in the school.

The next step was to design the training course programs, in terms of not only their content but also the technology of conducting classes. Within a year, every course was discussed in detail at faculty meetings. In doing so, we attempted to ensure that the instruction would stimulate the students' active participation in the training process and involve them in assimilating the material.

The third step involved retraining the instructors, developing their teaching abilities, and providing them with expertise. Three of the instructors were sent to the United States for training, two were sent to the IBM training center in Belgium, and one underwent on-the-job training at IMD in Lausanne. This made it possible to improve their professional qualifications considerably.

From the start, the Moscow State University School of Management was assigned four basic directions of activity, or, as we customarily say now, we decided to conduct four types of programs. Program 1 is a ten-week program to train middle-level managers in independent enterprises, economic units, cooperatives, and so on. The basic task of the program is to train managers to work in a market economy. Moreover, the emphasis is not placed on imparting particular kinds of knowledge or on improving their managerial skills; rather, it is on developing their entrepreneurial sense and developing particular attitudes toward conducting their activities. Which is to say, as a result of the training the manager ought to have a good sense of what a market economy is, develop a readiness and desire to work in market conditions, and prepare himself to serve in the role of businessman.

In connection with this task, the whole program was concentrated on two key aspects: (1) a market economy (and working in a market economy); and (2) entrepreneurial behavior. These two poles also defined the structure of the program. There are ten conceptual training modules that explain how a market economy works, how an enterprise operates in the market, and how to manage an entrepreneurial venture; ten skill-building modules are designed to develop the managers' communication skills, computer applications in management, behavior, and so on. Finally, the program includes ten modules of a general educational character, designed to develop managerial culture, such as statistics, ecology, foreign language, world economy, etc.

For all the modules, regardless of whether they involved theory or practical training, class work was designed to activate the trainees' maximum participation in the training process. For this reason, traditional lectures are virtually absent, and extensive use is made of discussions, cases, and so on. The students are supplied with all the necessary materials, which in effect relieves them from taking continuous notes and enables them to take active part in the discussion. And when you consider, moreover, that the class group includes a maximum of sixteen students, it becomes clear that we have attempted to create the necessary conditions for maximum participation by all students in the training process, in active form.

Class work in this program is conducted basically by the instructors of Moscow State University. Moreover, an important characteristic of the faculty of the School of Management consists of the fact that, to a greater or lesser extent, they are similar to courses conducted in the leading business schools of developed countries. This applies, in particular, to such courses as the market economy, strategic management, communication, finance, marketing, and a number of others. We believe that the opportunity that our school's instructors have to undergo training in Western training centers constitutes one of the basic factors accounting for our school's successful work.

The ten-week management training program is already being offered in both day and evening programs. Program 2 is a two-year program that is comparable to Western programs leading to a master's degree in business administration. Begun in September 1991, it is the first such program in the Soviet Union. Two curricula have been developed for the two-year program. One calls for conducting the program jointly with an American university; the second is designed to employ only Moscow State University instructors and enroll only Soviet students.

Program 3 is designed to provide ten-month training for foreign business people. At the present time, eleven young Japanese business-men are enrolled in Moscow State University's School of Manage-ment. According to an agreement that has been reached, starting next year businessmen from South Korea will also be enrolled here. For us, these programs represent a major source of hard currency, which we can use to purchase equipment for the School of Management.

Programs of the fourth type are short-term goal-oriented seminars or symposiums for top-level managers. The basic task of programs like these is not just to teach managers how to run a business under changed conditions but also to offer additional opportunities to develop business. One example of this kind of seminar was the first sympo-sium, held in September 1990—a meeting of Soviet and Japanese busi-nessmen at the Moscow State University School of Management. At this symposium there was not only an exchange of experience in the form of discussions of papers by Japanese businessmen but also meet-ings that made it possible to establish direct business contacts between participants in the symposium. It is planned to hold such seminars regularly, both with Japanese businessmen and with businessmen from Spain, Finland, and South Korea.

The Moscow State University School of Management is a young institution. Formally, it has been in existence only since 1990. But it already has a history going back several years, when we were prepar-ing training courses and classrooms, developing instructional methods, and developing an extensive international network of contacts with the leading centers of the West. The school had already sent two students to Boston in the United States to take a two-year MBA training pro-gram at Northeastern University's College of Business Administration. Some of the school's students, along with instructors from the school, went to Prague to attend the World Management Congress. A group also traveled to Switzerland for orientation training.

It is not easy to predict the future of the School of Management. What is most difficult is to avoid the temptation, under pressure from people who want to enroll in the school, to use its training programs to expand the training process. The school's motto, "Top Quality," can be realized only if it is faithful to the style of work and the criteria estab-lished at the outset. For this reason, the most immediate tasks facing the faculty is to improve themselves and, in this way, to strive to improve the training. In our school, we teach managers that the client's satisfaction is the main criterion of their own work, and that all their efforts in a market economy should be oriented toward this. But we are not only teaching this to them; we are attempting to realize this principle in our own work. The students evaluate every class and every training course, and this keeps us from becoming complacent.

5

The Western Executive and the Soviet Executive

A Talk with Nikolai A. Kaniskin

What does the head of a Soviet industrial enterprise do? Anyone in the know will most likely ask in return: What does he not do?

Nikolai Alekseevich, you are one of the few people attending management school in the Federal Republic of Germany. I think that the readers will be interested in learning about your impressions and the way in which their executives differ from ours. But let us start from the beginning. How did you come to attend this school? What is it all about?

During Chancellor Kohl's visit in 1989, an agreement was reached to train about a thousand Soviet executives in the FRG. The Bureau for Machine Building formed a group of trainees from enterprises in machine-building branches. We were trained at Rund EM, a private firm. Most people in our group were directors of large enterprises and associations from various cities and were about forty years of age.

The training program is in several phases. The first lasts three weeks. There are three days of study in school, followed by three days

Russian text © 1990 by "Nauka" Publishers and "Ekonomika i organizatsiia promyshlennogo proizvodstva." "Zapadnyi menedzher i sovetskii direktor," *EKO* [*Ekonomika i organizatsiia promyshlennogo proizvodstva*], 1990, no. 5, pp. 16–26. *Ekonomika i organizatsiia promyshlennogo proizvodstva* is a publication of the Institute of the Economics and the Organization of Industrial Production, Siberian Division, Russian Academy of Sciences. Translated by Arlo Schultz.

each in all types of firms. We were initially dissatisfied with this diversity, but we later realized that it was necessary not to examine kindred types of production but to study the principles of the manager's activity. The training program, which included market analysis, sales planning, marketing, training organization, and labor incentives, was very interesting. But our hosts expected us to be totally unprepared, and we were therefore occasionally instructed in things that are common knowledge. Naturally, three days of training did not provide a deep knowledge, say, of marketing. But we were able to get an idea of what it was, to study its basic principles, and to draw conclusions. Classes were held from 8 A.M. to 10 P.M. We are now working according to individual programs, and every six months for two years we will spend two weeks in internship and training in the firm.

It came as a revelation to our teachers that we are able to conclude a contract with them for the delivery of our output. They were used to the idea that we are conservative, that we are controlled from above, and that we are not independent. Our country interests them as a sales market or as a testing ground for hazardous types of production, atomic power plants, for example, which have been shut down on the Rhine. But they are not interested in us as executives, specialists, and competitors. There is no niche in the FRG that we could fill with our output. Nor do they wish to use their firms' trademarks to deliver our output to third countries. . . .

A creative situation developed in the school. For days we worked for the future. We did what an executive is supposed to do and gave no thought to where to find materials and components. Unlike our system, training in the FRG is in the hands of practitioners. For all the respect I have for economic scholars, they can hardly teach us where to obtain money. We were taught by executives or presidents of West German and mixed (FRG–U.S.) firms, some of whom had forty years of work experience. These specialists received 250 Deutsche marks an hour.

Nikolai Alekseevich, you have had personal contact with West German managers. What is your impression of the level of their training and erudition? How do they differ from our managers?

The FRG has a well-organized manager training system in both state and private firms. Executives are trained at the beginning of their careers, and the best are singled out. It is considered that a good manager can be trained in ten to fifteen years.

I was struck by the following. We have absolutely departed from humanistic education and have begun training technical specialists who do a good job of addressing design and technical problems. But a manager needs to have a better and a deeper vision of man, to know his psychology and the principles that are the basis for interpersonal relations, and to scrutinize the system of management of both people and processes in the broad sense of the word. We are, as a rule, self-taught. All this is built into their preparatory system, and greater emphasis is placed on intellectual development.

Our managers were sent abroad for training in the 1920s and 1930s. I think that this is also necessary now. Managers have sufficient knowledge and intellect to perceive everything that is good there and to attempt to put it into practice here. The laws governing the development of the economy and of production are the same. It is simply that there, the organization of production is on a higher order of magnitude. They went through the stretch of the road we are now on much earlier without being isolated from the rest of the world. We, on the other hand, stewed in our own juices and are reaping the fruits of this. We have little contact with one another even inside the country. Therefore, all informal avenues for bringing us closer together—executives' clubs or associations and management schools—merit support. The principal task of an executive today is to transfer the attainments of humankind in the area of economics and management into our practice. Only we can accomplish this task. We must decide how to make money and realize a profit. If we are enriched by modern knowledge, we will cope with this task. If we continue to stew in our own juices, we will again attempt to invent a bicycle that is not the easiest to ride.

Of course, it is the manager's business to make a profit. In our country, personnel policy is the prerogative of party organs. The ability to make a profit is by no means the most important personal quality of a prospective manager. Nor does the election of executives make professionalism the main consideration. Therefore, even if you obtain knowledge, you will be forced to confine yourself to the framework of what is possible. . . .

Yes, the party carries out personnel policy because it is the ruling party and realizes its tasks through this powerful lever. But after all, the party, as the political leader, is interested in the well-being of the people. Both the Soviet government and enterprises are interested in this. It would appear that everything favors this. So it is not necessary to shut the door to people who know how to make money. I think that the views of our leaders—both soviet and party—will change. After all, profits do not increase because an executive is to the liking of the party apparatus.

But as regards moral qualities, there, too, much importance is attached to them. A person cannot be an effective manager if he is arrogant and rude. I think that we will sooner or later return to an understanding of the fact that the executive's activity is purely professional, and that there can be no coarse interference with it.

The task of increasing the well-being of the working people has become political. But political tasks are constantly changing. . . .

No matter how they change, profit is the basis of a successfully functioning economy. We must learn how to extract it. We have transformed enterprises into social security departments. We have lost the growth of labor productivity. . . . We have been talking about the training and erudition of the chief executive officer (CEO). But what of executives at other levels? Initially we literally "cut down" foremen-practitioners—the bearers of the best production traditions—through low pay and began replacing them with yesterday's students. We assigned them to experienced workers who "broke" the young men. As a result, we did not produce either foremen or full-fledged engineers. In my organization, I forbade the appointment of college graduates as foremen. Then the shortage of shop chiefs developed like a chain reaction. Old employees retired and new ones were not trained. We are now actively working with thirty-year-old engineers. We are greatly hindered by the lack of training of executives of all ranks. Our organization has to enter the foreign market, where our turbo-generators are two or even three times more expensive than they are inside the country. However, we do not know how to organize business relations or advertise our output. But the saddest thing is that the CEO's attempt to learn causes grumbling among employees: "Where has he gone if there are no components at the plant?"

The attitude toward executives is generally guarded. Perestroika *even started with a campaign against executives.*

The persecution of the negligent is understandable. But all executives came under fire. Their authority is undermined. Many enterprises are now spinning their wheels because of intraproduction democratization. Western democracy is accompanied by the scrupulous fulfillment of obligations, by the highest performance discipline. There is no place for demagogy at their enterprises. You receive an order and you carry it out. And not just because you will be fired if you do not. This is not so easy to do, and, moreover, an unemployed person receives more than a thousand marks in unemployment compensation. If he works somewhere else for three hours or so, he has his 3,000–4,000 marks. There is a shortage of skilled workers, as in our country.

We have confused democracy with anarchy. The revolt against enterprise management, however, has turned against the worker. Declining profits mean a decline in funds for social development and material incentives. If the initial processing sector at our plant sits idle for a month, we will all lose a million rubles. Our kindergartens will go without repairs, and we will all be without wages.

Of course, we deduct 65 percent of our profits. What remains is hardly enough for maintaining the social sphere. And if we were to fulfill all demands of the district city council, there would be no funds left even for this. But this is no longer under the executive's jurisdiction. Let these questions be decided by the higher level of management. But in production, it is necessary to work. . . .

What then, Nikolai Alekseevich, is the difference between Western and Soviet executives with respect to indicators of professionalism?

A Western executive is a specialist who knows how to make money. A Soviet executive, on the other hand. . . . I remember how we started telling people in the FRG what we do. I described the structure of management of an organization. It is a trio: the chief executive officer (i.e., the general director), the party committee, the local [trade-union] committee, and ties that proceed downward from the chief executive. I said that the organization has 800 persons who deal with social issues; that I have seven preschool institutions, two schools, a hospital, a stadium, two gymnasia, two recreation centers, etc., under my patronage; that I am now building an apartment house, production buildings, a polyclinic, and a district hospital. They heard me out and replied: "You should be a mayor. Those are the functions of a mayor, not a manager." This is our professionalism for you. A Western manager is oriented toward the main task, and he is trained to perform it like a professional, while everything is the opposite for his Soviet counterpart.

If I do a little of everything, the principal effort suffers. When there are no funds either in the district or in the city, we are told: Mr. Manager, you are responsible for everything. For building houses, for childcare institutions, for growing cabbage. Hence, plants get many appeals, departmental letters, and checkups. Our executive "drowns" in meetings, in activities, and mountains of paperwork. They, on the other hand, do not have anything of the sort. At best they have a personal computer. The manager sits at a clear desk. He is virtually inaccessible even though the firms are small (99.8 percent of the firms employ between 100 and 200 persons). In the FRG, it is of fundamental significance that everyone know the executive. Firms merge to form consortia and corporations while remaining financially independent. Our organization has a work force of 5,500 persons and scientific research institutes. We produce everything from turbo- and hydrogenerators to consumer goods. In such a situation, it is impossible to know all people, even though I rose from worker to CEO at our "Turbinka." It is impossible to control our giants, to cope with all the functions assigned to the CEO.

You said that the Western manager is inaccessible. Why?
Evidently because the firm employs professionals at all levels. While everyone says hello to the manager, can go up to him and talk to him, production questions are decided at a lower level, with foremen, with sector and shop chiefs. Managers have their own tasks: they are paid for formulating strategy. The qualifications of personnel are high because the system of training is continuous. They do not require overseers. Everyone works reliably and is responsible to the customer. The loss of the firm's prestige is a serious restraining factor. With rare exceptions, enterprises in our country do not have their own face because their output is sold by ministry foreign-trade firms. The transition is now being made to leasing. Who is seriously training people to make the transition to leasing?

Some enterprises in the construction industry have made the transition to leasing on favorable terms. What is to be taught here and how? One of the largest enterprises has received a subsidy of more than a hundred million rubles upon making the transition to the new model of cost accounting. Thus the "new conditions of management" continue to vary just as they did in the old days. Some are promoted to the utmost without determining whether this should be done, while others are "drowned" by being reduced to the common level. The same all-seeing uncle gives each sister an earring. What kind of economy can survive this?

You are right. We are working on the first model of cost accounting. We want to convert large production facilities and shops to a lease basis. This is difficult; there are not enough funds, and a large part of the profit is taken away. Incidentally, West German enterprises are also left with almost no money. They believe that it is good if they retain a profit of up to 15 percent. But this money is truly left to them at the production facility. The money that is left to us must be spent on social programs. Development in such a situation is extremely complex. The growth of the volume of production for the five-year plan period is set at 55 percent and labor productivity, at 62 percent. The increase in volume in our country must be accompanied by a reduction in the size of the work force. We have no other sources of growth. But workers leave anyway. We ask people to work overtime. And all this because we used all reserves in previous years and were among the leaders. The result was that we found ourselves at a dead end. There was a social explosion at the plant and a new election for CEO was held. . . . We are now trying to stabilize the situation because it is basically impossible to raise the enterprise under the new conditions of management. We cannot keep up with the progressive norms indicated in the new draft laws. The draft law on taxation called for a maximum deduction of 60 percent from profits, but after discussion it was raised to 65 percent for us and there is no plan to lower it. Our social sphere only takes funds. How should I keep people at the enterprise? With kindergartens? But 40 percent of the places in them belongs to the district council. . . .

Here is another way in which the Western manager is different. He pays everything to the worker, who personally resolves [his own] social problems: housing, placing his children in kindergarten, etc. The Western manager does not have a headache over this. But I have the biggest headache. I must provide the working person with everything he needs: I open stores at the plant, I organize cooperatives, I conclude contracts with collective and state farms for the delivery of meat, I build a consumer service center. We earn money here and also try to invest it here, at the enterprise. And what of our ill-fated construction? We transfer noncash money for it but we do not know how it can be spent. Everything has been centralized, taken away, and then dispensed from the top. Moreover, less reaches Siberia.

Let us talk about social protections for the Western and Soviet manager.

I shall cite several facts. The cost of a Western manager in the Western labor market is very high. Even in a small firm, he is paid from 300,000 to 1,000,000 Deutsche marks a year. For the sake of comparison, my earnings for the year in 1989 were 5,000 rubles. If we take the basic shops, I am in the third decile by level of earnings. In the FRG, the pay system is as follows: 3,000–4,000 rubles for a worker, a brigade leader receives 30–40 percent more, and a department head or foreman receives 6,000–6,500. A shop chief receives 2.5 times more than a worker, and a vice-president (i.e., a deputy director) receives 3–10 times more.

We have high responsibility and low pay. Most executives hang on by sheer enthusiasm and their sense of responsibility for their work. But matters cannot continue this way for long. We are already experiencing a shortage of executives, and it will grow. There is also a shortage of them in the West, but a different kind. Executives are prized and pursued. If a small firm has a good manager, big ones try to hire him away. This is profit! Social protections for Western managers, unlike our managers, are good. Five-year contracts are concluded with them. In order to dissolve a contract, the manager must be given eighteen months' notice and must be paid a large compensation. In one firm, it totaled fifteen million marks. One-person management is strictly adhered to even though problems are discussed in a wide circle in the initial stage. The manager alone makes the decision. Neither a council nor the owner of the firm has the right to change it, although they may influence it.

The work routine there is the same as in our country: twelve hours. But they know how to relax. They play sports twice a week and rest two days as behooves an affluent executive. But we think about our work both Saturday and Sunday. The organization of work and recreation there is very rational.

Creative potential is evidently widely developed under such conditions.

There are no instructions scheduling the executive's every step. A person must be free to make decisions. But we do not so much create as plow. We ourselves are a working tool. All this comes from our cumbersome, unmanageable system of management. It would seem that there is an executive, a single manager, at its top. But he is pressured from the side by the party committee, by the plant committee, by the employees' council, and behind them—city and regional party committees and the soviets. The ministry hovers over him, and his own employees "make it hot for him" from below. On the one hand, the executive is an elected person, and he must therefore implement the policy in which the employees are interested. Otherwise, someone else will be elected in his place. On the other hand, there are demands from the side and from above that he observe the state's interests (the stabilization of wages, prices, etc.), otherwise he will lose his job. And the local authorities expect him to contribute solutions to food and other programs and to assist in solving social problems. There are unique pressure tactics here. What protects against and diminishes this pressure? Laws? Not at all. The Law on Labor, for example, states in Article 234 that trade unions confirm the distribution of material incentive funds, development funds, and expenditures on housing construction. And Article 235 gives the same prerogative to the employees' council. The laws are like a pole connecting us to our cart and they do not protect us.

In general, there is an enormous distance between progressively conceived laws and practice. We are still bound by normatives. We cannot form funds as provided by law. Legislators mandated the Council of Ministers to bring normative acts into conformity with new laws before October 1, 1989, but we still have not received a single corresponding document from the ministry. According to the law, an organization's structure is confirmed by the organization itself. But we are creating a heating equipment plant and are not certain that an account will be opened for us. And if a ministry clerk does not change the normative document, the clerk sitting in Gosbank will not allow us to build anything with our own money.

Don't make waves—this principle remains dominant in our lives. Those of us who are somewhat younger rose up and now we are breathing heavily and noisily through two holes. . . .

Let us proceed to more pleasant reminiscences. What theoretical disciplines were a revelation to you or have made the greatest impression on you?

We have incentives, they have motivation. An incentive, as is well known, is a stick with a pointed end. They have a different system. A special lecture, "The Art of Motivation Management Is the Guarantee of Future Success," was delivered to us. According to Maslow, the American psychologist, human needs are divided into five levels. The first consists of physiological needs (food, housing, clothing). The second is certainty about the future. The third is social contact. Fourth are self-respect and recognition on the part of others. The fifth is the individual's realization of his potential. We are stuck on the first level of this model.

Let us assume that a firm wants to appoint one of its work force to a high post, but that he is not very keen on the idea. Management calls his wife in and tells her that if her spouse accepts the job, he will receive a high-class car and other material goods. Executives' wives and children frequently receive holiday gifts and bonuses and participate in prestigious lunches and joint weekends. People have everything in the FRG; nevertheless, if on your birthday everything required to host a party is delivered to your wife, it is very touching. This creates a special microclimate and inspires a person to work better.

We once asked, "What do you do with a worker if his work is flawed?" "We talk with him." "And if it happens again?" "That does not happen. But if it did, we would talk with him once again." We saw a benevolent attitude toward personnel in all firms. Motivations behind actions are determined, a person's good intentions are aroused, and his abilities are revealed. They are far removed from an authoritarian leadership style, from both gross and mild coercion. In all the firms we visited, management with the participation of the work force predominated (support by the work force, its recognition of the rightness of your idea, and its deliberate implementation). There are firms with two equal senior executives—commercial and technical. And this does not pose any problem. Of course, the Germans' discipline and their high level of personal interaction (loyalty, tactfulness) are very important in collegial management. In all firms that we visited, there were no loungers, nor was there haste on the part of managers, engineers, or workers. The number of skilled workers employed was lower than in our country. To be sure, the Germans are not as dynamic as the Americans. But punctuality and discipline produce no less an effect than American enterprise and tenacity.

So you got something out of the management school, didn't you?
I admit that at first there were many of us Soviet managers who

asked why we were being told all of this, because it cannot be applied in our country anyway. But time passed and I thought it over and came to the conclusion that all this is very useful—even information about marketing, which no one is engaged in as yet. I remember that when I was elected CEO, one of the points in my platform was the establishment of independent cost-accounting units that would engage in selling the finished product. I wanted to break the huge plant into separate little plants. I pondered and agonized. . . . But I came to the FRG and saw that they did this ten to fifteen years ago when they abandoned unmanageable firms. If I could use the experience of people who found the solution a decade ago, it would not be necessary to think up anything. Therefore, when we were leaving, we asked that the next meeting be devoted to finance, the currency system, the market, the stock exchange, to things we know absolutely nothing about. They promised to fulfill our wishes.

And we will apparently be able to talk with you after your next visit to the FRG.

Of course, if it is of interest to your readers.

6

The Woman Manager

Evgenii I. Komarov

Introduction

Today the term "businesswoman" has become very widespread. The fact is, however, that it has a number of meanings that substantially enlarge the theme of concern to us here.

Businesslike qualities are possessed by housewives and mothers who are occupied with various concerns in the home and family.

The term business or businesslike has been applied to women working in various sectors of the economy. Today, women engineers make up 58 percent of all representatives of that profession; they make up 45 percent of all agronomists, animal specialists, and veterinarians; 67 percent of all doctors; 87 percent of all economists; 89 percent of all bookkeepers; and 91 percent of all librarians. The greatest percentages of women are working in trade and public food services—82 percent; health care, physical culture, and social security—81 percent; and in public education—75 percent.

And, finally, the term business (businesslike) is applied to the woman manager. In this meaning the term "businesswoman" first

Russian text © 1989 by "Moskovskii rabochii" Publishers. "Vvedenie" and Ch. 3, "Kachestva i stil' zhenskogo rukovodstva," in *Zhenshchina-rukovoditel'* (Moscow: Moskovskii rabochii, 1989, 175 pp.), pp. 3, 66–92.

gained currency in the early 1920s when women communists, workers, and peasants began to enter management work in the party, soviet, and economic apparatus. V. I. Lenin once remarked that a woman can carry out organizational work on a large as well as on a small scale. Soviet rule is striving to ensure that "all working people, nonparty as well as party members, and not just men but also women, take part in building the economy."[1]

The qualities and style
of women in management

> *There is no doubt that there is a great deal more* organizational talent *than we are aware of among women workers and peasants, people who possess the ability to run a practical business.*   V. I. Lenin

The writers of works on management have been so accustomed to "letting the man call the tune" that for a long time it was considered unnecessary to attempt to define the qualities and style of women in management. A typical argument was that managers of either sex would have to do the same thing. Does the question of differences even come up? Is there any point in exploring them?

If we wish to explore the character of the manager, especially that of a woman, there is no way to avoid taking account of certain gender characteristics. The music of management is the same for everyone. But a man and a woman will play it differently.

In order to make an objective evaluation of the quality and style of management, as is well known, it is important to consider different views of it from above and from below.

Men evaluate the woman manager

In order to determine whether there is any difference between female and male styles of management, the author utilized sociological research methods such as interviews, questionnaires, and conversations. A determination was made of what is most highly appreciated and, in particular, what is not appreciated, in the specific female or male manager. Four types of positive and negative evaluations were obtained:

- men's views of the qualities of the female manager
- men's views of the qualities of the male manager
- women's views of the qualities of the female manager
- women's views of the qualities of the male manager.

Since this book deals with women, we will examine the first, third, and fourth types of evaluations. Another variety is represented by evaluations of "higher-level manager—lower-level manager" relations, which will also be discussed.

At the present time, the science of management has formulated more than eighty positive qualities, each of which has its opposite. There is no point in citing more or less complete lists of qualities, especially because they include many that are universal human qualities. It will be sufficient to point out those that are most often singled out by both men and women.

Moreover, it would be inappropriate to prioritize the qualities. Every person has his own perception of a specific manager. But in the aggregate, many opinions create a generalized picture with its own set of properties.

Men put femininity, good looks, and charm in first place. They do not like slovenliness and untidiness in a woman in general, and in a woman manager in particular. They do not like women who are not tastefully dressed or wear excessive makeup and jewelry.

No self-help books are being published for managers concerning facial expressions, gestures, smiling, business speech and apparel, and the etiquette of communication. For some reason it is thought that our management people have no time for this. Yet managers themselves—especially those of the new generation—say that these attributes of management are very important. Incidentally, a woman has an excellent intuitive sense of the rules of etiquette. But suppose some particular Eva Ivanovna lacks this intuition? In that case, she will have to learn it step by step, in practice, any way she can.

You sometimes hear, "Why are there so few beautiful women managers?" I think it is difficult for a very beautiful woman to be a manager. Beauty, as one might guess, requires a great deal of time and effort, as well as many admirers and amusements. A beautiful woman, if the author's observations have not deceived him, lives for her beauty, and for this reason remains a woman, ever a woman, in all respects. A businesswoman, it seems to me, is likable rather than beautiful, and is a manager who is also a woman rather than a woman who is also a manager.

The second group of qualities that men most appreciate in women managers consists of competence (knowledge of business) and professionalism.

Professionalism in business is defined as goal-directedness, practicality, good organizational skills, the ability to see things through, unity of words and actions, precision, duty, and industriousness.

Certain manifestations of professionalism, such as industriousness, are linked to feminine psychology and physiology. As a rule, a man who is doing a lot of work does not know how to relax. In principle, a woman has a better mastery of the alternation of the pace and rhythm of work and uses a variety of techniques for relieving stress, not least among which, especially in critical situations, are tears, confessions, and sometimes just heart-to-heart talks.

Considering the fact that a manager is constantly having to deal with a very powerful irritant—human beings—and that his is one of the most risky professions in psychophysical terms, the ability to relieve stress must be classified as a professional skill.

Men evaluate women's professionalism with various reservations. Whereas aloofness, brevity, and even sternness in business interaction are considered more or less normal in male managers, the same qualities in a woman tend to be perceived by them as callousness. What women need from a female boss is kindhearted, compassionate efficiency that is free of metallic components and sounds. In other words, the best feminine style of management, if we generalize the opinions of men and women, consists of a flexible combination of unlike qualities—kindness and strictness, femininity and efficiency, calmness and exactingness, gentleness and a strong will.

The particular nature of male and female efficiency leaves its stamp on relations with workers. People expect decision making accompanied by understanding from a man; from a woman they expect first understanding and then a decision.

The exact opposite of efficiency is bureaucratism or red tape. It is believed that a woman manager is capable of greater compassion and empathy—and therefore it is easier for a man to become a bureaucrat. A woman's heart is less tolerant of paperwork. Nevertheless, it can still become hardened.

In one of his letters, Lenin remarked: "All the work of all of our economic organizations suffers most from bureaucracy. Communists have become bureaucrats. If anything is going to kill us, it's that."[2] We can interpret Lenin's idea this way: When a woman becomes a bureaucrat, female management begins to die.

The third group of qualities comprises the ability to deal with people.

Representatives of the stronger sex cannot stand it when a woman manager, copying men who are not of the best sort, acts coarse, shouts, pounds her fist on the desk, and swears. It is best to remain what you are and not lose the good qualities that are inherent to your nature.

A special quality of women managers is emotionality. Men understand that without emotions there is no woman. But they will not accept purely emotional methods.

In one of her letters, N. K. Krupskaia wrote that from her girlhood on she learned from Pushkin's Tat'iana the ability to "master herself": "And she not only did not shiver / Or flush, or suddenly turn white; / I swear, her eyebrow did not quiver; / Not even were her lips drawn tight. . . ." In Krupskaia's own words, this ability served her very well in later life. Her contemporaries emphasized her restraint and her strength of character along with mildness and feminine behavior.

Today also, of course, there are women who know how to control their excessive emotionality, to curb their natural desire to fall apart or flare up in a difficult situation.

Now a word about authoritativeness.

When conducting role-playing business games with college students, I noticed that it was easier for young women playing the role of plant director to become authoritative. The young men played this role in a somewhat embarrassed manner, as if apologizing for the rights suddenly conferred on them. Most of the young women, however, discussed things in a businesslike manner with their male subordinates, conducted meetings, and shaped their own course.

I advised the managers (both male and female students) who began to play their role timidly and indecisively to get a feel for their rights and even to overplay them, using a more metallic voice and independent mannerisms. This instruction to be more authoritative was picked up and implemented more quickly in the business game by the young women. Some of the young men remained indecisive and timid until the end of the game.

Observations of managers and talks with men and women have shown that women managers develop authoritativeness for a number of reasons.

First of all, women have the idea—to a greater extent than men— that the manager is invested with authority and consequently *is obli-*

gated to deal with the appropriate range of problems. Authority without decisions is not authority at all. A manager who does not know how to exercise his rights is someone women consider to be . . . (here follows a long list of unflattering definitions). Another reason—paradoxical as it may seem—is women's natural gentleness.

This, in brief, is how men relate to the woman manager.

Women evaluate the woman manager

The woman turns out to be the stricter judge.

She is also attracted by femininity, charm, and good looks. At the same time, she tends to see the technical and financial sides of what it takes to be attractive, to notice individually winning and losing aspects. If a woman lets herself go in appearance, a man merely takes note of it. But another woman will try to understand how it happened, seeking deeper causes.

Women hold in high regard the ability to deal with people and to create a friendly and harmonious work group.

Just what goes into such a valued skill as dealing with people?

First of all, it is a special gift. No matter how much you train a manager, if he does not have this gift he will remain aloof from people, trying to have as little contact with them as possible (a clear sign of being professionally unfit). Such persons turn into high-class office-bound souls who are partitioned off from everything by a pile of paper.

Now let's take a look at Table 1.

A manager who knows how to deal with people is nothing like the kindly uncle or soft-hearted aunt. He can be stern, demanding, and brusque. His subordinates do not think that sociability, caring, and courtesy are merely techniques for securing a cheap authority.

Having generalized the experience and mistakes of many managers, the author has compiled a memorandum that may, at some time, prove useful to the reader.

Memorandum
How a Manager Should Deal with Subordinates

1. There are many ways to turn someone against you. The most reliable and subtle way is to insult his dignity.
2. The way to keep employees is, above all, not to say anything unfair to them.

Table 1

Qualities characteristic of people who know how to interact	Qualities typical of those who do not know how to interact
Ability to listen to and understand a person	Inability to listen to and understand a person
Respectful, polite treatment of people	Disrespectful, impolite treatment of people
Manners that do not debase a person's dignity	Manners that debase a person's dignity
Good will, attentiveness, sensitivity	Ill will, inattentiveness, insensitivity

3. He who hath ears to hear, let him hear—this is more than the gospel truth; it is a wise rule of interaction.

4. The worst thing a manager can do is turn into a kind of managing machine, a robot who can't see people. He then becomes something like a island whose living inhabitants have abandoned it.

5. Anyone who does not know how to find an approach to people becomes isolated. The isolated manager is one of the most pathetic of all managerial situations.

6. Dealing with people means giving them the best rather than the worst that you have.

7. Consider people to be more intelligent than yourself and you will begin to talk with them as equals.

8. One quality begets another. Indifference to people leads to bureaucratism, bureaucratism to self-aggrandizement, and self-aggrandizement to despotism.

9. It is possible to improve relations with people indefinitely. The main obstacle to this is our unwillingness to be more flexible and sensitive.

10. "*Connection with the masses.* Live in the *thick of things.* Know people's *moods.* Know *everything.* Understand the masses. Know how to approach them. Win their *absolute* trust. Leaders must never become detached from the masses of the led. . . ."[3]

Every manager has his or her own personal manner of interaction. Is it possible, nevertheless, to generalize what it is in a woman manager that evokes the antipathy of both men and women?

"*The lady in the white gloves.*" Outwardly she plays at propriety, respectfulness, and honesty, but in fact she indulges in dirty tricks and insults the dignity of others, using "acceptable methods."

"The cold and haughty lady." She is interested only in the work and uninterested in anyone's emotional state; she avoids informal interaction with her subordinates, takes no account of their worries or needs, talks down to them, does everything to emphasize her managerial superiority, and is quick with a hurtful word.

"The awful gossip." A woman manager may be spoken very well of by her subordinates. But, they emphasize, she has a very damaging weakness—gossiping, making catty remarks, and hanging out other people's dirty laundry.

"The capricious dame." Her distinguishing trait is being all wrapped up in herself, accusing every one of malicious intent and ill will toward her. She also displays a lack of tact toward her subordinates and eternal dissatisfaction with their performance.

"The bluestocking." People have different attitudes toward this type of manager. She is, as a rule, a single woman who makes categorical judgments about everything. She is persistent and industrious. Because typically feminine pursuits do not play a key role in her life, work is her number one priority, work and nothing but work, which takes the place of anything else for her. In this respect she is the ideal businesswoman who confirms the idea that the profession of manager demands great devotion, hard work, and the male ability to distance oneself from domestic concerns.

There are managers who have what is known as a wishy-washy style that reflects little, if any, of their individuality and uniqueness. The main reasons for developing such a style are to attempt to make oneself into some kind of ideal and to attune oneself to the style of higher-level executives.

In a manager of their own sex, women highly appreciate the ability to create a friendly and harmonious work group, an ability that is rooted in interacting with people and the desire to create good working, living, and leisure conditions for them. It is not by chance, therefore, that women link the ability to rally people together with the resourcefulness, energy, practicality, and organizational ability of the manager.

In their opinion, the ability to organize primarily entails bringing people together, directing group efforts toward the accomplishment of some task, and achieving mutual understanding. In other words, sociopsychological values come to the forefront.

The qualities of a manager are not set in concrete. They may take on

Table 2

Qualities of a Woman Manager That Are Not Acceptable to Subordinates

High degree of unacceptability	Medium degree of unacceptability	Low degree of unacceptability
Lack of restraint	Loudness	Pettiness
Hysteria	Nervousness	Jealousy
Impoliteness	Hot-headedness	Talkativeness
Coarseness	Moodiness	Tendency to gossip

other coloration and become their opposites. And evaluations of them change accordingly.

Why will a woman sometimes categorically give preference to a male manager?

As a rule, this results from a specific unhappy experience, some unpleasantness with a specific woman manager.

Table 2 groups together certain qualities that do not do credit to any woman manager. We can only hope that the managers will draw the right conclusions themselves.

No matter how highly people are recommended, what is most important is their self-assessment, their critical attitude toward themselves and their self-development.

True, managers don't like to dwell on this. What is the reason? It seems a manager who attaches importance to self-development does not want to appear naive.

For some reason it is considered somehow shameful and inconsequential. But that's wrong.

Here are the most widespread methods of self-development and self-control.

The reminder method. Being aware of his own shortcomings, the manager constantly reminds himself about them. Some even do it in writing. For example, they may have a list on their desk with entries like "Restrain yourself!"; "Don't speak harshly!"; "Don't get uptight!"; "Bosses don't have the right to get uptight!"

The earlier the manager becomes aware of his own shortcomings and undertakes self-development, the greater the likelihood that he will get rid of them. With advancing age, shortcomings become entrenched in work style and methods.

The shut-off valve method. As soon as passions flare up, the manager cautions himself, "No, this can't go on. I need to behave differently and find more flexible approaches." Used abruptly in this way, the shut-off valve halts the storm and forces the manager to take a different view of himself, other people, and the situation.

The restraint method. In tense situations, when passions are heating up, the manager starts to tell himself earnestly that any further "heightening of tension" is not going to lead to anything good. Sometimes it is difficult to restrain oneself. One would rather answer blow for blow. But he deliberately restrains himself and his own emotions, removes himself from the situation and immerses himself in other matters, goes someplace and vents his feelings, etc.

The "explain-before-acting" method. This is quite an effective method because it also forces the other side to recognize his own behavior. Generally, the manager will say to his subordinate, "You are aware that you are not behaving correctly and you know my usual reaction. Why bring things to the point of tension?" This kind of explanation encourages both sides to understand the causes of extremely emotional relations. The method emphasizes once more how much depends on the willpower, reasonableness, and patience of the manager in particular.

Methods of self-development should be neither underrated nor overrated.

There is no getting around the question, "Does the woman manager have the right to fall in love?"

Men have different answers: "That's all we need," "There are plenty of other problems without that," "She might, but she doesn't have the right," "Let her fall in love as long as the plan is met and we get our bonuses," and "An enterprise is no place for people in love," and so on.

The women answer without any zigzagging whatever: "She does have the right, she can, and she must!" There are some who believe that in former times people with a heavy, sanctimonious hand would write in letters of references the words—uncomplimentary and even belittling to a normal woman—"morally straight."

While reading about the women in the Lenin Guards, I came across the following episode. In the 1930s, one of E. D. Stasova's acquaintances, who had spent time with her in exile back in tsarist days, was slandered by enemies who accused her of various transgressions and "immorality." In an official message sent to the Presidium of the Society of Old Bolsheviks, Stasova wrote: "Nor do I agree that (she) is an 'immoral' character, because I don't think that an inclination to get carried away and fall in love is 'immoral.' " So there you have it, ladies and gentlemen!

The art of compatibility of styles

Management is the art of mutual understanding, of acting and pulling together on the part of the one who leads and those who are led. Without reciprocity there can be no results, only one-sided movement with great obstacles.

Of particular interest in the study of compatibility of styles is the relationship between the upper-level and lower-level manager. When gender is involved, it has the following varieties: male–female, female–male, male–male, and female–female.

In practice, a great variety of situations can come about between them. The range of these situations, even when they are classified by type, can be rather broad. In order to get an idea of the characteristics of managers of both sexes, I will quote samples of their opinions about each other (see Table 3).

Whenever the subject of the art of compatibility of styles comes up it is necessary to reckon not only with the characteristics of female and male management but also with existing patterns governing their evaluation. And it is extremely important here to be aware of and overcome typical mistakes that derive from preconceived notions, stereotypes, and sometimes simple unwillingness or inability to understand each other.

Anyone who becomes a manager instinctively senses how the special telephone operates that persistently transmits information about the merits and the shortcomings of the boss or his subordinate. It is a grave mistake to rely on information of that sort. It is more difficult to overcome a prejudice than to make up one's own mind at the outset on the basis of personal observations.

Analysis has made it possible to systematize typical mistakes in evaluating styles and methods of management (see Table 4).

One of the key factors is the effort to understand the other person, his character, the motives of his actions, his way of thinking, work methods, and so on. It is here that the possibilities of compatibility start.

The way a manager perceives another manager, as indeed the way

Table 3

Female and Male Managers about Each Other

Women about men	Men about women
Leadership	
A man is ambitious and tries to gain leadership. To ignore this is to increase the possibility of being "crushed" in office dealings with him	A woman is not as ambitious as a man and is more easily reconciled to the lot of a manager who is never promoted, deferring to the man. But among her female colleagues she wants to be the leader in terms of position, appearance, and attention paid to her
Public opinion	
A constantly encountered view is that woman was created not to manage people but to manage a household	The psychologically dominant opinion is that to work for a woman manager is somehow demeaning to a man
Contradictions	
If a man treats a woman as he would treat any manager, she sometimes takes this as somehow abnormal	A woman wants people to perceive her as a good manager—yet when she is in charge of people she will at times regret that they treat her only as a manager
Behavior	
As a rule, a male manager will not attempt to get people to like him, but will compel them to reckon with him	A woman is emotional, but this does not prevent her from finding more flexible methods of interacting with a male manager
Compromises	
Men make compromises mostly at the expense of such concepts as principle, honor, and dignity, and it is primarily the human side of managing people that suffers from this	Women are less predisposed to making compromises and are frequently unaware of the tactical need for them. By standing firmly on principle, they may cause stress to themselves, the work group, and their superiors
Effectiveness	
The male style is intended to achieve effectiveness in management; combining it with female style may yield even better results	It is more difficult for a woman manager to ensure steady job performance, because she functions on two fronts —the office and the home. But her efforts and persistence are to be admired
A word of warning	
There are three sure ways to spoil a male manager's career. The first and most repulsive is to take to the bottle. The second, also most insidious, is to take everything personally. And the third and most pleasant is to fall in love with his female subordinate	If a woman is a manager that's perfectly normal. But if the woman in the manager frequently awakens, it takes a special art to deal with her

Table 4

Typical Mistakes in Evaluating the Style and Methods of Management.
Measures to Improve the Objectivity of Evaluations

Typical mistakes in evaluation	Measures to improve objectivity of evaluation
Categorical judgments of the style and methods of management on the basis of "narrow evaluation" (one-sidedness)	Determining the causes of categorical judgments and striving to view style and methods more flexibly, less one-sidedly.
A biased attitude toward the style and methods of management (prejudice)	Shaping one's own opinion on the basis of a variety of managerial situations
Constantly negative assessment of style without determining positive traits (negative evaluation)	Determining the causes of negative evaluation of the style and methods of management
Inflated evaluation without paying attention to negative traits and negative methods of management (liberalism in evaluation)	Critical evaluation of the style and methods of management

any person perceives any other person, depends on their individual characteristics. We can single out *three typical situations*:

• compatibility of styles and methods of management,
• incompatibility of styles and methods,
• an effort to find points of contact through reciprocal concessions.

Just as in mathematics, simplifications are also used in the science of management to explain certain phenomena. If we reduce all varieties of individual styles to three varieties—the authoritarian, the democratic, and the liberal—we can obtain correlations to evaluate their compatibility or incompatibility (see Table 5).

I suggest that the reader make his own evaluation on the basis of his understanding of each of the styles, utilizing such designations as compatible (C), more compatible than incompatible (CI), barely compatible (BC), and incompatible (I). These designations can be entered in the right-hand column of the table, on top of the dotted line followed by the question mark.

In real life, everything is much more dialectical than simplified formulae and tables. Take some of the correlations, for example. In the first of them, as in the fourth, which fairly begs to be evaluated as "barely compatible," compatibility is quite possible. The fact is that

Table 5

Style of higher-level manager	Style of lower-level manager	Evaluation of compatibility and incompatibility of styles
Authoritarian	Democratic	...?
Authoritarian	Authoritarian	...?
Authoritarian	Liberal	...?
Democratic	Authoritarian	...?
Democratic	Democratic	...?
Democratic	Liberal	...?
Liberal	Authoritarian	...?
Liberal	Democratic	...?
Liberal	Liberal	...?

any lack of certain qualities that a higher-level manager may have (and he may recognize this himself) is compensated by the fact that a lower-level manager does have them. The autocrat is complemented by the democrat, and the democrat by the autocrat. A liberal may have a stern (authoritarian) deputy, while the autocrat's influence in his own sector of work is subtly restrained by the liberal. One manager's democratic character is not especially sensed, because around a liberal people tend to manage many processes on their own. And, conversely, the liberal's indifference to the life of the work group is replaced by the democrat's sympathy and caring. Which is to say, the phenomenon of *compensation of qualities* plays an important role in the compatibility of managers, their styles and methods.

Naturally, every higher-level manager will seek to find someone who is like him in style. However, not everyone who seems to be similar outwardly really is. For this reason, the compatibility even of styles that are called identical is problematic. What mostly happens with respect to them, incidentally, are correct guesses.

Similarity in the designation of styles does not at all mean that they will be compatible, because every manager has his own way of manifesting authoritarianism, democracy, and liberalism. One may encounter an authoritarian democrat, a democratic autocrat, and a liberal who is nowhere when it comes to democratism. A great deal is determined by the characteristics that are typical of the activity of the specific manager.

Thus it happens that the more deeply you explore the problem of

Table 6

What Subordinates Prefer or Do Not Accept in a Manager

Preferred qualities	Rejected qualities
The ability to take charge of a situation	Authoritarian-pressure methods of management
Delegation of powers when necessary	Constant distrust. Butting in on lower-level managers and interfering in their business
Ability to help and support people in times of need	Stinginess with praise, constant rebukes and chewings-out
Unity of word and deed	Negative attitude toward initiative
Creation of conditions to foster normal work by lower-level managers	Imposition of his own work routine

compatibility and incompatibility, the more difficult it becomes to make an unequivocal evaluation. And the most valid answer will be a table that is not filled in with evaluations!

There are specific things that influence the compatibility or incompatibility of styles. Male managers, as a rule, do not ascribe any special importance to how they influence female managers subordinate to them. The concentration of shortcomings in style and methods constitutes one of the most serious obstacles to compatibility. In contrast, a woman manager will reason, quite rightly, "Why should I maintain a style that people condemn?"

A woman might not be happy with the way a higher-level manager deals with her. Women, for example, especially do not trust affectedly gallant male managers—that is, those who are courteous and attentive around other people, but one-on-one are offensive and cynical.

One thing is for certain: the more attractive the style of work of the higher-level manager, the stronger and better his influence will be on the style of the lower-level manager, especially the beginner. On the other hand, subordinates will have to deal somehow with a manager's unattractive traits, fight them or get around them, adjust to them, and so on.

There are qualities of men and women toward which people's attitude is unequivocal—they are either welcomed or completely rejected by managers of lower rank (see Table 6).

When studying the problems of compatibility of styles it is important to determine just whom it is difficult to work with, find a common language, and build relationships in general. For it is here that the character of what is known as the awkward, or embarrassing, manager emerges, referring in equal measure both to the higher-level and the lower-level manager, male or female.

Among higher-level male managers the "Bluebeard" is considered to be the most difficult type. He demands unquestioning performance and the support of his own actions (even if they are wrong) in any situation, makes use of methods of command and pressure, and imposes his own line of action regardless of the opinions of other people.

These traits are also characteristic of female manager types such as the "Empress," "Proprietress," and "High-born Lady." The repellent trait is administrative coldness.

The "Hot-tempered Woman" is the other extreme.

In general, types such as the "Little Tsar," "Petty Tyrant," "Gung-ho Administrator," and "Boss Lady" are the least popular types, the one that are the least accepted by today's lower-level managers.

In the opinion of higher-level managers, the most difficult to deal with, for them, are those who tend to get into conflicts and constant clashes. People like that (whether male or female) are upsetting, arbitrarily demand a great deal of attention, and create an unhealthy climate in the work group. There are those who are oppressive; there are those who keep things bottled up inside for a long time, and then begin to get into fights and vent their resentment, disagreement, and spite.

There are also those who are awkward in another sense. They are the ones who, so to speak, are disturbers of the "managerial peace"— seeking, restless, out-of-the-ordinary natures. Clever and experienced managers who have witnessed many things in their time will try not to restrain awkward people but rather understand them and offer them as much leeway as possible.

Organizational ability

Good organization is highly appreciated both in everyday life and in the business world. Just how is it manifested?

The organized manager is distinguished from the disorganized manager (just as in the case of any person) primarily by a particular system of work. It does not represent someone's whim but rather a necessary method of imposing order on the work. Better an elementary system than the lack of one. It is possible to improve what exists, not what does not exist.

Managers use a system with the daily work routine of preparing and holding conferences and meetings, working with documents and personal correspondence, reading literature, receiving guests, monitoring and verifying implementation, preparing speeches, self-development, and other types of activity.

Any one of these needs to be backed up by industriousness. A system multiplied by industriousness yields results. To put it another way, consider the formula of organization: system—industriousness—results.

In order to make our assertions more convincing, let us refer to the experience of some highly organized women.

E. D. Stasova (Comrade "Absolute") always kept to her systematic habits, even in prison. She established her daily routine within the framework of the prison routine. Just as she had on the outside, she allotted six hours to sleep. She devoted three hours in the morning to studying law. She developed for herself a body of legal knowledge of the kind necessary to a revolutionary, which enabled her to stand up to prosecutorial and judicial chicanery and tyranny. Her intellectual labors were followed by sewing, mending, and keeping the cell in order. Then she studied languages and read the works of English, French, and German authors. In the evening she studied newspapers and political literature, which were passed to the prisoners inside the covers of scientific or religious books.

Her day was filled to the limit, and in this way a "prison university" resulted.

In her old age, after she had lost her sight, Stasova continued to work and maintained an iron-clad routine. From ten o'clock to two o'clock she and her secretary dealt with her voluminous mail. She would listen to a letter and immediately dictate the answer. After dinner she worked again. As evening approached, comrades would come by and take turns reading her the newspapers, using the Stasova system, which employed a definite sequence of the newspaper material. She continued to assign herself daily chores, as she was afraid of losing her taste for work.

Another brilliantly organized woman was N. K. Krupskaia. She had developed the habit of getting up at six o'clock and going through her "intellectual exercises"—writing articles, answering mail, and preparing speeches. She would work fifteen to sixteen hours every day.

A schedule was drawn up for each day. At the end of the day, a summary was made, consisting of entries in a special notebook on what had been done. A similar approach was used at the end of the week, the month, and the year. Here, for example, are the summary data for 1938: articles prepared—112; speeches—172; meetings—120; letters written—2,500. This large number of letters was due to the fact that she used to receive around 400 to 500 every day. In January of 1939 (one month before she died) the tallies were as follows: articles—20, speeches—16, meetings—12, and letters—240.

Krupskaia's coworkers in the People's Commissariat for Education greatly admired her organizational ability. She attempted to teach them how to plan and keep track of their personal efforts. Some of them would take up plans but then abandon them and work as they pleased. It is easier to be enthusiastic about other people's accomplishments than to correct one's own shortcomings. Good organization requires a person to overcome what is disorganized in himself and establish a firm framework in his work.

Acquaintance with people who follow a system inevitably suggests that self-torture and self-coercion are useless. It is indeed very difficult to be well organized, because one is constantly having to deny oneself something, to curb one's desires. There are those who, as they attempt to adopt a daily routine, get tired of organizing and believe that it fatigues them and deprives them of their freedom. But it is the "free artists" (as Stasova ironically termed those who are disorganized) who are most frequently inefficient, disorganized, and undisciplined. The lack of any key quality has its own negative consequences.

Of primary importance to the self-inculcation of good organization are the goals that we set for ourselves. In order to attain them we need to be systematic—that is, to have order and rationality in our life and labor. Spontaneity is irrational and therefore more "human," but in practice it does not yield results.

The chief enemy of good organization is routine, in the whirl of which the manager, without noticing, gradually forgets about rationality. Here he can be helped by various well-known organizational *techniques of overcoming routine*:

• coordinate the work among managers within the framework of a single daily routine;

• delegate less important matters to subordinates;

• blitz trivial matters at certain intervals;

• separate things by priorities: important matters should be dealt with at one time, routine matters at another time;

- complete certain tasks immediately, as soon as they come up;
- establish a morning rule that no one is to bother the manager for a certain amount of time, so he can accomplish his duties in peace.

In addition to systematicity, good organization is manifested in the rational use of time. Time literally infuses the formula of organization adduced above. System entails ordering the work in time. A person's industriousness reflects his possibilities within the limits of time. Results depend on time: it will relate to us as we relate to it. In generalized form, the results of a manager's labor are measured as follows:

- the number of tasks accomplished in a particular interval of time (day, week, month, year);
- the extent to which goals have been attained, the accomplishment of tasks relative to the management's goals over a specified span of time.

There are those who believe that a woman cannot make rational use of time and that any rationalism just tires her out. Try to substitute the word "man" for "woman" in that sentence, and him for her, and you will produce an assertion that is no less valid. Everything depends on the specific individual and his position in regard to time and possibilities.

In the St. Petersburg prisons, E. D. Stasova was an unimpeachable authority for the political prisoners with regard to the rational use of time. Under her influence, cell inmates worked out a tight daily routine. For a certain period of time, collective studies were carried out, with reading aloud and individual work, and hours of silence were observed. One of Stasova's cellmates wrote, "We would have liked to be as collected, efficient, and organized as she. Her indefatigability was astonishing. She was always busy reading, writing, or sewing."

While in prison, Stasova wrote a school textbook on the history of primitive culture. She set herself a daily "output" quota and completed it without fail. The prison warden boasted to his acquaintances, "That's the kind of inmates I have—they even write textbooks!"

N. K. Krupskaia made productive use of her time and accomplished an enormous volume of work. One index of her "labor productivity" is the number of articles she wrote—around 3,000 titles.

One time at a conference of the lecturers' group in the Party Central Committee apparatus, which she served as a consultant, people began to ask who had given the most lectures and written the most articles in the past half-month. Krupskaia led all the rest. One of her contemporaries paid her this compliment:

"You have Lenin's industriousness and methodicalness in your work. That's what training does. . . ."

Good organization will not tolerate a wasteful attitude toward time or the performance of needless functions. In terms of content, it tends toward what is rational and economical. In order to raise the level of rationality and, consequently, good organization, managers utilize the following techniques.

Evaluation of past labor: from memory or from notes they reconstruct the past day in terms of work (tasks) accomplished and take note of any superfluous or unneeded things that can be omitted in the future.

Evaluation of future labor: a planned list of things for the day or the week is weeded in order to root out anything that is not essential.

Analysis of time losses: for example, on the average every meeting in the manager's office starts five minutes late. Let's say fifty conferences are held per year. In this way, yearly losses of time add up to 250 minutes, more than four hours. This is like a stealthy theft of time from oneself—one of the most widespread of managerial diseases. Any analysis of time losses involves not only finding the time leaks but also getting rid of them.

The female manager differs from the male manager, but one of the similarities between them, as professional workers, is their ability to make use of time. This ability is the same for everyone, but does not have the same meaning for each person. The organized individual values time a hundred times more than a disorganized person. Generalizing the opinions of business managers, we can state that their attitude toward systems and time makes these the hallmarks of good organization.

Organizational ability: systems and time

1. The most accessible method of understanding the importance of systems and time consists of setting one's goal and attempting to accomplish it. It is easier for the person who has no goal, because he does not need to be well organized.

2. It is not the tools of management that save time but rather the system by which they are organized.

3. At first glance, a precise daily routine appears to be an ordinary and innocuous system. In skilled hands, however, it "offends" any waste of time and disorderly use of it.

4. A truth that has been validated many times over is that beginning planned measures on time not only constitutes an indicator of the manager's level of sophistication but also a strong measure of the inculcation of good organization in people.

5. The value of time is reflected in good organization, good organization is reflected in the performance of obligations, performance is reflected in reliability, and reliability is reflected in work precision.

6. The disorganized individual squanders his own time and that of others. The organized person not only "earns" time but also gives it to other people. Time is one of the most valuable and unnoticed of gifts.

7. Good organization has a special relationship with time. It increases time where there is not enough and shortens it when more is needed.

8. Many people would like to be well organized. But very few are willing to sacrifice their habits and entrenched work methods.

Professionalism

The quality of professionalism refuses to be separated into masculine and feminine. It is the same regardless of gender.

There are some business values that compliment any person. The most significant manifestation of business professionalism is one's unity of word and deed. It is the businesslike manager (woman or man) who is always faithful and dedicated to his obligations, his word, the letter of the agreement. Keeping one's verbal or written word constitutes a business zeal comprising honor, prestige, conscience, and professionalism on the part of the manager.

Deviations can happen with anyone, including business people. In principle, a woman may be forgiven more readily than a man. A woman is more reliable, so to speak, in terms of the future. She may not get things done by a stipulated time, but she will get them done at some later time because it is in her nature to be more obliging than a man.

In business, one's word is not a means of putting something off until later and soothing people's feelings; rather, it is a method of finding a practical solution or speeding things up. If the business-like manager is not able to do something immediately, he will not promise it. A promise is made only when there are realistic grounds that it will be kept. Rather than speaking and not doing, it is better not to speak but to do.

A person's professionalism is manifested in his ability to present the essence of a question in a succinct, clear, and understandable manner. Businesslike people view protracted speeches as a waste of time. Longwindedness is the enemy of business. Businesslike people are distinguished by this practical rule: avoid talking a lot and saying nothing concrete.

A businesswoman's word is distinguished by emotionality. There is no such thing, even in well-managed organizations, as a woman lacking in talkativeness and strong emotions. A woman is less predisposed to masculine mechanicalness and succinctness and more sensitive to words and deeds. A woman's word is multifunctional. Engrossed in talking, a woman may forget about the business at hand—words let her down. By talking more about a matter, she will resolve it more quickly—words help her. Having received a dressing-down from above, a woman will sound off—words heal her. Giving way to her mood, she will not give any thought to what she says—words hurt her.

Nevertheless, despite all zigzags, impulses, and emotions, the unity of word and deed is the hallmark of the manager's professionalism, whether woman or man. It is not without interest, in this connection, to examine typical manifestations of discrepancies between word and deed, which cause suffering to the side that counts on businesslike reliability.

Forgetfulness: The manager is quick to make a promise and assure people that everything he has to do will get done, and no less quick to forget his word.

The questioning monologue: "Oh, yes . . . so, um, did I promise that? And haven't I done it yet? Did I really promise? How could that have happened? Me, of all people? You think it will happen again?" And this is a monologue that takes place repeatedly. . . .

Endless promises: The manager assures you that he really will remember his promise. And the next time, for the umpteenth time, there are more assurances of his good memory. The individual's circumstances change in such a manner that no more promises are required. "But you see," they tell you, "things just happened that way. But, believe me, I always kept that promise in mind."

A businessperson's word has practical resonance. It does so especially in the babbling of the chatterboxes and windbags who love to produce oratorical effects, and so on.

First of all, if a final decision is taken in the process of discussions, exchanges of opinion, and explorations of points of view, the decision is going to be placed on the right track—that is, it is going to start being implemented. Good business practice is not typified by making decisions for decisions' sake, where one decision that is not carried out is followed by another also never carried out, and so on. The credo of the business professional is quite different: words that are turned into decisions are backed up by deeds in order to accomplish practical results.

Second, if someone appeals to the manager for help in the course of implementing decisions, he will take account of the circumstances and attempt to respond with action—providing materials, people, and finances. Not to wave sufferers away, not to delude them with verbal sleight-of-hand, but to give them practical help—this is the hallmark of sound business practice. It attracts people like a magnet. Whenever something happens, people turn to the businesslike person, the manager. Those who are not businesslike have it easier; hardly anyone ever appeals to them. A professionalism increases one's workload. Yet it is this burden that validates all its genuine values.

One clear manifestation of effectiveness is the manager's ability to complete what he starts, to accomplish tangible results. And the most difficult psychological barrier is to force oneself to do what is necessary rather than what one wants. A. M. Kollontai called this effort by a rather strange term, "buttoning all one's buttons."

There are some managers whose style is such that they typically start something and then abandon it half-done or forget about it. The main problem of such managers is that they are easily distracted, get carried away with fanciful schemes, lack a sense of reality, and shrink from difficulties. Strictly speaking, all of their professionalism is manifested in some kind of idealistic management. The person who gets things done looks for realistic ways to do it; the person who makes excuses for his failures tries to find "objective causes." For the effective manager, the yardstick is the practical result.

By referring to practice, we can discern *certain rules for accomplishing results* in the activity of skilled managers.

The rule of reality: It is better to set realistic but attainable goals than goals that are attractive but, for a given period of time, unrealistic.

The rule of focus: Not to tackle twenty jobs simultaneously but to select the most important of them and carry them through, not abandoning them half-done.

The rule of struggle: Results are a strong opponent that will not give up without a fight. In order to beat the opponent it is necessary to use a variety of means. If one is to fail, it is better to be conquered than to give up.

The rule of acquiring experience: Only by completing jobs that have been started does one gain the necessary experience of learning the "price of results." The higher the price, the more valuable is the experience.

A woman with good business sense has a particular advantage over a man when it comes to completing what she starts—she knows how to stop in time. A man ordinarily strives relentlessly toward the goal. Any stop or delay offends his self-esteem. He gets tired more quickly. The woman takes a different tactic: if the job is not getting anywhere, she stops, gradually regroups her powers, and seeks out more effective means of attack. Using flexible tactics to accomplish results is one of the key factors in management. And women can teach men a great deal in this regard.

When examining the advantages of a male or female manager, un-questionably, it is difficult not to idealize. But the image of the male manager has been praised to the skies for dozens of years. Why not, then, say something good about the businesswoman?

Yet another characteristic of managerial effectiveness is an under-standing of facts and figures, and the ability to evaluate and to take the situation and circumstances into account. The business-woman has her own special advantages. If in her everyday activities she is, in addition, "armed" with real facts, then she becomes simply unbeatable. How many men have been burned because of their male habit of trusting just one source of information rather than rechecking data, at least in casual conversation?

It is said that facts are like air for the scientist. But this saying needs to be made more precise by applying it to a woman also. And she is certainly ahead of the scientist, to whom she gives a big headstart on this count. There are frequent cases when male scientists, using the latest methods, prepare the "world's most well-substantiated" manage-ment decision for the woman manager. Having looked over the pro-posal, she may very well make an entirely different decision, heeding a barely perceptible inner voice—her intuition. And she will turn out to be right, because one woman always has more information and feel for a problem than a dozen men. . . .

The inculcation of sound business sense, it is very sad to note, was carried out in a rather peculiar manner in the recent past. Enterprises would be given obviously inflated plans that were not in accord with production capacity or the allotted material resources. Economists wrote millions of letters to the ministries asking that the "air" (inflated indicators) that was smothering the workforce be eliminated. In general, sound, statistically based economics was not held in esteem. Everything was decided by the all-powerful will of higher-level authorities and their views from their own bell tower.

And now this ability to conduct oneself professionally in business has proved to be very useful in converting to cost accounting. It has served to protect the rights of workers as stipulated in the USSR Law on the State Enterprise (Association) and to substantiate results. Professionalism in business requires real rather than artificial economic relations.

A very widespread management method, one that comes in many varieties, is *persuasion*. The manager needs to be able to persuade both himself and others. The method becomes effective if it is based on facts and figures. The professional manager is distinguished by well-argued persuasion because he knows how to translate any phenomenon into the language of interests and incentives, activeness and passivity, winning and losing, expenditures and results. There is nothing that cannot be demonstrated or repudiated in the business world. Everything is susceptible to some kind of measurement. But this is an art that needs to be learned; and one should make oneself use the method of persuasion.

At this point, an essential factor needs to be emphasized: the art of persuasion can be mastered only by someone who is dedicated to the job. Unless the job and the manager constitute a single whole, it is useless to expect any conviction from him. He will not be able to fathom what is happening.

Business will not tolerate an attitude such as "I'll give a little of myself to the cause and keep something for myself." To submit to a cause is to be totally in its power. Only in this way is it possible to fight for a cause, to stand up for it, to advance it and carry it through to completion—that is, to be a business person.

Notes

1. V. I. Lenin, *Polnoe sobranie sochinenii* [Complete Collected Works], vol. 39, p. 204.
2. Ibid., vol. 54, p. 180.
3. Ibid., vol. 44, p. 497.

Part II

NEW METHODS IN
MANAGEMENT EDUCATION

Introduction

Part II focuses on some of the new methodologies being used to teach management skills. These novel subjects and innovative instructional methods are dramatically different from those that prevailed before *perestroika*. In particular, they are worlds away from what I experienced as the only non-Soviet participant in an executive management program at the Plekhanov Institute of the National Economy in Moscow in 1979–80.[1] The one hundred executives from all corners of the Soviet Union who attended the three-month in-residence program listened to lectures for five hours a day on management subjects such as planning, production, and business law, as well as international communism and civil defense. While some managers stated that they benefited from the program, many others said that the material was not new: they had to know it in order to have been appointed to their positions.

Given the huge demands placed upon them to transform their organizations to become competitive in a market-driven economy, managers in the former Soviet republics cannot afford in the 1990s to sit passively listening to lectures about the old ways of doing things. Rather, managers must become actively engaged in the learning process in order to change their thinking and master the skills of market-based management. Fortunately, the alternatives to lectures, such as case discussions, business games, and role plays, which were just beginning to be used in the early 1980s, have been refined and tested.

Part II showcases some of these innovative techniques. Some are the brainchild of management experts in the former USSR and will be new to Western audiences. Others are adapted from well-known methodologies developed in the West.

Overview

In chapter 7, "Managerial Diagnosis: Practical Experience and Recommendations," Rapoport describes the method of managerial diagnosis of an organization. Readers will find it very similar to Western methods of assessing an organization's problems. Two themes are evident in Rapoport's article. First, like his Western counterparts, Rapoport observes that too often there is a tendency to try to solve problems before understanding their causes. To counteract this reaction, he stresses the importance of using specific techniques to ensure the systematic analysis of problems. Second, Rapoport emphasizes the importance of employee involvement. He describes several methods for getting employees involved such as the game "If I were the company president," and various innovation games. The involvement of employees in diagnosing and solving problems is similar to total quality management programs that are widespread in the United States. These programs can produce dramatic results in improving organizational effectiveness, but they require a heavy time commitment and sensitivity to employees' concerns about trusting management to respect their needs.

The themes found in Rapoport's chapter are also taken up by Prigozhin in chapter 8, "Game Methods of Collective Decision Making in Management Consulting." Prigozhin describes business games whose goals are team building along with problem solving and implementation of changes. Management consultants oversee six-day games, with forty to fifty participants from a single organization. The key feature of the game is that participants alternate working in homogeneous and heterogeneous groups. The objective is to let them founder in homogeneous groups (e.g., individuals at the same hierarchical level or in the same functional area) so that they then can appreciate the benefits of being in heterogeneous groups to solve complex problems that cross functional areas. This should be a valuable lesson for managers because historically Soviet organizations have been managed vertically and decisions have been pushed up to the top manager (*edinonachal'nik*). Horizontal and diagonal communication and collaboration have been underdeveloped. According to Prigozhin, these game techniques have two benefits. First, the importance of hierarchical rank is reduced and therefore the most capable people in the game may be identified for advancement in the real organization. Second, healthy competitiveness is fostered through intergroup rivalry between heterogeneous groups, and this competitiveness overshadows conflict within homogeneous groups. Prigozhin cautions that these potential benefits need to be weighed against other considerations such as the capacities of the participants and their psychological health and the danger of unquestioningly adopting game methods in daily operations or unwittingly replicating bad practices such as unproductive conflict and rude behavior.

Chapter 9, "Personnel-Technology: The Selection and Training of Managers," is devoted to an innovative set of games and exercises developed by Tarasov to select and train managers. These techniques, which comprise Tarasov's managerial assessment method called personnel-technology, are of interest to Western management educators for two reasons. First, some of the games and exercises may be adapted for use in Western managerial assessment centers. Second, the techniques provide great insight into the types of issues that managers dealt with in the former Soviet Union, as well as common managerial practices and their associated problems. Among the exercises created by Tarasov that may be new to Western readers are paratheater and duels. Paratheater is a sophisticated role play in which the manager plays three roles—scriptwriter, director, and manager. Duels consist of role plays in which participants take turns being the boss. The object of the exercises is to provide opportunities to assess the managerial ability of participants.

The insights that Tarasov's exercises provide into managerial activity in the former Soviet Union include the following. In the slalom game we learn about the wide range of activities in which managers have been involved. The number of apparently trivial issues that were pushed up the hierarchy suggest that managers need to learn how to delegate and to encourage subordinates to make more decisions themselves and be accountable for the outcomes. Other exercises show that managers had to coordinate activities that extended beyond the organization and the job itself: they had to send workers to the collective farm to bring in the harvest, they had to deal with the needs and concerns of employees' spouses and extended families, and they had to clear certain activities with the Communist Party organizer. Several of the exercises give a picture of a managerial style based on punishment, control, and manipulation. In one role play a manager who wants to get rid of his deputy sets him up for failure by sending him unprepared to a meeting with the president. The same type of manipulation is evident in the young specialist exercise in which managers make self-serving power plays at the expense of young staff members. In the dueling role play participants are egged on to be tough and abusive in the role of manager, as though people who do not appear tough and controlling do not fit the image of a manager and are perceived as too weak to be in charge. In the self-control exercise individuals playing the role of subordinates are expected to maintain their self-control while their "boss" tries to unnerve them by forcing them to say something wrong and then punishing them for it. Finally, in the promotion exercise we learn about the problems that arise when a formerly unprofitable section of an enterprise becomes successful once it is leased to the employees themselves. The success breeds conflict and jealousy on the part of employees in other parts of the organization, rather than a desire to learn how to emulate this success.

These exercises, games, and role plays are very powerful learning tools. Because they have the potential to cause participants to become emotionally charged and explosive, they require a skilled facilitator as well as a thorough psychological screening of participants. Some are reminiscent of T-group and sensitivity-training methods that gained popularity in the United States in the 1960s and 1970s. Management educators in the former Soviet republics would be advised to avoid the pitfalls of these techniques by consulting the literature on the American and European experience.

The essence of Tarasov's personnel-technology method appears to be to confront people with the old ways of doing things, to get them to realize the dysfunctionality of these old ways, and to teach them new ways of managing. Ekaterinoslavskii takes a similar approach to training entrepreneurs in chapter 10, "Diagnosis, Destruction, and Creation: A New Conception of Training Managers for the Market Economy." He argues that entrepreneurial ventures are currently dominated by unscrupulous opportunists, many of whom got their start in underground (black market) businesses. He wants to create a new breed of entrepreneurs who will behave in a professional and knowledgeable way. Ekaterinoslavskii has developed a three-step method. First, participants are given a battery of tests to assess their psychological profile. This is followed by a program to root out stereotypes and dysfunctional behavior, which is accomplished through exercises, business games, and role plays. The third step consists of implanting new knowledge about the skills and attitudes required to be a professional entrepreneur. An innovation in Ekaterinoslavskii's program is the goal of developing the complete individual. Participants receive instruction in physical fitness and stress management as part of the program. This comprehensive approach to business education is very promising in the long run because a major clientele is young people with little prior work experience. It will be much easier to train them in professional entrepreneurial methods without having to untrain them in old methods.

Zhezhko provides a review of the open game movement that has gained popularity in the former USSR over the last ten years. In chapter 11, "Open Games as a Method of Personal Transformation and Motivation," she describes the features of this uniquely Russian technique and compares it with other types of business games. Open games are a means of solving weakly structured problems that have no ready solutions. They are much more fluid than traditional business games in that there are no strict rules to be followed. Open games are conducted in conditions of isolation from daily tasks and can last several weeks. The goal is to bring about deep personal, organizational, and social transformation by having participants question the values they hold in these domains. In successful open games participants become emotionally involved, achieve self-determination, and learn the principles of democracy, responsibility, and openness. Open games have produced tangible outcomes such as new organizational structures. As with Ekaterinoslavskii's training program for entrepreneurs, open games are time intensive and require a strong emotional commitment from participants in order to be effective. Open games also require facilitators who are skilled in managing conflict and who can ensure that the outcomes are constructive rather than destructive.

Part II concludes with "The American MBA Program: A Russian Student's View." This is a first-person account by a Russian of his first year as a full-time student in an American MBA program. Shekshnia's observations about studying at Northeastern University compared to Moscow State University highlight the large differences in American and Soviet approaches to college education, as well as differences in students' assumptions and study habits. Shekshnia points out that his romantic notions of America and American business schools were quickly dispelled once he launched into his studies. He came to realize that, in spite of its general educational value, an American MBA degree is not a panacea. The number of individuals who have access to such an education is too small to make an impact. Shekshnia believes that a more practical approach is to send faculty members to the West for shorter training programs. They will be in a better position to adapt the information and disseminate it widely in the republics. Shekshnia also comments on some aspects of the American educational system that he was unaccustomed to, for example, the heavy academic workload, the high value placed on competitiveness and individualism, and the preoccupation with grades. These are important factors in shaping the way managers think and act, and managers need to take such differences into account when they interact with their counterpart in other countries.

As the chapters in Parts I and II attest, management educators in the former USSR are hard at work redesigning their course offerings and instructional methodologies. These individuals have wisely chosen to develop methods that demand a large investment in time and psychological commitment on their part and on the part of their students. There are no short cuts to radical organizational and personal change.

Note

1. Sheila M. Puffer, "Inside a Soviet Management Institute," *California Management Review*, 1981, 24, pp. 90–96.

7

Managerial Diagnosis: Practical Experience and Recommendations

Valentin S. Rapoport

Instant diagnosis of an enterprise

Instant diagnosis with written survey of personnel

In the work of a broad-profile management consultant (what is known as a "generalist,"), it is extremely important to know how to diagnose correctly actual problems and bottlenecks in an organization's management system. Whereas designers of management systems can sometimes afford to work on the basis of precedents and standard decisions, the generalist consultant cannot afford to do so, because what people typically expect from him is quick and effective help. And the effectiveness of this help is directly proportional to the actual weight of the problems to be dealt with in the enterprise's functioning. We can discern here considerable similarity to the work of the physician. In the same way that it requires a correct diagnosis of the illness for the physician's prescription to be useful, all of the consultant's accumulated experience will be useful only on condition that the enterprise's problems have been correctly diagnosed.

Another characteristic that distinguishes work in the management

Russian text © 1988 by "Ekonomika" Publishers. "Ekspress-diagnostika problem predpriiatiia," Ch. 5 in *Diagnostika upravleniia: prakticheskii opyt i rekomendatsii* (Moscow: "Ekonomika" Publishers, 1988), pp. 113–26.

consulting mode (compared with the planning and design mode) is the pace of the work. As a rule, the consultant does not have a great deal of time to do the diagnosis—about five to ten days. In such a short time it is difficult, obviously, to organize any complete array of information for an in-depth independent analysis. All that is possible is to mobilize the knowledge and ideas about the enterprise's problems as seen by the collective, with further refinement. It needs to be taken into account, at the same time, that a correct diagnosis of problems can be made only if the systemic approach is applied. Generally, an enterprise's problems are interconnected. Among them are *cause-problems* and *effect-problems*; together they form a complex "problem tree," and any attempt to examine and solve them in isolation from one another is rarely going to be effective.

In addition, an enterprise will have many problems. According to the infamous "eighty-twenty rule," about 20 percent of them produce 80 percent of all breakdowns and losses in production, and vice versa. The ability to single out these 20 percent of key problems is extremely important in the diagnosing of an enterprise.

Working in the consultation mode requires diagnostic methodologies that meet all the requirements listed above. One such methodology is *the methodology of constructing a problem tree of the enterprise based on data from a short survey.* In essence, it consists of asking the enterprise's personnel just one question: "Where does it 'hurt?' " The personnel are told to write down their problems on problem cards (one problem per sheet). The formulations of the problems are edited, classified, and utilized to construct a problem tree. We use two versions of this survey, depending on the purpose that the consultant has set for himself at a given moment.

If the consultant's purpose is to single out the enterprise's problems, he makes use of a methodology that requires the minimum intervention on the part of the consultant. The consultant poses the question rigorously, as shown on the problem card (Figure 1). In this case, people are to list only those problems that "hurt," and we thereby obtain a "microscopic section" of collective consciousness that is not distorted by our intervention. This provides a clear picture of the urgency and content of the problems (compared with other enterprises) and the problems to which workers ascribe the greatest importance.

If, however, the consultant's purpose is to diagnose the state of the enterprise, this survey will prove incomplete. In that case, a second

Problem Card

Surname _____   Position _____

Content of problem _____

Causes and the service that is at fault _____

Consequences of the problem _____

Attention: You are to formulate the problem itself rather than make any proposals or recommendations (measures).

Evaluate on a scale:

	0	5	10
A - the importance of the problem to the organization	low	medium	high
B - feasibility using the organization's resources	0	5	10
	low	medium	high
C - tendency of the problem to get worse in the future	0	5	10
	declining	no change	getting worse

A=	B=	C=

Figure 1.

version is used, which differs in that the consultant makes use of a systematic questionnaire designed to "suggest" to the personnel just what spheres of activity require an analysis of how production is going, in order to reveal the entire system of problems. A questionnaire of this sort is constructed in the form of a chart, as proposed by the Estonian consultant Erik Terk.[1] For the construction of such charts, it is best to make use of the methodology of functional-purpose analysis. Figures 2, 3, and 4 use the feature of decomposition with respect to incoming resources. Criteria have been developed to evaluate the state of each resource, followed by the feature of decomposition with respect to the managerial cycle, in order to attempt an answer to the question, "What needs to be improved in the organization of management in order to solve these problems?"

Having constructed a "tree of purposes and functions" on the basis of the subsystem being investigated, we gain the possibility of presenting the employees with detailed questions with regard to each of the purposes and functions: "Is this purpose being accomplished?"; "Is this function being performed satisfactorily?" Failure to accomplish a particular purpose or unsatisfactory performance of a particular function also gives us the problems of the enterprise.

For example, in the process of an innovative game that was conducted in the city of Iaroslavl′ in March 1986, to reveal problems

86

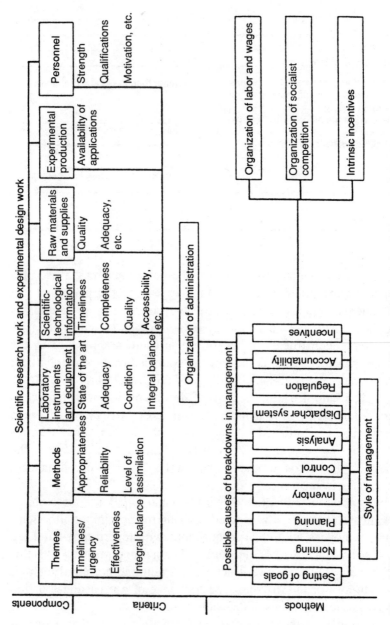

Figure 2. Chart of diagnostic questionnaire for scientific research work and experimental design work

87

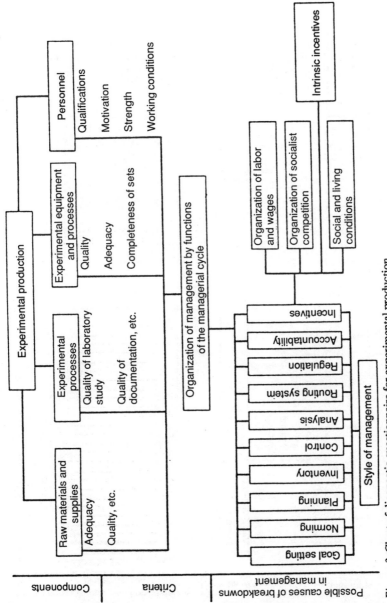

Figure 3. Chart of diagnostic questionnaire for experimental production

88

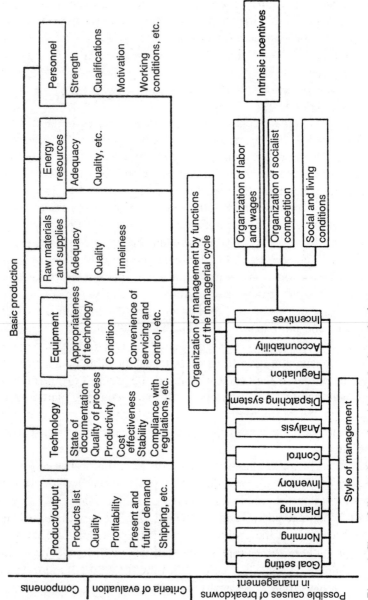

Figure 4. Chart of diagnostic questionnaire for basic production

relating to the intensification of production, functional-purpose analysis was used to produce the chart shown in Figure 5.

Once he has the problem chart, the consultant organizes a survey of the personnel, preferably in groups of twenty-five to thirty persons; the groups ought to be representative of the organization. In addition, the management and key specialists ought to be represented as completely as possible, while rank-and-file specialists, office employees, and workers should be represented by the biggest sampling possible under the specific circumstances.

For example, in the mechanical repair shop of the Pavlodar Tractor Plant Production Association, the following were included in the group to be surveyed: the entire management of the shop, all the shop and department chiefs, some of the bureau heads and their deputies, some of the leading specialists, leading foremen, brigade leaders, and workers. The survey generally takes one hour and thirty minutes and proceeds as follows. Having acquainted them with the purposes and methods of the survey, the consultant explains the problem chart and asks the participants to add to it. After clarifying and perfecting the chart, the participants are asked to look at each branch of it and note what problems, in their opinion, are taking place (one problem per card).

In the course of his work, the consultant looks through the cards, consults with the participants, and, with their consent, reads aloud the most successful formulations, or else points out typical methodological errors in the formulation of problems. After all the participants have set down all the problems they can call to mind, the group is dismissed, and the consultant, with two or three of the most qualified participants, reads through the problem cards. If several cards deal with identical problems, they are replaced by one that fully reflects the formulation of the problems.

The next stage in the diagnosis is to construct the problem tree. To do this, the cards dealing with the problems are classified in terms of their pertinence to the functional spheres of activity, laid out on large sheets of Whatman paper, and connected with arrows to reflect the interconnectedness of the problems. At the top is placed a generalized "output" problem of the enterprise (most often, it is the consultant who has to formulate it), and, thereafter, from the top to the bottom of the chart, "from the effect-problem to the cause-problem." The full chart of the enterprise's problems, as a rule, has the following structure: the generalizing problem on top, followed by functional problems branch-

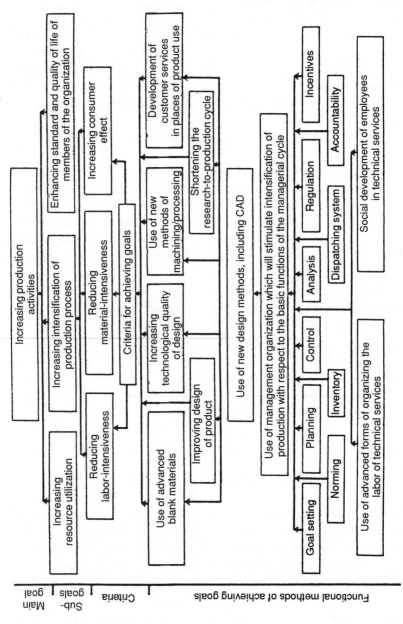

Figure 5. Chart of problems of increasing production (fragment)

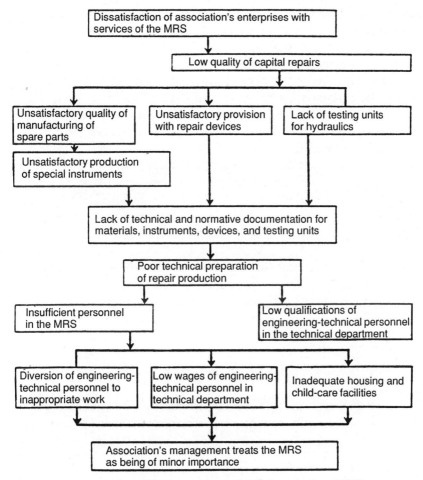

Figure 6. Fragment of problem chart of the mechanical repair shop (MRS)

ing downward from it and general problems descending lower—these are generally sociopsychological problems, those relating to social and living conditions. The chart concludes with problems of the organizational-managerial, general-systemic type.

A fragment of the problem chart is shown in Figure 6.

The problem tree serves as a tool for analyzing and solving problems. It does not make sense to undertake to solve an effect-problem until the cause-problem has been solved. In management practice, nevertheless, this erroneous and unsystematic approach is widespread.

To a certain extent, a problem chart that has been constructed on the basis of questionnaire data reflects the organization's collective consciousness and frequently gives a distorted picture of reality. For this reason, the consultant's next task is to *analyze the problems in terms of the validity of their formulations.* As a rule, not all the problems are subjected to this verification, only those that are crucial or seem doubtful to the consultant.

In order to analyze the problems for the validity of their formulation in the "quick-mode," the consultant asks appropriate workers of the enterprise four groups of questions relating to each problem that is to be verified.

1. The presence of a problem

• Is there an indicator that characterizes the problem quantitatively or qualitatively?
• Are there any figures and statistics reflecting this indicator?
• Are the figures and statistics reflecting this indicator reliable?

2. Sociological aspects

• Which social groups take part in generating or resolving the problem?
• How do their interests affect the resolution of the problem?
• How is their participation in solving the particular problem encouraged?

3. Resource aspects

• What resources are necessary to solve the problem?
• What resources are actually on hand?
• How are the available resources being utilized? Are figures and statistics being kept concerning their utilization? To what extent are they reliable?

4. Managerial aspects

• What organizational documents regulate management with respect to the function that relates to the particular problem?
• Are these documents in keeping with the rules governing a rational technology of management?

• How well is the management actually carried out with respect to this function?

• Is the actual management in keeping with the rules of the rational technology of management?

In the process of such an analysis of problems, the consultant not only makes use of the survey or interview method—he also studies the particular problem on the spot, and in difficult cases he organizes partial investigations using more complex methodologies.[2]

As a result of such an analysis, a certain portion of the problems receive new—sometimes fundamentally new—formulations, and the entire problem tree is more reflective of reality.

> For example, these problems were selected from the fragment of the problem tree of the mechanical repair shop shown in Figure 6 because they represent crucial problems needing in-depth analysis: "Insufficient personnel in the mechanical repair shop's technical department" and "low qualifications of engineering-technical personnel in the technical department." During the discussion of the problem tree (held at a meeting of the management and active personnel of the mechanical repair shop in the form of a game titled "if I were the company president . . .") it was revealed that:
>
> (1) the head of the technical department had no grounds whatever for claiming insufficient personnel;
>
> (2) the planning and accounting of the utilization of worktime and the monitoring of execution in the technical department were at an extremely low level;
>
> (3) no work was being done to improve skills;
>
> (4) available incentives were not being utilized effectively.
>
> This was how additional problems arose (Figure 7).
>
> Such an approach does not eliminate all the problems in the technical department that were noted by the shop's personnel, but it does show the possibility of substantially improving its work by means of internal measures.

After finishing the construction of the problem tree the consultant organizes a conference or a series of meetings (dealing with thematic portions of the problem tree), during which a thorough group analysis of the problems is held, and the formulations, interconnections, and priorities are specified. As a result, the diagnosis offered by the consultant is accepted by the employees and becomes a part of its organiza-

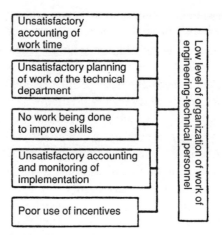

Figure 7. Chart of additional problems of technical department of mechanical repair shop

tional consciousness and a stimulus to successful solutions to the problems. At this point, the diagnostic stage of the consultant's work is complete, and if necessary he will turn to the job of consulting on processes of solving the problems.

Involving employees in problem solving

More than any other endeavor, effective management depends on the human factor, on the extent to which managerial ideas and decisions are accepted by the organization. The conception of management consulting is structured in consideration of this factor.

In contrast to the designer or researcher, the consultant takes account of the fact that even the most progressive managerial decisions, when dictated from above or brought in from outside, are generally rejected by the work group and therefore are hard to adopt. It is for this reason, as well, that the consultant's task is to structure his work so that he is neither above nor outside of the enterprise's personnel but rather within it, not a lecturer expounding *ex cathedra* but rather the mentor of groups of organizational staffers working to solve their own problems. This is the kind of goal that today's manager should also strive for. The timeliness of this approach is even more obvious to the extent that the democratization of management is expanded, involving as many workers as possible in management.

At the present time, there is an ongoing, active search for methods to involve personnel, including those developed by the present author. Thus, the technological process of management was created as follows.

Having determined the primary diagnosis—the existence of a problem—and having outlined it, the consultant and the director together determined the set of persons involved in it and created a working group of forty people. They included the deputy director for production, the heads of the main and auxiliary shops, a number of brigade leaders, and heads and leading specialists of the departments. The form of the work was the problem conference, consisting of two two-hour stages with a one-day break.

The conference was held in a classroom, with a blackboard and posters. There were two rows of tables at 45-degree angles, as shown in Figure 8.

On the consultant's right was a "team" of production workers; on the left was a "team" from the auxiliary shops and the plant administration departments.

On the *first day*, having presented his opinion briefly about the basic problem, the consultant obtained the participants' confirmation that the problem was indeed of prime importance to the collective. After that, the following slogan was written on the blackboard: "We are all in the same boat." It was met with approval, and they set themselves the task of constructing a chart of the problems that would have to be diagnosed and dealt with.

The consultant drew a rectangular "workplace" on the blackboard showing the appropriate product at the output end and then asked people to name all the inputs. The chart was constructed by means of the consultant's leading questions. During the discussion, special attention was focused on the criteria of quality with respect to every input, and possible means of influencing them, both organizational and those relating to resources. After that, a brainstorming session was organized to promote diagnostic thinking. Each group consisting of four persons seated at the same table was told to make use of the problem chart, discuss all the problems, and appoint someone to report. The speakers took turns presenting their group's opinion (the reports were allotted one minute each). In this way, all forty persons were given the opportunity to take active part in the work for twenty minutes. The directions of the work and the rules governing the formulation of problems became clearer (thanks to dialogue between the speakers and the consultant).

After a brief recess, during which there was discussion of the problems in the hallways, the participants tackled the main task of the first

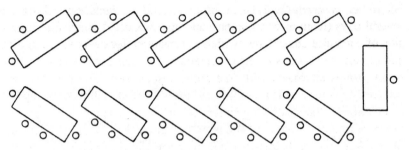

Figure 8. Chart of placement of conference participants

round of the conference—filling out the problem cards, which took about twenty-five minutes. On this note, the first round of the conference ended.

On the *second day*, the consultant, working with a close group of five people, constructed a problem tree on the basis of the cards turned in, sorted in accordance with the problem chart's branches. In this way, the problem tree became similar to the aforementioned chart and its basic shortcomings became obvious. For this reason, the following was noted to be the main problem: "Not everyone in our boat is pulling his weight."

For half of the second day, the consultant discussed the problems and ways to solve them with the main members of the working group, gradually providing expertise and possibilities for making use of it.

On the *third day* the second round of the conference was held. Fifteen minutes were spent in inspecting the problem tree, after which there was a brainstorming session to find ideas for solving the problems. This resulted in an "idea portfolio," which became the object of discussion. The debate led to the selection of the basic ideas for working out the technology of managing workplace servicing. The final formulation was carried out by a small working group that added the finishing touches after the conference was over, taking several days to do so.

In this way, most of the workers who were interested took part in all phases of the process of developing solutions to the problems, having understood the origins and the content of the decisions that were made. As a result, they had a sense of involvement in it, which had a positive influence on the adoption of decisions in the life of the enterprise.

An even more effective instrument for involving personnel (one designed to deal with general, weakly structured problems) is what are known as "innovation games." Strictly speaking, they are not games but rather *problem-conferences using special methodology.*[3] They last several days (from three to seven), and are conducted under the supervision of a team of consultants (with one consultant for every seven or eight participants or sections in the conference). At such conferences, work in small groups alternates with intergroup discussions. The handling of a task at the conference is accomplished using the following technology: (1) elucidation of the task; (2) construction of an ideal situation; (3) analysis of the normative situation; (4) analysis of the real situation; (5) detection of retrospective problems (the gap between the normative and the real situations); (6) detection of prospective problems (the gap between the ideal and the real situations); (7) search for and selection of ideas to be dealt with; (8) formulation of a rough plan to deal with the problems; (9) formulation of a mechanism to accomplish the plan; (10) determination of one's own role in accomplishing the plan.

In the process of working in small groups, we use a large set of sociopsychological methodologies of involving every participant under the general slogan, "Everyone's opinion may prove useful." We will not describe these methodologies here; that is a subject for special publications. In addition, extensive use is made of systems analysis, functional-purpose analysis, morphological analysis of phenomena, and so on.

> *From a plant's in-house newspaper* (concerning the results of holding such a game-conference):
> We had thought that there was no innovation that our famous plant would be surprised at—but one like this? During days of feverish excitement at the plant, its managers and employee council members get on an Icarus Bus and ride out into the countryside to a recreation center. What for? To play! And the fact that these games were called *business games* did nothing to reduce a certain skepticism or ironic astonishment on the part of those who went and those who remained.
>
> *From the program of a scientific-practical seminar:*
> . . . the seminar is being held, by decision of the management and the party committee, as the concluding stage of a lengthy management consultation. Its participants are the most thoughtful, farsighted, and creative representatives of the basic groups of employees. The basic method of the seminar comprises *innovation games* as a technique of group problem solving, a technique for training the participants and making maximum use of their experience, knowledge, and creative and intellectual potential.

The consultants helped to solve a large number of problems of great importance to the plant: they helped determine the causes of the plant's prolonged crisis and found specific ways to solve them. In addition, they taught managers how to think together and inculcated skills of collective searching for solutions. . . .

The consultants also faced another supertask: that of bringing together those who have to manage the plant, on whose shoulders lies the responsibility for realizing the strategy of enterprise development that was worked out during the seminar.

The seminar participants' intensive working days lasted thirteen to fourteen hours each. . . . Participants in the games were divided into three working groups that discussed plant problems of most concern to them. In addition to these groups, there were arbiters who evaluated all aspects of the work during discussion. Later on, a polishing group got involved. Its task was to bring the decisions that were made up to the level of authoritative documents.

From the seminar program:

All forms of the work are designed to develop new things—new ideas, decisions, forms of organization, and methods and techniques of solving problems. . . .

It should be emphasized, moreover, that the consultants never suggested solutions to the participants in the seminar-game. They merely helped them to evaluate proposed solutions and directed the movement of the general thinking. . . . And, again, their task was to involve every "player" and all those in attendance to take part with maximum output and interest in formulating and solving problems. I had occasion to witness a number of clever psychological methods and techniques as I observed the work of the organizers. . . .

Well, the results of this all-encompassing collective "brainstorming" are at hand. The problems that plague the plant have been determined, the tasks requiring solution have been mapped out, and the ways to solve them have been proposed.

In conclusion, it is worthwhile to quote excerpts from the seminar participants' response to the question, "What is the most valuable thing you have accomplished at the seminar?" It is familiarization with the method, a better understanding of what is taking place in the plant, new information about the enterprise, opportunities to take part in a useful endeavor, and so on.

(The author must remind his readers at this point that, in accordance with the ethics of management consulting, he cannot cite the information obtained, indicate address, names, titles, and so on, without the client's consent. Such publication can be authorized only by internal consultants at their own discretion.)

* * *

I have attempted to set forth my own experience of management consulting, singling out diagnostic problems. Although I do not consider it above reproach, I hope, nevertheless, that it will prove valuable to my colleagues and, in particular, beginning consultants. For my part, I would be grateful for readers' reactions—comments, proposals, and their own solutions as well. An exchange of knowledge among specialists is essential for general success in consulting activities.

Notes

1. Erik Terk, *Priniatie upravlencheskikh reshenii. Metody prikladnogo sistemnogo analiza* [Management Decision Making. Methods of Applied Systems Analysis] (Tallinn: MIPK ESSR, 1983), pp. 29–33.
2. V. Sh. Rapoport, "Sistemnyi podkhod k upravleniiu proizvodstvom" [The Systems Approach to Production Management], *EKO*, 1980, nos. 10–11.
3. V. S. Dudchenko, et al., *Programma innovatsionnoi igry* [Program of the Innovation Game] (Iaroslavl: Iaroslavl Affiliate of IPKNeftekhim [Petrochemical Industry Training Institute], 1987).

8

Game Methods of Collective Decision Making in Management Consulting

Arkadii I. Prigozhin

The social character of today's restructuring of society is such that it cannot be accomplished without involving managers and employees in the process of management decisions and procedures for implementing them. It is for this reason that in recent years management consultants—specialists in dealing with organizational problems—have begun to make more extensive use of social-psychological methods—especially game methods—in the joint search for fundamentally new solutions and accelerated development of organizations.

Characteristics of management consulting

Intensification of economic development is possible only if managerial caliber is substantially enhanced. At the same time, most managers are engineers and economists by education and tend to master the skills of management empirically. This accounts for their notorious technocratism and stereotypical managerial thinking, their inclination to use standard solutions, the familiar methods they mastered at one time or

Russian text © 1988 by "Moskovskii rabochii" Publishers. "Igrovye metody kollektivnykh reshenii v praktike upravlencheskogo konsul'tirovaniia," in *Kak i kem upravliat': opyt, problemy, mneniia. Sbornik* [How and Whom to Manage: Experience, Problems, and Opinions. A Collection] (Moscow: "Moskovskii rabochii" Publishers, 1988, 230 pp.), pp. 74–94.

another to deal with new tasks. All of these factors constitute a perceptible brake on restructuring the national economy, which is a reserve of conservatism.

The system of management development programs via the appropriate institutes and courses goes only part way in improving the situation. In the sectorial management development institutes, the management cycle is allotted an unacceptably small number of hours, and even that time is filled generally with college-type material that is frequently detached from managerial practice, with excessive theory or popular oversimplification. Even active methods of classroom training (primarily business games) deal only with abstract situations.

Nor can the extensive network of scientific and project-planning organizations solve the problem completely. Why? First of all, they are oriented toward standard recommendations, while management consultants adapt such solutions to the specific conditions of concrete client organizations. Second, consultants frequently undertake to solve purely local, sometimes unique, problems of individual organizations. Third, the present widespread system of interorganizational contracts is designed primarily to implement large-scale and long-term research and development projects carried out by whole collectives, whereas management consulting makes it possible to find efficient solutions to problems of varying significance using the efforts of one to four consultants in a comparatively short time on the basis of labor agreements.

Hence, any substantial upgrading of the professional level of managers and the quality of management effort is possible only if scientific and project development, and institute training, is supplemented by management consulting in the actual workplace, in the everyday practice of managing production and the work group.

The development of management consulting services in our country is also important from the standpoint of the effectiveness of international economic and scientific-technological ties. The most typical situation, unfortunately, is that we build whole plants and mines in foreign countries and then bring in specialists from Western countries to manage them.

In our country, professional consultants—practicing specialists in the improvement of management—began to appear in the mid-1970s. The first among them were given the opportunity to study the forms and methods of management consulting abroad. By adapting these methods to our conditions and successfully practicing them in enterprises and institutions and publicizing their experience at conferences and in the specialized press, they created a steady demand for their services among leading managers. In response to this demand, a number of individuals in scientific and educational institutes and the enterprises themselves began to specialize professionally in this field. Seminars and conferences are being held to exchange methodological experience. Pamphlets and articles in journals have appeared. A specialized commission has been created within the framework of the USSR Union of Scientific and Engineering Societies. The most highly qualified specialists in management consulting are working at Moscow State University, the All-Union Scientific Research Institute of Systems Research (USSR Academy of Sciences), the International Scientific Research Institute of Management, and the Moscow Institute of Management; in the Estonian SSR, in Tbilisi, Novosibirsk, Cheliabinsk, Voroshilovgrad, Saratov, and elsewhere. Today, several thousand specialists are involved in management consulting all over the country, and their number is growing.

The necessity of organizing a management consulting service in this country has been addressed by *Pravda* (August 19, 1982) and *Sovetskaia Rossiia* (February 6 and June 28, 1985). Similar initiatives have also originated among consultants themselves.

But why is it that the development of this type of professional activity is becoming so urgent today?

The professionalization of intermediary functions is a worldwide tendency. In all the industrially developed countries, and in ours as well, supply firms, design firms, information firms, and other types are coming into being. We have definitely lagged behind most other countries as far as management consulting is concerned. The experience of a number of European socialist and capitalist countries, as well as our own, indicates that the activity of management consultants can substantially influence the acceleration of scientific-technological progress, activization of the human factor in production, timely renovation of structures and methods of management, and so on.

Management consulting constitutes expert aid to the managers of organizations in dealing with tasks of restructuring management under changing conditions at home and abroad. A management consultant is a specialist in improving organizational structures, decision-making processes, management style and methods, employee selection and deployment, and so on. Some consultants specialize in general problems of management—formulation of an organization's strategy, restructuring of its components, improvement of relations in the collective, intensification of innovation work, and so forth. Others specialize in relatively specific yet universal tasks such as setting up a system of document circulation, employee certification, monitoring order fulfillment, and so on. The expert nature of this kind of help means that as a rule it is provided at the request of the manager concerned and has the character of a recommendation.

Generally, those who serve as management consultants are experienced production workers who know management theory, as well as workers in scientific and design organizations and higher educational institutions who are thoroughly familiar with production. At present they are providing consultation work mainly on a contractual basis or on the basis of an individual agreement with the client.

Our own experience as well as experience abroad shows that whereas initially management consultants tended to be former managers, as the forms and methods of consulting increasingly improved they included more and more research organization personnel. The latter have even tended to be in competition with the former, inasmuch as they are not so much resorting to direct recommendations as involving clients in the process of recognizing the real problems of their organizations and searching for ways to solve them. This approach makes it possible to find solutions that are most appropriate for local conditions while enabling management personnel to feel they are participating in the consulting and to perceive the result as their own. They become more involved in implementing the solution that has been determined, thus increasing the effectiveness of the consultant's work. At the same time, managers and specialists of the client organization are learning new methods of analyzing the situation, detecting problems, looking for solutions, and cooperating with one another.

The management consultant starts with the local problems of every specific organization (department), beginning with a diagnosis—that is, detecting the most urgent problems—and then seeking ways to solve them.

Management consulting is a vital tool in the dissemination of modern scientific accomplishments and advanced experience in the field of management. Conducting its work in a variety of organizations as it does, it not only implements the recommendations of science there but also accumulates local findings, improvements, and ideas that it passes on to other clients.

The activity of the management consultant, as a rule, is concerned with improving executives' managerial qualifications. The consultant introduces new ideas, shakes loose stereotypes in their thinking, and brings in professional training drills.

Methodologically, the basic types of management consulting are divided into:

• consultation on a project, in which the consultant, on the basis of diagnosis and his own knowledge and experience, himself works out and offers to the leadership of the organizations (departments) a plan or specific solution to an actual problem;

• consultation on a process, in which the consultant uses specialized means to organize the group work of the client organization, in order to seek the needed solution (for example, in the form of problem-oriented conferences or practical business games);

• consultation via reflection, in which the consultant, based on his diagnosis, presents the management with a picture of the latter's activity in order to encourage it to realize its own mistakes and, in the future, strive to correct its behavior;

• consultation via reciprocal instruction, in which the consultant, using a special program, organizes the direct exchange of skills and accomplishments between managers in the services and organizations;

• training consultation, in which the consultant, in a lecture-room situation, demonstrates to management personnel tested ways and means of dealing with a variety of nontrivial tasks.

In practice, consultants use a combination of these methods, depending on the character of the task and the situation in the organization.

A practical business game

Among the social methods of management consulting, increased attention has been focused on those that enable the consultant to collaborate actively with different groups of personnel in the client organization and to involve the segments of the collective in accomplishing their shared tasks.

This applies to cases where the consultant cannot immediately offer the client organization a solution to a vital problem. He has made a diagnosis and determined the difficulties, but neither the scientific recommendations that are familiar to him nor his own or his colleagues' practical experience enable him to formulate recommendations.

At that point, the consultant advises the managers to conduct a business game.

The history and overall purpose of business games are well known, of course. They are called business games to distinguish them from athletic and military games, amusements, and so on. We are talking about those that are most widespread today, the training business games. The essence is to simulate (generally on a model or some kind of formalized basis) certain actual or imaginary situations in order to develop the game participants' decision-making skills under similar circumstances. In games of this sort, the emphasis is on the hypothetical: the situation is "someone else's" and the decision, however right it may be, is not intended to be carried out.

But the management consultant offers his clients a completely different type of business game. In contrast to training business games he may single out a relatively new, independent direction of what might be called practical business games—which, although on a different methodological and methodical basis, are designed to shape the actual process of formulating new management decisions at a radical level. At the same time, the development of personnel and intraorganizational relations is also taking place. What is important is that the practical business game does not simulate anything but is dealing with concrete problems in the particular organization; the solution arrived at in the course of the game is not intended for the purpose of evaluating its authors' abilities (although the factor of evaluation may be overtly or latently present) but rather for use in subsequent practice by the game's participants themselves. This definitely changes attitudes toward it on the part of all those involved, because this is what constitutes the main interest of the majority of the organization's personnel.

In addition, it does not call for consultation on a project but rather a process of working out a solution, for which it provides the game tools to the organization.

The practical business game is intended to produce a twofold result: the formulation of concrete recommendations for dealing with a task at hand and the development of participants' skills of cooperation and finding collective solutions to shared problems.

The game is preceded by an organizational diagnosis, conducted by the organizers of the game in order to map out its specific tasks and goals.

The intensiveness and productiveness of the game are a result of its combining methods of management consulting and group dynamics.

The management consultants provide the game participants with analytical thinking charts and specialized questionnaires; they encourage the most promising of the ideas expressed, inform participants about advanced experience and scientific principles of management, emphasize differences in viewpoints and help integrate them, and so on.

They also take steps to activate the game participants by stimulating the allocation of roles assigned to them ("generator of ideas," "critic," "organizer," "person who gives report," and so on), the exchange of roles, self-reflection (reexamining one's work techniques), mutual reflection (recognizing the interests and problems of one's partners), uniting of groups of participants for common purposes, and so on.

Thanks to methods like these, participants begin to exchange information intensively, immerse themselves deeply in the task, and view it in a more integrated fashion. By means of competition, increased motivation to deal with tasks, and emotional involvement in group work, the game participants achieve a high level of activization of their abilities (knowledge, experience, thinking), which—given the specialized methods by which they are put together—yield a high level of performance.

Effective group work is also ensured by the fact that:

• within its framework, intensive working ties are established between people who otherwise would not be in direct contact with one another;

• in addition to people who generally make the decisions in a particular field, competent employees who generally do not take direct part in making such decisions become involved in formulating decisions on an equal footing;

• during the game, the participants are brought out of their everyday organizational relations and surmount the barriers of the concerns and interests of their own departments and organizations.

A practical business game takes five to six days, with forty to fifty people participating. In the process, group work alternates with plenary sessions during which results are presented and critical remarks and proposals are exchanged. A special role is played by the expert group. It formulates the precise goals and tasks of the game, draws up evaluation criteria and the "shape" of the final result, works out its own solution variants, and sees to the implementation of the final result in the specific organization.

The game is structured simultaneously along three lines:

• the logical structure of the game calls for concentrating the participants systematically on analyzing the situation, delineating the complex of urgent problems, formulating a plan of desired and possible changes, and mapping out a program for implementing the plan;

• the group structure of the game calls for dividing participants into different groups and subgroups with respect to different characteristics in order to obtain the most effective combination of sections dealing with specific tasks; it is also possible to create one-time (summary, initiative, and so on) groups to deal with specific tasks for a briefer time;

• the temporal structure of the game stipulates the distribution of the work and forms of organizing it within a definite rhythm that is as constant as possible (the combination of small group and plenary sessions, rest breaks, preparation and presentation of intermediate results, and so on).

The practical business game is designed chiefly to deal with integrative tasks. They comprise a rather broad class of tasks that reflect widespread problems of what are known as horizontal connections, because organizations are structured according to the division of labor by departments, shops, and services. This gives rise to the development of a subunit mentality—an inevitable exclusiveness focusing on local concerns, an exaggeration of the significance of one's own functions, and so on. The centrifugal forces that arise in this process bring about conflicts and dysfunction in the organization.

For this reason, games of this sort are structured on the principle of "positioning." Positioning consists of a particular form of isolation of the group interest in the organization on a subunit or personal basis, and consequently the shaping of a number of subgoals that are either mutually contradictory or cannot be reduced to a common goal. Even during the diagnosis stage, it brings to light the basic lines of demarcation, the various organizational and sociopsychological groups that are oriented primarily toward their own interests. Then they are assembled for the game in order to deal with the most urgent specific task of management. When the participants are assigned to groups having a homogeneous makeup on the first day—that is, in terms of their actual positioning, they come up with ways to solve the task that are strongly inclined toward local interests. In the course of the game this positioning is revealed to be unpromising in terms of accomplishing the common goal and is discredited in the eyes of the participants, which leads to a crisis in the game. Then mixed groups are formed to deal with the same task, and through the use of special game techniques new groups are formed in competition with one another, so that the game positioning that develops in this way proves to be stronger than the actual positioning that is inherent to the game. In combination with the technique of intellectual mobilization, this makes it possible to work out a new, mutually acceptable decision that each one will consider to be his own.

Proceeding on this basis, the overall structure of the practical business game is constructed as follows.

The first day. Analysis of the situation—problem formulation—draft plan of changes (short version).

Work in homogeneous groups (monogroups), each of which includes representatives of a single professional, departmental category of participants.

The task: Reproduce a concentrated picture of the existing reality and demonstrate the impossibility of effective solutions from any narrowly departmental position.

The expert group specifies the purpose of the game and works on the "shape of the results."

The second day. Analysis of the situation.

At this point and henceforth, work is in heterogeneous groups (polygroups), each of which includes an equal representation of all categories of participants, taking account of their subjective characteristics (competence, activeness, psychological vulnerability), to be determined by the methodologists based on the results of the first day.

The task: By means of exchanging information, generalizing it, and critically studying differences in interpretations of it, to come up with an integral picture of interrelationships within the state of affairs. Single out manageable and unmanageable factors of the situation, both those of a departmental character and those of significance to the national economy.

The third day. Determination of the problems.

The task: Drawing upon the analysis of the situation, formulate and systematize the complex of fundamental problems that cause difficulties and obstacles, singling out key factors.

What is meant by "problem" is any contradiction in the system of various relations between the interests and goals of the collectives, organizations, and departments.

The problems must be specific and divided into those that are solvable and those that are not (under current conditions). It is essential to separate the systematic-organizational (impersonal) aspect from the human (interpersonal, psychological) aspect. Demonstrate the sources of these problems and their consequences.

The fourth and fifth days. Formulation of a draft plan of changes.

The task: On the basis of the problematization carried out before, draw up proposals for restructuring the mechanism of the participants' interaction under actual circumstances in order to find solutions to the problems.

The plan of changes should be an integrated one—that is, it should establish the interdependence among its organizational, economic, social, and engineering aspects. The plan will have to track the positive and negative consequences of its implementation. Demonstrate the possibility of implementing the plan of changes. Take note of its novelty and radical character.

Other indications with respect to formulating the plan of changes are oriented toward the results of the previous day's problem formulation.

The sixth day. Formulation of a program of implementing the plan.

The task: Map out the sequence to fully adopt the plan of changes in practice.

Who is to revise the plan in accordance with the clients' comments? Who is to take charge of seeing to it that it gets to all the departments? What should foster its implementation? What might hamper it? What objections to the plan are expected and from whom? How should they be responded to? Evaluate the advisability of using the experimental method.

Within the framework of each day, this work procedure is followed:
- nomination of the director of the game (the task for the day);
- work in groups;
- plenary meetings (discussions of the results presented by the groups, the opinions of the expert group, the conclusion of the game's directors).

Starting on the second day, the expert group conducts parallel work on the overall themes, focusing on evaluation of the results being presented by the groups. After the game, the expert group sees to the implementation of the final plan under actual conditions.

The psychology of business games

First let us examine in detail the outward, procedural side of practical business games, and then their principles and possibilities, not addressing the differences between them.

Let's say the consultant urges the managers of an organization to undertake such a measure, explaining it by the necessity of finding a nontrivial alternate solution to a problem in such a way as to take maximum account of the specifics of the concrete organization. For his part, the consultant offers methodological support and supervision of the game, and at the end, in collaboration with the expert group mentioned above, he will attempt to formulate the result achieved in this manner.

On obtaining permission, the consultant undertakes to make up the personnel composition of the participants.

In doing so, what needs to be kept in mind?

Although there are a great many differences in the methodologies of conducting games of this sort, the total number of participants, as has been mentioned, ought to range between forty and fifty. The consultant determines the principles of the selection in a concrete manner applicable to the task at hand. Generally he strives to ensure the positioning and representation of the offices and social groups involved. Frequently, however, the following relations are taken as the basis for grouping participants: managers with subordinates; designers with technologists and mechanics; technicians, economists, and administrators; and so on. For example, if the focus is on intensifying innovation, they may include positional groups like these: organizers, developers, designers, manufacturers, users. Most important, the groups must be problem-oriented and include competing points of view and divergent aims.

The consultant draws up a program for conducting the game, which includes a justification for it (the findings of the diagnosis and the particular need for just this way of finding a solution), a statement of the overall task (which may develop during the course of the game), and a brief explanation of the rules and schedules of the game conduct. The participants acquaint themselves with the program before the game begins.

The question of where the game is to be held is not a trivial one. The fact is that in the course of in-play interaction between participants a particular psychological climate is formed (enthusiasm, strong mutual feelings, immersion in the range of problems, a feeling of community), which is absolutely essential for the success of the undertaking, but at the same time extremely fragile and vulnerable from without. The appearance of an outsider on the "playing field," the diversion of any of the participants to other matters, even the announcement of information from outside will introduce embarrassment and awkwardness to the game environment, will interrupt the process, and may even create a setback. These possibilities are difficult to prevent if the game is conducted in ordinary office facilities (the plant administration offices, for example, or a shop). For this reason, the game ought to be conducted in a building far from the enterprise or institution, such as a recreation or cultural center or a vacation facility.

Just what is the strategy of supervising the game?

Various strategies are possible. Let us examine one of them, a strategy designed for problems of intensifying innovation. It is to be implemented by a brigade of four or five consultants.

As mentioned above, the consultants separate participants into groups two times: first, each group has a homogeneous professional makeup (monogroup). One group, for example, consists only of organizers—that is, individuals who make decisions about any innovation and allocate funds and staff members for it; another consists only of innovation developers; and so on. At the end of the monoday, the consultants evaluate every participant in his group on a three-point scale that takes account of the following features: competence, active involvement, and psychological vulnerability. In consideration of their uniform combination, the groups are restructured on a different basis—multipositioning (polygroups), in which one or two representatives from each of the previous groups are brought together. Six to eight monogroups are therefore formed in the first case, and three or four polygroups are formed in the second.

What is the purpose of this sequence of groupings? After all, the groups in both cases face a single common task, for example that of developing a substantially more effective mechanism for the creation and development of innovations.

The restructuring of the game has an important purpose. The course of an ordinary game is characterized by the participants' thinking and searching along lines of improving what already exists, but this does not provide an opening for radical change. As they pursue that route, the participants, as a rule, soon come to a dead end, become disillusioned with the game, and are even inclined to quit. A crisis arises that constitutes a logical stage of the game's development.

Stereotypical thinking, naturally, is enhanced by the homogeneous makeup of a group. But, from the standpoint of the strategy of management consulting, it is essential to provide the opportunity to exhaust paths of partial improvement long before the game time runs out, in order that dissatisfaction with this state of affairs will encourage a revision of customary ideas. It is at this point that changing the composition of the groups noticeably activates the quest. From the very beginning, of course, the consulting proceeds on the basis that a solution can be found in the polygroups. But the game has its own logic—or, more accurately, its own psychology. Unless it runs aground it can hardly return to the main channel.

It is quite probable that this point in the entire system of practical business games will be controversial. This technique of activating participants may be termed manipulation. But this is the kind of case in which participants manipulate themselves, so to speak. Any appeal to discard entrenched ideas at the outset may be greeted politely, but it will soon turn out that even following this appeal decisively will be perceived by many as just the same old "improvement. . . ." And from the beginning they always want to be convinced that simple solutions are impossible.

It is for this reason that, at the crisis stage of the game, the consultants may resort to the "shift" procedure. This is a kind of psychological guarantee of restructuring of the groups. The consultant initiates extreme points of view, questioning things that seem obvious. For example, if participants are discussing how to improve the foreman's work, the consultant may ask, "Do we need a foreman at all?" The purpose is to encourage participants to rethink tasks, to focus their attention on the basics.

And now, let us address the role of consultants as a whole. As is clear from what has already been said, consultants provide the method of inquiry but also take active part in it. At the start of the game, an expert group is formed, generally by means of a vote, to which participants nominate those to whom they entrust the selection and accomplishment of the result. The leader of the consultants' brigade works with it. Its basic purpose is to evaluate ideas; when the groups disperse to separate rooms, the "experts" intensively review the positive aspects of what has accumulated.

But the consultants also take part in the group work, with a consultant assigned to each group or, more rarely, to two. What is his pattern of behavior there?

First of all, he scrupulously avoids the role of leader, even though there are expectations that he will do so, at least during the initial stages. He merely catalyzes the group's movement in a direction that yields results. Primarily, however, the consultant is supposed to ensure that all of the principles and rules of the game are complied with. Another object of his concern is the dynamics of interaction. For example, if one of the participants applies pressure that inhibits other participants' judgments, the consultant may attempt to "erode" the person's leadership, for example using questions of this type: "Is there really only one opinion among us?" Another time it may be necessary to encourage those on the psychological periphery of the group. Again, however, the most important thing is to pick up on promising statements of problems and encourage their elaboration.

Meanwhile, intensive interaction is taking place in the groups; at times it may wane, but at other times it may rise to a level of excitement. Activity may intensify due to the anticipation of the next report (once or twice every day) at plenary meetings, due to competition among the groups, and due to the inevitable insertion of professional, collective, and personal interests and attitudes from without.

The phenomenon of "unfreezing" takes place, followed by "disclosure." The former is essential to ensure full self-manifestation and contribution; the latter is not required at this point but is difficult to avoid. It is at this stage that the participants' emotional vulnerability rises. The probability of interpersonal tensions becomes stronger.

The consultant's vigilance in this regard must go into operation at the very first incidence of "getting personal," even remote ones. The kind of exchange of evaluations that is natural in this kind of interaction must here be confined to what is known as "internal speech" that is not allowed to be manifested behaviorally. In order to avoid a breakdown of the group, it may be necessary to change its composition somewhat. The expert group conducts its own game as well. In the optimal version (especially if it consists of a sufficient number of participants), the expert group simultaneously views itself as one of the polygroups, with the same tasks. Inasmuch as it is primarily occupied with its basic duties of regulating the game, it is not expected to present results at each plenary meeting but only during the final days.

Nevertheless, in order to ensure psychological balance in the game and the satisfaction of the others, it is essential to emphasize that none here are "more equal." Advancement in the game depends only on personal contributions to the content of the work.

The technology of the game also calls for another energy source: periodic reflection by the participants. What is the essence of this?

During the course of the game, the consultants will have many occasions to remark, "Everything that has been produced by the group so far has been well known a long time. There are no results yet." This is an appropriate moment for self-awareness: How well are we working? Essentially what have we done so far? Some variations of the game call for an independent consultative reflection group, which evaluates the actual character of the activity it has been observing, in the groups or during the plenary meetings. For example: "the majority have tried to recall literature they have read"; "we are slipping in the struggle for influence"; "there is a predominance of stereotypes"; and so on. In this way, the participants are steered toward a conscious selection of ways to advance toward success. From time to time, the game "sloughs off" the encrusted residue of passions and clichés and gets its second wind.

Up to now we have examined its processes and main components while ignoring its conceptual aspects. Let us move on to these.

As a rule, there are stable mechanisms in organizations for making management decisions. With greater or lesser success they also serve to encourage and find ways to make radical organizational changes as the need arises. In that case, then, what is the purpose of another method that is so complicated and does not come cheap?

Routine methods of individual or collective problem solving (meetings, conferences) have their own limitations. Persons who are formally responsible for particular sectors are invited to them, and general organizational relationships are reproduced (the final word goes to the senior executive, competing offices "divide the field," and so on). In addition, these methods are good when there is already sufficient thinking about the problem itself rather than its secondary features.

All of this is overcome in practical business games. However, the issue requires a more elaborate response.

Problems of organizational innovations are made substantially easier by one of the most important principles in such business games: the connection between the development and the implementation of innovations.

This kind of connection is accomplished, first of all, by the composition of the participants, because such a game involves the work, simultaneously and on an equal footing, of both those who plan and monitor changes and those who implement those plans. Second, this connection is accomplished by the content of the decisions: they accept what they themselves are to implement and are not about to undertake anything unrealistic. Third, being involved in the birth of an innovation makes people interested in making it a reality.

Another principle is that of relating work on a solution to the development of organizational relations of the personnel themselves. After all, the game also brings together people who otherwise are never in contact: practical cooperation is established along many horizontal and diagonal lines of the organizational structure, genuine entry into the collective across subdepartmental boundaries. An important point is that the game makes it possible for employees engaged in it to bring out capabilities that could not be utilized in their actual jobs.

Now it is easier to see the value of the game techniques themselves. Just what are they?

According to the rules of the game, differences of rank, which are so important in the organizations, are erased. The game groups, of course, shape their own structure—even a hierarchy—but it is of an informal, sociopsychological type made up of elements of leadership, prestige, coalitions, and so on. Hence the possibility for the participants' role mobility, of initiatives relating to not only content but also status (it is worth noting that the distribution of participants' influence in the groups and in the plenary meetings frequently diverges from that in the administrative network). It has yet to be demonstrated, but we may assume that this is also the source of job promotions in the organizations that are as yet unforeseen.

Competitiveness is also a game factor. It deserves special comment.

As has been mentioned, the selection of participants ought to be problem-oriented—that is, it ought to reflect fundamental difficulties in actual organizational relations. Designers and technologists, shops and suppliers, makers and users of innovative products—there are many such differences, even opposing goals and interests, which, of course, are inserted into the game. But in fact the function of the game is to adjust these lines of tension and set other, more constructive ones.

At the conclusion of the monogroup period, the consultants need to be able to show participants the futility of external demarcations (the task will not be accomplished). In the process of subsequently recombining participants in the polygroups responsible for working on a shared task, the mechanics of the game incorporate new, intergroup rivalry, which is constantly nourished by plenary discussions.

Benefits of the game, then, begin only when in-group solidarity forms a united interest to the extent that rivalry between the polygroups becomes stronger and prevails over the contradictions, introduced from without, between the professions, subunits, organizations, and departments in the monogroups. This constitutes a categorical imperative of the game, and that is why we will discuss it further.

In the plenary group meetings, situations of competition take shape quite objectively: there will probably be as many solutions as there are groups, but the game should have only one result. Naturally, the expert group will hesitate to accept even two variants as equal recommendations.

It would be totally wrong to leave out motives of duty, conscience, and the interests of the endeavor. And surely everyone would wish to improve the work of his own organization. In the game, however, there is almost a palpable feeling that keeping to a single method is not going to work; one must turn to reciprocity.

In short, there are incentives to productive competitiveness among the polygroups. And whereas within them the consultants strive not to allow differences to reach the point of demarcation, the plenary polemics come down to how the problems themselves are approached. The difficulty is that there must be no losers at the finish. It is essential to find integrating points between groups, even if one of them is obviously running ahead in terms of the result. Although, to be sure, it is always possible to resort to the "you're right too" method, but it is best to work on interesting all the participants in helping to carry out the option that has been adopted.

The props of the game can also be supplemented by special options, for example addressing people by their first name. The participants themselves suggest a number of rituals. The consultants ought to support this to the extent that it fosters the creation of a community, a "we" feeling.

And so, what is the purpose of practical business games?

Clearly, they cannot abolish or weaken routine mechanisms of decision making. Even where the game has come to a completely successful conclusion, moreover, the results are submitted to the top officials of the client organizations—not to be developed, but to make decisions. But in big doses it is too strong a medicine. Consultants experienced in this matter say that the method itself is becoming "worn out" from frequent use, and there are those who are beginning their own "game within a game." In short, it will not do to exaggerate. The method is by no means universal but is specifically goal-oriented.

But what kind? Primarily that relating to a felt need for major organizational restructuring, in order to plan radical innovations on an organization-wide scale: a change in the style of leadership or job assignments, personnel policy, and so on. A typical cause for appealing to consultants for that kind of help is a case when ample funds are being spent and people are enthusiastic, yet goals are not being reached. Naturally, "failure to reach the goal" is just an excuse, not a problem or a task of the game. Organizational diagnosis is also needed. But unless the client is consciously ready for required changes, the game is not going to be viable.

Modification of the game is also used for complicated but local tasks of training managers and specialists and creating bonus and in-plant transport systems where the essence of the problem and the formulation of the tasks are determined prior to the start of the game. Also possible, very likely, are what might be called variations for renewal—designed to activate personnel involved with urgent tasks, improve intragroup relations, develop workers' managerial abilities, and so on.

Among the most fundamental aspects of such games, mention should be made of their special importance in and of themselves as a vital social innovation. In effect, they create a kind of alternative mechanism parallel to the main one for making decisions and developing organizations. They represent a new phenomenon in our managerial culture. It is difficult to predict their fate, but they carry far-reaching possibilities.

Questions do arise, however, which even the most decisive proponents of practical business games find difficult to answer. We are talking about common exaggerations that enthusiasts are inclined to make. It is more interesting to take a look at genuinely substantiated doubts. And they have to do mostly with the results of such games.

Let's start with the fact that the organizers of such events do not guarantee any results. Obviously, results depend on the composition of the group. Although participants are selected by the consultants, they come from the actual "material" that the clients have at their disposal, and the selection is based on the information that can be obtained about employees' personal qualities. To no lesser degree, the result depends on the task itself, the problem that has been singled out. Let's say, for example, that a solution to the problem is beyond the capabilities of the organizations represented in the game but requires a revision of certain linkages and norms on the macro level. From the foregoing it is also clear that, compared to routine methods, the game process has a great deal more indeterminacy and variability, hence the probability of unanticipated events and turning points that can in fact affect the result. Breakdowns can also result from simple failure to comply with the rules of the game. Participants are not supposed to quit the game until it is completely finished, but during crisis stages such as those described above someone is bound to try it. Another unanticipated occurrence: no one who is not included in the game is allowed on the "playing field," but along comes the director to enquire whether he can help the consultant, who was not able to prevent the appearance of the director, whose subordinates spontaneously begin to report to their boss. This is followed by his kindly guidance and well-meant directives. But the game has broken down.

Furthermore, this method of making recommendations may deserve to be accused of conformity. Indeed, the recommendations seem to come from the employees of the client organization themselves. One might think that the consultant is just knuckling under. There is that danger. But a well-qualified consultant is not going to take the result of the game to constitute recommendations; he is not going to lose sight of the difference between them. He is going to scrutinize the results through his own knowledge of the science of management and his consulting experience.

On the subject of knowledge: it used to be said that the consultant resorts to the game procedure when he wants to test one of his own proposals or give participants the opportunity to arrive at it themselves. In doing so he takes account of the usual tendencies of the development of organizations in general, standard solutions that have already been found, and so on. He then introduces them into the game via the consultants in the groups, in the "shift" procedure, and even in the formulation of the task.

To some extent, the result depends on one's viewpoint. Among methodologists of games of this type one can even hear this answer to the question being discussed here: "The result is the game itself." What is meant is that the social effects that the technology of the game produces (the establishment of new relationships, the development of the employees' role-playing and thinking abilities, participation in critical decisions, and so on) constitute such a high value for people, for organizations, and for society, that this alone fully justifies the expenditure of time and money. To be sure, a pragmatic director does not call upon consultants for this purpose. Indeed, an overly pragmatic director will probably not call upon consultants at all.

In fact, contacts with a potential client also constitute difficulties of the method. Executives' perception of the information or a proposal of such a measure—especially in a subordinate group—reflects all shades of "for" and "against"—and probably not necessarily in favor of the former. What are they wary of? The unusualness, the riskiness, of course. But mainly, obviously, the fact that a certain alternative may be difficult to control. There are concerns as well among ardent proponents. There was a case when one of them got carried away and declared to the consultants that he would henceforth conduct his management meetings using that method. That's the danger of fads. There have also been instructive examples of related initiatives such as brainstorming and expert evaluations.

It is also necessary to develop a plan that takes participants' psychological health into consideration. The emotional states and in-group and intergroup tensions that were discussed earlier must somehow be restricted methodologically to within reasonable limits. Naturally, in the everyday routine on the job, cases of overreaction may be worse. But it is wrong to consider that stress is an acceptable price to pay, even for a good result. In addition to ethical considerations there are also what might be called strategic considerations. The introduction of a higher level of business culture into the practice of management ought not to copy the vulgarisms that are entrenched there. A nervous and conflict-laden atmosphere and raised voices can rightly be categorized as features of work that has not been properly organized. Finally, tactical factors are also very important. If relations between participants of the game worsen, that will cast a long shadow on the reputation of the method. For this reason, the game needs a reliable psychological foundation.

The application of the proposed method, like any kind of management consulting, requires that formalized, methodologically tested techniques be combined with the consultant's special art. The success of the latter depends not only on the mastery of science and experience but also on the consultant's development of the necessary personal qualities within himself.

9

Personnel-Technology: The Selection and Training of Managers

Vladimir K. Tarasov

Program and methods of training

One of the most important of the declared principles of the Tallinn School of Managers is the absence of a training program as a normative document. Teachers (or, more accurately, instructors who conduct the training) do not have the right to decide in advance what material they will be giving the next day, what training exercises or games they will be conducting. The prohibition of exact syllabi or curricula throughout the training period should orient instructors to be flexible in their teaching, to take account of the specific makeup of their audience, of the students' reactions and moods and their ability to assimilate various material.

Nevertheless, it is possible to single out five blocks that constitute the basis of instructional improvisations: writing a business letter, communication, taking and maintaining control, production and operations management, and product distribution. The emphasis falls on one or another of these blocks depending on the makeup of the audience. The number of people in the audience is also important, inasmuch as business games—a basic methodological tool—are geared to a specific number of participants.

Russian text © 1989 by "Mashinostroenie." "Programma i metody obucheniia," Ch. 19 in *Personal-tekhnologiia: Otbor i podgotovka menedzherov* (Leningrad: Mashinostroenie, 1989), pp. 307–18, 321–35.

In elaborated form, the training program can be represented as follows:

writing business letters, orders, and instructions;
formulating regulations, charters, and directives;
labor legislation and labor conflicts;
communication;
acting skills for the manager;
public speaking;
taking and maintaining control;
strategy and tactics of competition;
fostering employee loyalty and motivation;
evaluating applicants for jobs, and hiring;
analysis of technologies, time-and-motion studies, rate setting;
incentive and compensation systems;
production and operations management;
marketing;
credit and banking;
forecasting of solvency;
currency issue and commodity coverage;
pricing and tax policy;
company values and company style;
marketing and market niches;
inventory and inventory control;
auditing and control (preventing economic or commercial abuses);
foreign trade transactions;
business negotiations;
mixed forms of property ownership and joint ventures;
organization of stock companies;
economic support of political activity;
organization of election campaigns;
organization of public relations;
advertising;
how to use consultants.

The character of the Tallinn School of Managers is determined by its training methods. The four basic methodological blocks that make up the training day are: business games, management training exercises, game techniques, and illustrated lectures.

For training purposes we use the same business games as in competitions, except that the emphasis is shifted from evaluating the results to the cognitive process. Another difference is that the trainees are rewarded not with points but with play money that actually has commodity value. In particular, it can be exchanged for management books.

During the training, the instructor gradually removes himself from the role of the game leader, turning it over to one of the trainees. Leading the game is important in mastering practical management. This is a particular instance, then, of the creation of a social technology—an aggregate of actions that have specific social consequences and that are designed to accomplish a specific social goal. The leader, taking account of the makeup and motivation of the training group, uses his authority and the characteristics of his managerial style to convert the social technology into a personal technology. And this transformation is the most difficult element of management training.

The "Organizer" business game

The "Organizer" business game was played as follows. Six persons were designated as managers of mock production organizations and had the right to "hire" persons whom they considered essential. Every mock organization numbered six persons.

The job of the mock organizations was to assemble blank materials into candy boxes of the Kalev Confectionery Factory. The organizations were given time (about one and a half hours) to set up production—in other words, to master the technology, do a time-and-motion study, plan, draw up requisitions for components and packing materials, and deploy employees. The preparations were followed by a thirty-minute production period.

Our task was to create conditions under which the organizations would have to adopt "an intensive but realistic" plan. We were well aware that for several five-year periods now appeals to enterprises to take on intensive but realistic plans have sounded hollow. Enterprise managers were perfectly aware of what can result from following this appeal in a period that is to be planned "from the present level" of output. But in the game this problem could be solved more easily.

We provided for three types of product—three types of candy boxes—and set the prices for each of them. The participants were supposed to determine the actual labor-intensiveness during preparations for production. Moreover, we set the "mandatory" part of the plan—that is, the minimum number of products of each of the three types that each of the six organizations was supposed to turn out. In contemporary terms, it was a "state order" taking up approximately 30 percent of the production capacity of each organization.

The organization was supposed to take upon itself a plan obligation for the entire period of production. Upon completion it would be rewarded, provided that it also filled the "state order." The compensation formula for fulfilling the plan was as follows: *the actual results plus the plan, if the plan is fulfilled.* It is this kind of formula that compels participants to adopt an intensive but realistic plan automatically, without impassioned appeals.

Let us examine an example of the mechanism by which it works.

Let's say you planned to make forty boxes but made only thirty-five. You are credited with thirty-five because the plan was not fulfilled.

If, however, the plan called for ten boxes but thirty-four were made, the score will be $34 + 10 = 44$ boxes (because the plan was fulfilled, we added it to the actual results).

Finally, let's say the plan called for making thirty boxes but thirty-two were produced. The score would be $32 + 30 = 62$.

And so, although the least number of boxes were actually made in the final case, the team took first place because its plan proved to be not only realistic but also intensive.

The participants took all of this into consideration as they strove to plan and prepare production as efficiently as possible.

The beginning of production is arranged like an athletic race. Everyone is removed from the game zone until the start. The components are laid out on the tables of the mock production organizations in accordance with the requisitions that have been submitted.

The managers of the organizations sign a paper affirming that they have been "supplied" exactly according to requisitions. Otherwise, there might be a big fuss in the event of "underdelivery" of components. And even if the shortage of materials were to be made up comparatively quickly, the team would still claim that it had lost time due to the delay and demand compensation. But the other teams, even if they did not object to such compensation, would dispute its amount. A situation might arise in which the teams could not come to an agreement, and then you might as well replay everything. But one of the teams might not agree to this radical solution either. A crisis would arise and nullify the whole competition, and everyone would be unhappy about the waste of time. In my several dozen competitions, fortunately, I have never been in this predicament, although I have been on the verge of it. I don't wish going through that on anyone: it takes experience to get out of it.

And so, the managers have signed a statement that they have received all they requisitioned. At that point, all the participants are given permission to enter the zone. The atmosphere heats up with the cues: "Everyone stand behind their chairs! Do not touch the tables. Hands behind your backs! Begin!" Everyone rushes to his place and things really get moving.

Versions of the "Organizer" game

Almost half of every training day is taken up by the main business game, "Organizer." The optimal number of a group undergoing general management training is thirty to thirty-five. This number of participants enables five mock organizations to be formed. The selection of the product to be manufactured is limited only by the instructor's imagination. The organizations may be engaged in the assembly or disassembly of items made with a children's erector set (ranging from very elementary to complex; an electromechanical device demonstrating the normal functioning of a finished product such as a telegraphy set, a watch, etc.), or the sorting of a variety of small objects (for example, the parts of cut-up postcards), or the production of images on paper (crosses, circles, and so on), or calculations of varying complexity.

The instructor must find a way out of any situation and organize realistic production work literally from nothing. One example: without materials or time to prepare a game, the instructor bought three dozen copies of the same newspaper and organized the sorting of lines in a newspaper column in accordance with the decreasing frequency of the letter "b" in the line.

The instructor has to organize properly the participants' motivation in the game; this is not easy, especially when the play money has no commercial value.

Given the lack of commercial value, it does not make sense to set up a play store. It is best to organize an auction, assigning the sale of every unit of goods to the game participants. This will make it possible to demonstrate the variations of the personnel-technology of auction sales.

If there is not even a small quantity of goods, it is possible to make some. For example, it is possible to compile and type three or four copies of a list of the trainees in the group, indicating their addresses, phone numbers, place of work, and date of birth, and auction them off.

Finally, positive incentives can be found in the actual course of the game. For example, you can organize a procedure of rewarding winners with information about their "image."

All of the participants, except for the winner (if there are several winners, they will receive awards in turn, individually), are removed from the classroom and then summoned one at a time. Each one is given the chance to answer two questions: (1) what was his initial opinion of the winner; (2) in what way did it change as he got to know him better?

For a manager, this kind of procedure is truly a valuable reward, if it is properly constructed psychologically and carried out successfully.

Having realistically evaluated the possibilities of rewarding participants, the instructor will have to present them in his introduction to the game. Like any valuable gift, the packaging needs to be attractive, reassuring, and opaque. It would be wrong to appeal to greed, curiosity, or some other less-than-noble feeling. The trainee must not only react appropriately to the stimulus but also respect himself for his reaction.

Video commentary

The effectiveness of the training can be increased substantially if the critique of the participants' mistakes is accompanied by video commentary. For this it will be necessary to play video tapes of the key points in the game process, those fragments of the game where the probability of visible mistakes is greatest.

It would be wrong to view the video commentary as evidence or proof that a particular mistake had been committed. It is needed in order to analyze the cause of the mistake. While viewing the video with the trainees it is essential to show how the mistake started, developed, matured, and was brought to a conclusion. In order to deal successfully with this task it is necessary to determine what motivated the action that is being viewed as a mistake and to point out the real possibility of correct action.

Let's compare two types of such commentary.

1. You failed to count the components in good time. When production started, there were not enough components. You had to spend time getting the missing amount from the warehouse. As a result, your organization missed fulfilling the plan by literally a minute, and instead of first place it came in fifth!

2. Look there! You did start to count the components, but not very eagerly. You stopped—obviously the amount of the work seemed too big. Instead of counting further, you slapped the pile of components like this, with careless approval. Your gesture could be interpreted as follows: "What's there to count? Everything's all right!" Now you've stopped. You're doing nothing, just standing there looking happy. All's right with the world, you like yourself. There's still time to finish the counting. Judging by your face, you don't want to bother with such "trifles." There you're nodding your head to someone. Clearly you mean that everything's in order. But as we know now, it isn't so. You are sitting on a time bomb. Am I right?

These two types of commentary differ in terms of not only content but also effectiveness. Hearing the first version, the participant will shake his head and his face will express regret: "That's all I needed! Who would have thought that there were missing components! That's what you get for trusting people! Formally, of course, I'm to blame, that's why I'm nodding my head and agreeing with you!" The second version gives no leeway for excuses.

From the foregoing we obtain the first rule of video commentary: *Pay as much attention to details as possible; the more closely you scrutinize what is taking place, the more reasonable the commentary will be.*

In addition, in the first version the commentator does not make use of the visual route but instead appeals only to the sense of hearing, consequently it cannot be considered properly a *video commentary*.

The effectiveness of the video commentary also depends on the game's characteristics. Its greatest possibilities are probably afforded by the "Personnel" business game. There, erroneous versus correct behavior is sharply distinguishable; the distinction is unambiguous. You can stop a frame: "Look there, you didn't want to ask again. Why didn't you ask again?" Or, "Look there, your partner wants to ask again, but he can't bring himself to do it. Why didn't you give him the opportunity to do so?! You failed to notice it. And why did you fail to notice it? Because you're not looking at your partner! You're gesticulating and looking at your own hands, explaining things to yourself rather than your partner. You've done your piece, and after that you don't give a damn!"

It is impossible to film absolutely everything. For this reason, it is not worthwhile to try to comment on the game in its entirety. What is important is for your commentary to be detailed and useful to all the participants, to reveal typical mistakes.

Let us formulate the second rule: *If the other participants are bored and just waiting their turn during the video commentary on the mistakes of one of them, it means that the commentary has not been properly constructed.*

It is said that winners are never judged. There is a grain of truth in this; it is much more convenient to judge the losers. But there is a danger here, namely that the commentary might turn into an indictment, in which irony gives way to incrimination and demands for repentance. It is also possible that the other participants will not be bored, that the execution by video will not give rise to any objections even on the part of the "sacrifice," who lapses into self-flagellation or uncontrollable jollity, or simply endures the video torture stoically. But it is not good to get carried away on this account!

When the commentator starts to "bog down" and begins to repeat the same things with variations just to please the crowd, it means he has "slipped" from commentary into condemnation.

And so, rule three: *If the commentary can be shortened considerably without damaging its value, it has not been constructed properly.*

In order to avoid this, just imagine that the video commentary itself has been filmed and is also to be subjected to commentary.

Duel

The duel—a basic form of managerial training—is a kind of one-on-one combat between two participants, each of whom must demonstrate his superiority to his partner.

On a chess clock the leader sets the time (for example, five minutes) of the participant, who begins by drawing lots or by mutual consent.

What follows is some managerial move, for example, the player forces his partner to play out some role dialogue, demands an answer to a number of questions, or proposes that he talk to the audience on a given subject and then interrupts him and criticizes him. The person in possession of the control time can assign his partner any structure of behavior that is permitted by the customs of home and office and treat him like a subordinate.

Everyone will probably find himself in a situation where the boss has put him in an awkward situation, not giving him the opportunity to show he is right, interrupting, asking questions that are not relevant to the case, refusing to answer questions himself. . . . Inevitably the idea occurs to us that if our roles were switched we would be talking differently. . . . This is exactly what the duel makes it possible to do.

The participants take turns having control time; they take turns being "on top." The duel is supposed to show who knows how to take advantage of the time allotted to him, and how well.

As soon as the one who started play senses that he has made a good move or, on the contrary, that there is no use wasting any more control time looking for a move, he turns the control over to his partner, presses the button on his time clock, and says, "I turn the control over!"

His partner, having been given control, makes a move. Then he also turns it over. Play continues in this way until the time allotted to both partners runs out.

In the course of the duel, the participants make use of a variety of game techniques, attempting to demonstrate their own superiority over their partner.

The duel is judged by members of a jury who are selected by the participants. Each participant in the duel selects one member of the jury as he sees fit. The two jury members thus chosen agree between themselves on the choice of a third.

After the duel is over, the leader advises the members of the jury first to make an "internal" decision. This means that every member of the jury, without regard to the leader and without talking to the other two, makes an "internal" decision as to which of the participants in the duel has won. In the process, no "draw" will be allowed. When the jury member lifts his head and looks at the leader it means he has made his "internal" decision. Then the votes are counted. The score can be either 3:0 or 2:1 in somebody's favor.

The leader proposes that the members of the jury comment on their decisions if there is a desire to do so. Then he invites the spectators to express themselves. The last ones to be allowed to speak are the participants in the duel.

Game techniques

In the duel, the same game techniques are used as in the training process as a whole. The only difference is that during the instruction they are used by the instructor, whereas during the duel they are used by the participant who has been given the control time.

Transfer of control. One of the trainees is given control of the audience. He can do nothing, speak, give permission to others to speak, ask questions of any of those present, interrogate the partner, conduct a confrontation, compel people to offer constructive proposals or to play roles, turn over any of his rights to any of those present, or turn over control of the audience to someone else.

Interruptions. If the person to whom the control has been delegated is wasting time without results, he will be stripped of his right ahead of time and must respond to a number of questions:
   What were you attempting to accomplish just now? Formulate it.
   Are you keeping this goal precisely in mind or have you lost it?
   Why are you pursuing this particular goal?
   What was your decision based on?
   Do you distinguish between a motive, a cause, and an excuse?
   What result would you like to get, and in what form?
   Do your partners understand what you want from them?
   Which of them do or do not understand the tasks? (point).
   Who is trying to take control from you?
   What immediate steps do you intend to take?
   Would you like to take a break in order to collect your thoughts?
   To whom would it be worthwhile now to transfer control?

Audience differentiation. The audience is to be divided into groups on the basis of a vote, the selection of groups by appointed or self-appointed leaders, a drawing of straws, on a sociodemographic basis.
   The groups are assigned particular roles. The following, for example, may be singled out: scenario writers, supervisors (those who set the goals), managers, submanagers, social technologists, consultants, experts, actors, objects of control, leaders, disturbers of the peace, and victims.
   A set of game techniques are to be used depending on the reaction

of the trainees in order to show them which of their life trajectories are most probable at the present level of development. This set of techniques forms a paratheater.

Paratheater

The technique of paratheater requires that the leader perform three roles—that of the script writer, the director, and the manager.

As the *script writer*, the leader maps out the scenes in the show and puts the various characters into specific situations. The actors (trainees) are free to act as they see fit, and they write their own scripts. For this reason, the script writer does not know just how a particular scene will end. Even the structuring of the scenes into events is not wholly under his control: unexpectedly for him, one of the characters might leave the stage or introduce a new character. However, the script writer does have the right to stop a given scene (to consider it completed) or to introduce a new event.

The stage is set by the script writer, using a number of elements from among the following: the characters, their objective relationships (conditioned by age, sex, position, and so on); their subjective relationships; the circumstances that have brought them together; their goals, aspirations, needs, and problems that govern their behavior; the prehistory that the characters may draw upon; an approximate content of the dialogue; and the result, on completion of which one of the characters may end the given scene.

The script writer utilizes only that portion of elements from this list sufficient to enable the characters to get an idea of what is going on and to advance the action. Naturally, the very first scene will require the greatest number of elements from this list—perhaps even all of them—while later scenes may need only two or three of the elements.

As the *director* the leader instructs the actors (interprets the script), keeps track of the actual flow of the scene, organizes it in space (determines the placement of objects and characters) and in time (making remarks to speed, slow, or stop the course of a scene), selects the actors, and assigns them their roles. At the end of the scene the director interprets what he has seen and heard, placing it in the broader social context, and assigns himself—as the script writer now—the task of composing a new (following) scene that will ensure motivated advancement of the plot toward the culmination and then to the dénouement.

As the *manager*, the leader must know how to perceive the trainees' managerial mistakes and, giving himself assignments as both script writer and director, know how to influence the course of events in such a manner as to:

• show graphically the weak points of the trainees' managerial activities by making them sufficiently vivid and visible;

• demonstrate, with the action itself, the possible negative consequences of these shortcomings;

• offer the trainees the opportunity to try out variations of managerial behavior that they have not managed to perform in real life and to perceive their consequences;

• make graphic the successful managerial moves of the trainees, adjusting the plot so that the course of events converts potential success into genuine success.

The leader can use brief remarks to suggest preferred moves (for example, "Tell your enemy where to get off!" or "Take the bull by the horns and you won't go wrong!" and so on).

Because the leader performs all three of his functions practically simultaneously as the show proceeds, he will have to work in "real time." He must not only watch the parashow but also create it as he goes along, which requires refined skills. The job is made somewhat easier by experience and the presence of "homemade components"— plots of paraplays that are used in the school but are not familiar to the particular contingent of trainees. Every leader will have his own set of favorite plots, enriched with the experience of having played them.

Conflict with a deputy. An enterprise director (i.e., the president) is dissatisfied with his new deputy and wants to get rid of him, but first he wants to discredit him (with a warning) in the eyes of the company's general director (the chief executive officer). With this in mind, he sends his deputy on short notice to confer with the general director without giving him the chance to prepare himself, so that he will look incompetent.

Roles: the director, his deputy, the deputy's wife, the general director, the secretary of the party organization, and the deputy's subordinate.

Possible scenes: (1) the director tells his deputy to go confer, but the deputy resists; (2) the deputy talks to his wife about it on the eve of the conference; (3) the deputy complains about the director to the secretary of the party organization; (4) during the conference, the general director can tell that the deputy is "not prepared"; (5) after the conference, the general director has a talk with the deputy; (6) there is a telephone conversation between the general director and the enterprise director; (7) the deputy tells the director about the results of the conference; and so on.

Possible course of events: (1) the deputy director doesn't even go to the conference, either pleading illness or showing lack of discipline; (2) the general director is irritated by the deputy's lack of preparedness and tries to apply a sanction; (3) the general director is irritated by the enterprise director and tries to get to the bottom of things; (4) the party bureau examines the conflict between the director and his deputy.

The shoe factory. Workers serving on the production line that manufactures men's shoes have decided to refuse to work any longer because the glue is substandard, they've had it with the many years of promises by the administration, and they are tired of turning good materials into junk.

Roles: a brigade leader, an instigator, someone who wishes the instigator ill, a young foreman, a shop chief, the director, the party organizer, the chairman of the trade union committee, the wife of the instigator, and the wife of the young foreman.

Possible scenes: (1) an *ad hoc* meeting of the brigade; (2) a dialogue between the shop chief and the young foreman; (3) a dialogue between the wives in a beauty salon; (4) a conference in the director's office, participated in by the shop chief, the foreman, the party organizer, the chairman of the trade union committee, and the person who wishes the instigator ill; (5) a tea in the home of the instigator, with the brigade leader taking part; (6) a dialogue between the instigator and his wife after the brigade leader leaves; (7) an *ad hoc* meeting organized by the person who wishes the instigator ill, in the absence of the latter; (8) a continuation of the meeting with the instigator present; and so on.

Possible course of events: a strike; a refusal to strike; unavoidable dismissal of the instigator; reelection of the shop chief; members of the brigade quit the factory *en masse*; and so on.

The young specialist. The director of an institute asks the young specialist to familiarize himself with a report that is objectively weak, without informing him who drew it up. After listening to a negative assessment, he unexpectedly asks him to repeat it in the presence of the report's author, a venerable section head who is in conflict with the director.

Roles: the director, the section head, the young specialist, the wife of the section head, the deputy director, the secretary of the party organization, and a friend of the young specialist.

Possible scenes: (1) the director tells the young specialist to familiarize himself with the report; (2) a dialogue between the young specialist and his friend, who was his classmate; (3) the director listens to the young specialist's assessment and summons the author of the report; (4) a dialogue between the director and the section head after the young specialist leaves; (5) a dialogue between the director and the young specialist after the section head leaves; (6) a dialogue between the section head and his wife; (7) a discussion, in the office of the deputy director (who supports the section head), of the young specialist's work plan, with the participation of the young specialist himself and the section head who is "one of the leading specialists in the institute"; (8) the director offers the young specialist the chance to speak at a meeting of the institute's staff concerning the problems of young specialists, the offer being made jointly with the secretary of the party organization.

Possible course of events: the young specialist does everything he can to avoid any "intrigues"; he is drawn into the conflict on the director's side; or he is drawn into the conflict on the section head's side.

Kolkhoz training exercise

The objective of the "Kolkhoz" [collective farm] training exercise is to force your partner to back down without coming into conflict with him.

An even number of participants sit facing one another across a long table. Every participant has someone opposite him, with whom he must engage in mild confrontation.

> An organization has been "granted" authorization to send some workers to work on a kolkhoz that it sponsors. Naturally, none of the subunit supervisors are delighted with the prospect of having to get along without workers for a week and they would like to minimize the

number of persons they have to send from their own unit to the kolkhoz. On the other hand, however, every supervisor's immediate superior strives to maximize the number in order to get along better with the supervisors of the other subunits. At the exercise leader's command, they engage in a five-minute dialogue during which they are supposed to agree on a final figure.

And so, one of the chains plays the role of the subunit supervisors, while the other plays the role of their superiors. For convenience in recording the results of the negotiations, small sticks can be used (or, if there are none available, matches). Every stick stands for one worker. The superior does not have the right to demand more than five sticks from his subordinate.

At the leader's command, all pairs of participants begin a simultaneous dialogue. In five minutes, the leader claps his hands to stop the dialogue. He tells all of them to stand up and tells those who have arrived at an agreement to pass the corresponding number of sticks from hand to hand. The pairs who have concluded negotiations sit down. Those who have failed to reach an agreement remain standing. The leader takes all five sticks from the subordinate.

Then people change places: one chain remains in place, while in the other chain every person shifts one place to the right. The rightmost person, who is left without a sheet, takes his seat at the extreme end of the left flank. Now the chain that played the role of the subunit supervisor is to play the role of the superior, and vice versa. This time, only four and a half rather than five minutes are allotted to the dialogue.

Everything is repeated, followed by people changing places. The time allotted for the next dialogue is reduced by another half minute, and so on. The dialogue is conducted an even number of times so that both chains play each role an equal number of times.

The results of the agreement between them may take the following form: 4:1; 3:2; 2:3; 1:4.

By the time the exercise is over, every participant will have collected a certain number of sticks. Participants who are vulnerable to pressure and give way too easily will have lost some of their sticks, while the more aggressive and flexible participants will have increased their original number.

The participants quickly come to perceive the truth that the figure that is named first, the anticipation of one's partner's argument, and the insinuation of new circumstances are all factors that promote success. Those personalities who are most argumentative are also quickly revealed. A person who winds up participating in more than three conflicts, as a rule, will also behave the same way in real life.

During a parashow in Kishinev, I was astonished by the audience's restrained reaction to the brilliant play of one participant.

What happened was that during the "Kolkhoz" exercise he deceived two partners in a row when he was playing the role of subunit supervisor. After he and his partner agreed on acceptable terms, at the moment of handing over the sticks he quickly withdrew his hand and sat down. His partner, who was not prepared for this maneuver, sat down out of inertia without getting the promised sticks. But then he was too embarrassed to stand up and attract attention as one who played the role of the deceived. He did not succeed in deceiving a third person: the warning had been passed along the chain.

This enterprising player acquired the reputation of a man who was capable of dishonest moves. He had thought that a game was just a game, but it turned out that it was also real life.

The "Prince" training exercise

There once was an ancient Chinese tradition, almost four thousand years old, for choosing a prince.

The elders of the clan proposed that the candidate for prince take that post. As a cultured man, however, he would refuse the princely title even though he desired it. He would say that he considered himself unworthy of such a high post. After a certain amount of time, the elders would again turn to him and make their offer. But the self-respecting candidate would again refuse. The offer would be made to him again. And so on.

After any one of his refusals, the elders might not repeat their offer but give it to someone else. Moreover, they might make the offer to him while counting on his refusal, so that later they could turn to someone else whom they really preferred to see as prince.

Both sides were taking a risk. The candidate, by refusing one more time, took the risk of not getting another offer. The elders, who might have some other pretender in mind, took the risk of getting his consent.

We made this situation the basis of a training exercise whose technology is similar to that of the "Kolkhoz" exercise: chain against chain, shifting of seats, and alternating roles.

When making the offer, the "elder" places a stick (or match) in front of the "candidate for prince," accompanying the gesture with various polite words. Responding courteously, the candidate places one more stick next to the first one. The elder accompanies a repeat of the offer with another stick. The refusal is accompanied by one more stick. In this way, a small pile of sticks builds up.

If the elder decides that he has made enough offers, he will say, "Well, what can you do, I'll have to turn to another candidate!"—and picks up the whole pile of sticks.

If, however, the candidate decides he has demonstrated enough good manners, he will say, "Well, what can you do, obviously I'll have to consent!"—and pick up the pile of sticks himself.

This is followed by a shifting of places, and those who played the role of elders become the candidates for prince, and vice versa.

The participants' aim is to collect as many sticks as possible. At the game's start, everyone is given the same number of sticks (for example, twenty). If an impatient participant picks up the pile of sticks immediately it won't be a big harvest. If the participants show restraint, the harvest will be abundant, but the risk is great.

This exercise serves to help develop managerial empathy—an understanding of what the partner is currently feeling and what managerial decision he is preparing to make. Probably in no other type of exercise do the participants watch their partner as intently as in the "Prince" game.

The "Slalom" training exercise

A manager is hurrying to a meeting; all the other participants have assembled and are waiting for him. On the way he keeps being stopped by staffers or petitioners presenting him with a variety of extremely urgent items of business, which he has to deal with literally on the run.

Several participants (from five to eight) in this "slalom" play the role of "obstacles"; all the others, who play the role of manager, have to get over these obstacles one after another.

Examples of obstacles:

1. The job trainee student: "They sent me to you in the shop, but everyone keeps sending me to someone else. I don't know who to turn to. Maybe nobody even needs me here?"

2. A planner (a woman): "Ivan Vasil′evich! I need your signature! I know you're in a hurry. Wait, that's not it! Here it is . . . No, no. . . . Wait a minute. . . ." (Rummages through papers while the "manager" stands and waits).

3. A young foreman: "Ivan Vasil′evich! The welder is drunk and there's no one to do the job. Shall I let him come to work?"

4. A worker: "Vasilich! Give me a three-day pass with pay! Such a mess, it's a long story, I have to go to my mother's in the village right away!"

5. A woman from Supplies: "Ivan Vasil′evich! The truck is here, the driver is furious, and there's no one to do the unloading. He says he's going to take the load and leave if someone doesn't unload it right away! What shall we do?!"

6. A worker from the main administration: "Excuse me, are you the shop chief? Good day! It's a good thing I managed to catch you before I left and I can get the information from the horse's mouth, so to speak. . . ."

7. A brigade leader: "Do what you will, Ivan Vasil′evich, I can't take any more! How long are they going to keep feeding us with promises?! What do we get out of this? Why does everyone on our brigade have to go out?! At best we'll manage to wind up with three rubles a day! What am I supposed to tell the guys?!"

8. A journalist: "Excuse me, could you tell me how to find Fedor Kuznetsov? They told me he works in this shop. But I forgot what his specialty is. . . ."

If the manager deals effectively with the problem, he gets a coupon from the obstacle person; if he brushes him off he gets nothing. The time devoted to the entire distance is five minutes. The more coupons the trainee gets, the better his score.

The "Intelligence-Gathering" training exercise

The exercise is conducted in the form of a dialogue between two participants. Practically any number of pairs can take part in it simultaneously. Each participant gets a note telling him to find out something about his partner (for example, whether he or one of his close acquaintances has a chess clock at home, whether he was a leader or Komsomol organizer during his school years). He must get an answer to the question of interest to him without letting his partner find out what he wants, and, in addition, he must try to determine what his partner needs to find out.

The exercise takes five minutes. It may be extended somewhat if the two sides wish.

After the dialogue comes to an end, the leader asks each side, "In your opinion, what was your partner trying to find out?" The one whose task has been guessed is considered to be the loser.

Then the leader asks the two sides a second question: "What were you able to find out in accordance with your assignment?" The more accurately the participant answers the question of his assignment the better his score.

The audience evaluates the extent to which the conversation was relaxed and the participants' questions were natural.

A more complicated version can also be conducted, with the participation of coaches and an analysis of the training.

The "Self-Control" training exercise

The participants pair off, facing one another, as in the "Prince" and "Kolkhoz" exercises. One of the partners plays the role of the boss, while the other plays the role of his subordinate. A general theme of the dialogue between the boss and his subordinate is assigned. During the course of the dialogue, the boss is supposed to unnerve his subordinate, force him to say or do something impolite, and then punish him for violating office ethics. The subordinate's task is to not give in to the provocation but to conduct himself appropriately, maintain self-control, and stay within the boundaries of office ethics.

Once the boss manages to achieve his purpose he punishes his subordinate by telling him to raise his hand. The subordinate has to continue the dialogue with one hand raised. After a second lapse, the subordinate will have to raise both hands. After that he has to stand up with both hands raised. The worst luck will be to have to stand on one leg with hands raised. In this way, the subordinate winds up being punished by the awkwardness of the pose in which the dialogue is conducted.

After that, there is the standard switching of places; those who played the role of the boss become the subordinate, and vice versa.

The results of the exercise can also be tallied in points (sticks). In this case it is advisable to use sticks of two types. One type is used for punishment. When punishing his subordinate, the manager takes one stick of that type from him each time. If, however, the subordinate believes that he has been punished unjustly because he had conducted himself correctly and did not violate office ethics, while the boss is of the opposite opinion, they must tell the leader about their conflict, and he will take from each of the participants in the conflict a stick of the second type.

If either one of the participants gets into many conflicts, he ends up having fewer sticks of the second type. After all the dialogues are ended, the conflicting pairs approach the leader in search of justice. They submit all their "conflict" sticks to him. The one who has the most sticks is right. The one who has the fewest sticks must turn one punishment stick over to the opposing side (for each conflict, if the same pair has been in conflict several times).

If they submit an equal number of "conflict" sticks, then in the first conflict this pair engaged in the boss is considered the winner; in the second conflict it will be the subordinate, then the boss again, and so on. If there was just one conflict, on the other hand, given an equal number of "conflict" sticks the boss is considered the winner.

Overall success in the exercise is evaluated by the total number of sticks of both types.

> *An example of a dialogue theme:* The subordinate has persuaded his boss to pledge to higher-level management increased obligations on one of the jobs that is within the competence of this subordinate. As the deadline for completion of the job approaches, it becomes clear that the subordinate is not in a position to fulfill it because he overestimated his abilities. The dialogue takes place at the moment when the boss realizes that the project that he himself asked for has fallen through.

The "Promotion" training exercise

The "Promotion" training exercise proceeds in two stages. During the first stage, several groups of trainees work in parallel dealing with the same assignment. The assignment that is given to the groups is a specific management situation. Each group nominates its own representative to give the report to the jury at the "plenary session" (second stage) concerning the decision that has been taken.

But the technology of the exercise does not consist of that alone: along with the general assignment, each participant also must deal with his own personal assignment, which has been formulated for him in a note handed to him by the leader at the start of the exercise. The success of each participant is determined by two factors: the place occupied by his group in the overall competition and the extent to which he has fulfilled his individual assignment.

Two degrees of fulfillment of the individual assignment are called for: minimum and maximum. Failure to fulfill the assignment is evaluated at 0 points, minimum fulfillment earns 1 point, and maximum fulfillment earns 2 points.

Evaluations for reporting for the group range between 0 and 3 points, depending on the place that is occupied.

Thus, every participant may be given from 0 to 5 points depending on his personal success and the success of the group. But the individual assignments are structured in such a manner that they make it difficult to accomplish the group's goal, as well as to attain mutual understanding among members of a single group (see the table).

> *Situation*: The manager of an enterprise has leased an unprofitable section to the employees of the section. Soon after, everything in the section improves, but the manager of the enterprise is not happy about it. He starts to think of the section as being like a cuckoo chick in someone else's nest. The section is getting rich, servicing its own and other enterprises successfully; but it's as if the enterprise were working for the section rather than the other way around: many workers in the offices of the enterprise are being "supported" by the section. Since they directly or indirectly get additional pay from the section, they have begun to pay more attention to the needs of the section than those of the enterprise. In addition, the fact that the wages of workers in the section are double or triple the average wages throughout the enterprise is irritating, stirring up, and distracting a substantial portion of the enterprise's work force. The manager does not want to use forbidden strong-arm methods but he sees that things cannot continue that way or he risks losing control over the situation.

The "Boundary" training exercise

This exercise is designed to develop skills of drawing the sociopsychological boundary between "us and them"; in other words, consciously tracing socially significant traits of similarities and differences between partners.

In terms of its technology, the exercise is similar to "Kolkhoz."

Individual Assignments

Participant	Task	
	Minimum	Maximum
1st	Your group's point of view must rule out the application of any prohibitive measures to the section	Your group must try to get the entire enterprise converted to lease
2nd	Do not allow the 1st participant to be elected to represent your group	Try to get the 3rd participant elected to represent your group
3rd	Your group must endorse the view that leasing is a form of economic relations that is unacceptable to our society which will lead to covert plundering of socialist property	Your group's point of view must envision the gradual conversion of the enterprise to the work group's cooperative ownership, with the tools of production to be purchased on credit rather than being leased
4th	The group's decision must call for using any means to liquidate the section's special position	Your group must demand that the enterprise's employees formulate and approve a provision to convert the enterprise's services and subunits to a lease footing, one which rules out any special position for the section
5th	Do not allow the 3rd participant to be elected to represent your group	Try to get the 1st or 4th participant elected to represent your group
6th	Do not allow your group to take lower than third place	Try to ensure that your group takes first or second place
7th	Do not allow the 1st, 2nd, 3rd, or 4th participant to represent your group	Try to see to it that you yourself are chosen to represent the group
8th	Try to see to it that the participant chosen to represent the group is the one who condemns prohibitive measures being applied to the section	The group's decision must call for immediate cessation of lease relations with the section and for inviting the OBKhSS [Department Against Theft of Socialist Property] to institute criminal proceedings on counts of bribery, embezzlement, and abuse of position benefiting the lessees

Each participant takes turns playing two roles: one looks for traits of sociopsychological similarity with his partner, factors that unite them in the community of "us," and the other looks for sociopsychological differences with his partner, reasons for categorizing him with "them."

In doing so, the search for traits of similarity and difference is conducted against the background of the specific training group: what is important is not merely what socially significant traits of similarity and differences there are but rather those that distinguish a particular pair from the majority or a substantial number among the training group.

At the leader's command, the participants engage in "polite conversation" and continue it for five minutes, jumping from theme to theme and making no written notes.

Then—also on command—they draw up lists: one participant draws up a list of features of similarity, while the other draws up a list of differences.

The leader draws participants' attention to the fact that any feature of similarity or difference needs to meet two criteria:

• it must be socially significant—that is, capable of uniting the portion of the group that has that feature or distinguishing it from that portion of the group that does not have it;

• the participants must have grounds for believing that this feature varies within the particular training group; someone in the group besides the particular pair has it, someone else does not.

The compilation of the lists should take two minutes. Then, on the leader's command, the participants compare their lists, checking one another to see that the features do meet the above criteria. After the comparison, the participant whose list turns out to have the fewest points gives his partner some sticks, the number of which equals the difference in the number of points.

This is followed by a switching of places. Everyone changes partners and roles: the one who looked for features of similarity before now looks for differences, and vice versa. As before, the main goal is to accumulate as many sticks as possible.

The "Role" training exercise

This exercise is designed to develop skills of monitoring the allocation of roles and controlling that allocation.

The exercise's technology is also quite similar to that of the "Kolkhoz" exercise, but it does not require changing roles. After each switching of places all that changes is the partner; the role does not change.

As in the "Boundary" exercise, the participants engage in polite conversation, going smoothly from one topic to another. Each pair is given five minutes for the conversation. During that time, the leader interrupts the conversation three or four times by clapping his hands.

Immediately after the handclaps, each of the participants quickly assesses the actual allocation of roles between him and his partner, judging by the last fragment of conversation immediately before the leader's handclap. If the participant believes that the advantage is on his side he raises his hand. At the same time, his partner might think that the advantage is on his side. In that case, each of the participants writes several words on a piece of paper that record the role allocation. If the partner does not dispute the other participant's advantage, he gives him one stick. A dispute between the partners as to the advantage in the role allocation may be decided both between themselves and by introducing "conflict" sticks.

> *Examples of role allocation* (the role that has the advantage is listed first): expert—dilettante, experienced—inexperienced, senior—junior, higher position—lower position, teacher—student, well-off—not well-off, witness—absent, formerly well-off—formerly not well-off, having prospects—without prospects, well-known—unknown, distinguished—ordinary, doctor—patient, request examiner—petitioner, host—guest.

The participant's task is to guide the conversation in such a manner that, as he and his partner move from topic to topic in polite conversation, he is attempting constantly to obtain overt or covert advantage.

The design of training exercises

Any instructor who conducts general management training needs to know how to add to the arsenal described above with new types of exercises depending on the specific makeup of the training group and the direction the training program takes.

The main consideration in designing exercises is to organize dynamic, discrete transition from opinions to action and back again. Determining precise maneuvers (working out an opinion, recording it, doing the action), recording the participants and role allocation accurately, providing for spatial-temporal organization, and, finally, designing the technology on this basis that will make it possible to achieve the goal of the exercise—these are the basic landmarks of the process.

For example, the audience must make an analysis of the possible consequences of any managerial decision. A simple questionnaire may also yield specific results, but it will not get all the trainees equally involved in the work. Some prefer to keep silent and listen to what the others are saying. Such a position will affect the leader's authority, as he cannot help looking as if he were paying attention only to the active participants; otherwise he will be openly acknowledging his inability to get all the trainees involved. Tricks of this sort are subconsciously noted by the audience, and even if they sympathize with the instructor they will begin to respect him less.

The problem of getting all the trainees involved will solve itself if, for example, they are divided into groups of four or five persons each, with each group assigned to determine the possible consequences independently. Then the trainees selected as hapless representatives of a group stand in a circle and take turns naming one consequence. Anyone who hesitates more than ten seconds, which are counted out loud by the leader, is expelled from the circle. Along with him, his group is considered as having lost. It continues this way until a winner is determined. In the process, everyone watches to see that nothing is repeated.

This will not have to be done if the atmosphere in the audience is such that everyone wants to express himself. It is simple enough to give everyone who wants to the opportunity.

But if there are too many who want to express themselves, it is possible to direct the audience's attention to searching for nontrivial judgments. The audience is divided into groups that record the list of consequences in writing and then read them aloud. If just two groups are found to have the same recorded note, they each get a minus.

Each time, the instructor must design a new exercise or modify a standard one in accordance with the situation that has taken shape. At first glance it seems that only a few are able to do this. However, all it takes is to know the school's standard technology, and it is difficult to keep from designing something. The main thing is not to be satisfied with what has been achieved and to be ready to "rejoice in failure" before it happens.

Illustrated lectures

This special form of teaching that is practiced in our school has features that are both similar and dissimilar to traditional lectures.

The trainees have the right to enter or leave the lecture hall freely. Being late to a lecture is not encouraged, but neither is it criticized. The instructor should weave every appearance or disappearance of a trainee into the fabric of the lecture.

Any trainee has the right to interrupt the lecture at any point with an objection, a question, or a skeptical or angry remark. The instructor is obligated to make use of them and give a new turn to the topic in a direction that is more promising.

The monologue should be constantly interspersed with answers to questions, some of which are provoked, by game techniques, exercises, paratheater, and by turning over control to the students.

Theoretical propositions absolutely need to be couched in specific techniques of social technology, anticipating reactions: "Well, and what do we get from this? How can it be applied?" These need to be accompanied by illustrations such as historical examples, playing with the trainees, mental experiments, and so on.

The instructor ought not to have a rigid lecture plan or class program. Only that which has taken place directly in the lecture hall should determine which direction the narrative will go each day.

The exposition of the material should be made in circles and loops: the instructor should constantly return to the same theses, recipes, examples, and questions, but each time from a different angle. New aspects are constantly being singled out, certain new details are brought in each time, the trainees learn to take note of the slightest shifts in emphasis. It is the task of the instructor not to have the trainees memorize material until it has been understood correctly.

A trainee's notes ought to be incomprehensible to anyone who missed the lecture. If the notes are comprehensible, what has been conveyed is knowledge rather than understanding and skill. Skill is imparted thanks precisely to a chaotic, disorderly exposition that does, nevertheless, represent a continuous, if tangled, thread.

The main point is not memorization but understanding and recognition, influence by example rather than through syllogisms.

The content of lectures is made up of stories, parables, incidents, principles (about 300), techniques, actions, models, and pictures of the world—that is, everything that relates to the social technology.

An instructor should not tell his audience everything he knows: at all times he needs to have in reserve something more than he has already told. Every time, the audience must be convinced that if it hadn't been for one of the trainees asking some question, or if some event had not taken place, the trainees would not have been given this very valuable piece of information. This creates a sense of the importance of every question that is asked, every event.

Even in hostile or stupid questions or remarks made by trainees, the instructor must know how to find a grain of reason and, to the surprise of the audience, present the good side of the author of the question or remark, without playing up to him but rather showing the possibility of cooperation. It is categorically forbidden to put hostile trainees down or hold them up to ridicule. In every case, it is essential to give the trainee the chance to "save face." However, the trainee himself, and the other trainees, must have a clear sense of how close he came to "losing face," a feeling of the breath of danger. Let the offending trainee retain a sense of gratitude even if he does not relate it to the instructor.

After the course comes to an end, the group ought to have a sense of mild dissatisfaction—because they were not told everything, there are things that remain unknown, there is no feeling of completeness and wholeness of the material, there is the desire to do more and read more on their own to make up for what the instructor did not do and did not tell them.

As far as the actual content of illustrated lectures is concerned, the reader will not find it in the pages of this book—neither the size nor the genre permit it. That is material for another book, if circumstances ever permit me to write it. Fortunately, there are still video recordings, which in time will probably lead to the appearance of a video school.

Conclusion

Through the ages, people who publicly proclaim malicious and immoral intentions have probably been rare. Most bad deeds are committed under the cover of nice words. There are a lot of people who live by a double standard. From the standpoint of pragmatics, this is convenient. To be sure, it is difficult to retain self-respect. In order to live in harmony with themselves, people with a double standard need to expand their ranks and argue constantly that any other kind of life is impossible. This is why they desire to provoke others to take on such high moral obligations—in order (by virtue of the obvious unfeasibility of the latter) to ensure that they are doomed to a double standard. That is the approximate picture of the mechanism by which people whose morality is not particularly high frequently look cleaner than people who are really decent, who have set their moral crossbar lower precisely because they can in fact jump over it every time.

We frequently come up against attempts to place our school, which is steadily (and, for many, inexplicably!) moving forward, between a moral Scylla and Charybdis: If you teach the good, what are your trainees going to do in the hard real world? But if you teach the bad, you ought to be ashamed of yourself!

Worshipers of the double standard are especially agitated by the study of the techniques of taking control and holding it, based to a large extent on ancient Chinese principles of the art of war (to say nothing of the principles of Machiavelli!). The subtext is approximately this: It's all right to train people like me (that is, vehicles of high morality), but what you're doing is training ordinary people (read: Neanderthals), who might foolishly use the knowledge they have gained for evil!

Social technology (and, in particular, personnel-technology) cannot be either moral or immoral. It is a weapon that can be used for evil or for good. A weapon is beyond morality. It merely enhances human potential. That any weapon demands a certain cautiousness in its use is another matter. But in fact this is the subject of study in our school.

You have now read this book, and undoubtedly it has evoked contradictory feelings. It's as if you went fishing, derived pleasure from it, but didn't catch a fish. It's as if the fish were swimming nearby but never took the hook.

You are not mistaken in this feeling. The fact is that we have yet to enter the age of personnel-technology. Man came down once from the trees and subordinated the environment to himself. Now he will have to come down from the trees again and adapt mankind to his needs.

10

Diagnosis, Destruction, and Creation: A New Conception of Training Managers for the Market Economy

Iurii Iu. Ekaterinoslavskii

Many years of domination by the administrative-command system in all spheres of life in the former Soviet Union have not only led to a crisis in the economy but have almost totally eliminated such qualities in our people as entrepreneurship, business acumen, and initiative. For many of us, unfortunately, these losses are irreversible in character. Our brief experience in the economy of the transitional period—from rigid centralization to a certain amount of freedom in market relations and entrepreneurship—reflects an ambiguous picture. On the one hand, the first results of the work of certain stock-company, lease-based, cooperative, joint, and outright private enterprises have graphically demonstrated the possibility of reviving entrepreneurship. On the other hand, any expansion of economic freedom is accompanied by a strengthening and spread of such negative phenomena as fraud, poor business practices, deterioration in interpersonal relations, aggressiveness, and rapid exhaustion of the physical and mental potential of the entrepreneurs. There is a growing number of unscrupulous entrepreneurs, people who have neither honor nor conscience, let alone the rudimentary knowledge necessary for entrepreneurship. Corruption and the rackets

Russian text © 1991 by Professor Iurii Iu. Ekaterinoslavskii. "Diagnostika, razrushenie, sozidanie: novaia kontseptsiia podgotovki upravlencheskikh kadrov dlia rynochnoi ekonomiki Sovetskogo Soiuza." This unpublished manuscript is translated and printed here with the permission of the author.

are flourishing, and there is the real danger that honest and capable entrepreneurs will either be forced to adopt these "rules of the game" or get out of business. It must also be kept in mind that the state of the socioeconomic crisis can only exacerbate this negative situation.

How are these problems to be solved? How can we get out of the crisis? How can we develop hundreds of thousands of entrepreneurs who are not only energetic and assertive but also knowledgeable and honest, as well as physically and mentally healthy? Every type of entrepreneurship, whether state, lease-based, private, or other type— has its own characteristics. But whereas the state economy (with all its shortcomings) at least has certain established rules and procedures, small- and medium-sized businesses are like an open field where both healthful and poisonous fruits are growing vigorously, sometimes side by side.

So there are plenty of problems here, and solutions to them must vary but be interconnected, just as all aspects of economic and social life are interconnected.

In this article I will deal only with the problems and solutions that relate to training primarily for small and medium-sized businesses. Many Soviet and foreign colleagues have asked us, "What can there be that's new? What problems are there? Just teach them using the same programs that have proved their worth in the West and the East in free-enterprise economies." The training of Soviet entrepreneurs is in fact proceeding according to that clear scenario in the former USSR and abroad. Numerous small, medium-sized, and large schools for managers have been organized in the former USSR. As one of the consequences of the strengthening of international trust and bilateral cooperation between the former USSR and the countries of the West, several thousand Soviet managers are now going to the United States, Germany, and France for classroom and on-the-job training. Not bad, you say? Well, I can't share that optimism. And there are solid reasons for this judgment.

First of all, new types of knowledge about economics, entrepreneurship, and management are being put into the consciousness of people who have been shaped by social and economic conditions that are quite different from those in a free enterprise economy. And these new types of knowledge are vigorously rejected by those who hold entrenched social and economic stereotypes. Naturally, certain knowledge and skills are being acquired, but for most "students" these are never going to be transformed into activities that correspond to Western ideas. The real way to arrive at a solution to this problem involves training entre-preneurs in their youth. As far as people in the middle and older age brackets are concerned, we're not going to get anywhere unless special methods to destroy old stereotypes are used.

Second, it is necessary not only to shape a new type of professional entrepreneur but also, essentially, to shape a new social type of worker. It may be that this problem is not so obvious at present either to Western or Soviet specialists. But unless it is taken into account, the consequences may be very destructive. What we are talking about, in particular, is the formulation of the social priorities of entrepreneurial activity. In "big business"—state business and management—these priorities are shaped, so to speak, "from above" by the government. But what about small and medium-sized businesses? Here the "rules of the game" of the era of the first accumulation of capital are flourishing. This could probably be stated in even stronger terms, because whereas an evolutionary process of creating professional entrepreneurship was characteristic of the West, what is taking place in the former USSR is a leap in a very short interval of time. And those who are the best prepared for this leap are the real or potential smart operators of the shadow economy who are accustomed to surviving in stiff competition and in a criminal environment.

I think that many of the Americans who are taking part in business with new Soviet partners have come up against astonishing discrepan-cies with respect to social attitudes, rules of behavior, and other attri-butes of entrepreneurship.

In the third place, the aforementioned amount of training of entre-preneurs in Western countries can in no way be compared with the needs of the economy. Meanwhile, the quality of entrepreneurial train-ing in the former USSR, with extremely rare exceptions, cannot be considered remotely satisfactory. This means it is of paramount neces-sity to train "teachers" for business schools in the same specialty that is found in the United States—as instructors in adult education. And it is equally vital at the same time to train entrepreneurs in a powerful and methodologically substantiated flow, recruiting for the process an in-creasing number of specially trained instructors in adult education.

And now let's turn to a description of our proposed conception of entrepreneurial training for the changing economy. It takes account of both the aforementioned issues of the shaping of training professional entrepreneurs as well as the qualitative and quantitative issues of operating centers for management training. The main focus is the content and sequencing of stages of instruction and of tailoring it to individual needs.

The following stages are proposed:

1. Evaluation of the personality of the potential entrepreneur.

2. Destruction of the stereotypes of socioeconomic behavior that were established under the administrative-command system.

3. Enhancement of the psychosomatic potential of the people being trained.

4. Offering of a course titled "Entrepreneurship" ("Market Economy") and concrete reinforcement of new skills and patterns of behavior for entrepreneurs.

What is new here are the second, third, and partially (in terms of the course structure and instructional methods) the fourth stages. There is a certain amount of novelty in the first stage as well. In what follows I will describe in detail the content of each stage and the instruments available for implementation. I will also note the problems that are being addressed, as well as what I see to be potential areas of cooperation between Soviet and American specialists.

Stage 1: Evaluation of the student's personality

In accordance with the aforementioned need to develop a new social type of entrepreneur I propose a whole spectrum of evaluations to determine not only professionally important but also socially meaningful qualities. These include five groups of qualities:

1. Basic personality traits (dominant qualities, thinking, motivation, sociability, self-esteem, self-control). In order to determine these traits, a broad range of instruments are available—from designing individual scenarios to Shmishek and Leary tests, MMPI [Minnesota Multiphasic Personality Inventory] subtests, the Freiburg questionnaire, and so on.

2. Qualities that are professionally important for entrepreneurial activity (independent thinking; motivation to achieve goals; risk taking; self-control; self-esteem; total amount of knowledge and skills in the field of economics, management, and marketing). This group of qualities can be assessed with nonverbal tests, expert assessments, modifications of the Raven and Liusher tests, a set of business games, cases, and precedents.

3. Evaluation of the characteristics of interpersonal relations (intergroup interaction; psychophysical structure of the team). Here again,

existing or modified instruments (the Leary Test, the "Motivation" Test, sociometric questionnaires, the test to evaluate the role functions of group members, etc.) can be used.

4. Evaluation of sociocultural characteristics of behavior (level of the individual's socialization; overall culture). The instruments used to evaluate this group of qualities are not so well developed. I think that it would be advisable here to analyze the following parameters: mastery of professional ethics; ethical components of the personality; vocabulary; and artistry in behavior and communication.

5. Evaluation of the psychosomatic state of the potential entrepreneur. I will not focus upon this in detail, but will simply note that there are ample diagnostic methods for a preliminary, premedical analysis of physical and mental health.

As can be seen from the above list, a considerable number of parameters are subject to evaluation. In the final analysis, what is most important and complex here is not so much the compilation of a person's general personality profile (it is entirely appropriate here to make use of descriptions in the form of frames) but rather the interpretation of this characterization, the evaluation of potential abilities for normal entrepreneurship. In any case, the proposed set of evaluations makes it possible to subdivide the group enrolling in the training into differentiated subgroups—on the basis of criteria to be chosen—or to decide to provide exclusively individualized instruction.

Stage 2: Destruction of stereotypes of socioeconomic behavior established under the administrative-command system

Without this stage, the instruction will not lead to the desired results. What this involves, in fact, is a stage of social technology designed to remake the individual's personality. And even if the future entrepreneur wants to reject the old stereotypes, on the subconscious level he will still be held prisoner by them. The life of people in the former USSR has been too strongly saturated with legal nihilism, the acquisition of goods by illegal means, the desire for unearned privileges, conformism of the totalitarian character, rudeness, disrespect for the thinking of others, and similar negative stereotypes of social and economic behavior that are incompatible with the concept of professional entrepreneurship.

We have developed an approach to solving this complicated scientific and practical problem. We propose a three-step procedure for destroying old stereotypes. The *first step* is to identify the stereotypical behavior of every student. This is done by comparing the student's general profile with the three-dimensional classification scheme "situations—behavioral stereotypes—negative consequences of using old stereotypes." To develop such a classification scheme, first socioeconomic situations are classified with respect to three features: the type of activity, the object of people's interaction, and the subjects of interaction. Then a description is made of the basic types of socioeconomic activity. Finally, a list is drawn up of possible negative consequences of entrepreneurial catastrophes— loss of capital, loss of reputation, loss of capable employees, and so on.

The classifiers described above are local. Combining them results in a three-dimensional classification scheme, "situations—old stereotypes—negative consequences." Such a scheme is currently in the developmental stage.

The *second step* in the procedure to destroy old stereotypes has a sound methodological basis: business games, cases, precedents, and other active learning methods. The only stipulation is to tie the results of the games, cases, and other methods to the list of negative consequences of using old stereotypes that were discussed above. It would be wrong to confine ourselves to computerized procedures for identifying stereotypes; what is needed is an analysis of practical examples. I think that the development of games and cases can have as its basis the modeling of a variant of the choice of strategy with respect to payments and probabilities.

The *third step* in the procedure for destroying stereotypes has a positivist nuance. It consists of shaping new psychological precepts of socioeconomic activity. For this we require the following guidelines, which are very rarely encountered in the practice of Soviet entrepreneurship: a long-term strategy of activity, integrative work tactics, well-defined goals, and psychological stability. It is advisable not so much to explain as to reinforce these guidelines using a variety of training exercises (such as "Risk," "Projecting the Future," "Communications Laboratory," etc.). We have drawn up a list of such exercises.

Stage 3: Enhancement of psychosomatic potential

Naturally, destroying stereotypes, replacing valued outcomes in social and economic spheres, and demonstrating the failure of previous strategies is inevitably stressful for people. But what is most important is the fact that the disappearance of the old atmosphere, of strategies that permit no alternatives, and of, in effect, economic irresponsibility, as well as the need for substantially more intensive and diverse activities (with successes and failures) are all capable of exhausting quickly the potential of the future entrepreneur. Moreover, the former USSR lacks the appropriate infrastructure to enhance psychological and physical stability. The remedy is not just to create and develop such an infra-structure but rather, in particular, to reorient and reinforce the internal needs of future entrepreneurs. Otherwise—and this happens frequently nowadays—what develops is asocial behavior, aggressiveness, and the loss of a humanistic orientation.

What is needed in order to deal with the problems that arise is to implement special programs along two directions. The first direction calls for developing specific psychophysiological functions to improve the body's defensive powers, actualizing creative abilities, and expand-ing the sphere of the conscious and the subconscious. For these pur-poses the following methods can be used: traditional oriental health and curative methods; modern methods of diagnosing and monitoring one's psychophysiological condition; individual computerized moni-toring methods, maintaining, and improving physical fitness; therapeu-tic exercise programs adapted to the social and emotional state of trainees, who are grouped by selected dominant characteristics.

The second direction calls for changing the inner orientations of the trainee: from an orientation of seeking help for himself from outside (from a doctor, coach, benevolent organization, and so on) to an orien-tation of satisfying the natural need to help others. This can be accom-plished by implementing programs of self-regulation and self-awareness. The following methods are being used: attractive and extremely popular methods of oriental health and fitness systems (individualized); involving the future entrepreneurs in working with sick people and participating in charitable activities. The existing methods for improving trainees' psy-chosomatic state will need to be adapted to the economic and social goals that are being mapped out as the Soviet Union proceeds along the path of joining the world community of free nations.

Stage 4: Teaching the "Entrepreneurship" course

In practical terms, the shaping of this new type of entrepreneur started at the end of the second stage. Only now, however, in the fourth stage, can we discuss professional training as such. Here the experience of business schools and universities in the United States would seem to be extremely fruitful. At the same time, an analysis of programs providing instruction in management and entrepreneurship in those educational institutions makes it possible to conclude that it is necessary, in training Soviet entrepreneurs, to structure the course somewhat differently and shift some of the emphases.

In particular, the training should be divided precisely into three parts.

1. Shaping new models of socioeconomic activity. What is necessary here are special courses, for example: "Humanitarian Values, Motives, and Ethics of Professional Entrepreneurship"; "The Life and Achievements of Outstanding Businessmen and Entrepreneurs"; "The History of the Rise and Development of Leading Firms"; "How Developing States Become Great." All of these courses are illustrations of the positive consequences of the new guidelines.

2. The "Economics, Entrepreneurship, and Management" course. In this course, which is quite traditional for American entrepreneurs, the emphasis needs to be placed on such themes as "Small Business Incubators," "Industrial Parks," "Stock Exchanges," "Corporate Ethics," and "Advertising." These are fields of knowledge that are least familiar to Soviet entrepreneurs.

3. Immersion of future entrepreneurs in practical activities by having them start their "own" business as well as participate in consulting and club activities.

This, then, is a brief description of the new conception of training Soviet entrepreneurs. Does it seem utopian? Yes, given present forms of training in Soviet management training centers, it is unquestionably utopian. Nevertheless, many elements of the proposed conception have been accomplished in a number of centers, although not systematically enough. The new approach also requires a new instructional methodology and new organizational forms. As far as the former is concerned, the only thing that would seem acceptable is to convert to intensive instruction, with workdays lasting twelve to thirteen hours that are spent away from the familiar, domestic conditions of life. As for organizational forms, they can vary depending both on the results of the evaluation (the first stage of the training) and many other conditions. But what appears to be most promising during the initial stage of shaping a corps of Soviet entrepreneurs is the creation of an Academy of Entrepreneurship—not purely as a training center, however, but a center that serves to integrate business, training, research, and club and commercial activities—a center designed to revive Russian entrepreneurship and integrate it with the entrepreneurship of the West and the East. The Russian Academy of Entrepreneurship is a nongovernmental organization recently set up by approximately two dozen founders— enterprises, educational institutions, and associations. The institute in which the author of the present article works is the primary founder.

11

Open Games as a Method of Personal Transformation and Motivation

Irina V. Zhezhko

Business games have recently received much attention in both academic journals and popular publications in the former USSR. These games have spread throughout the country and are used in many areas of economic and social life. Not long ago, game specialists had the burden of showing that the games deserved serious attention. Now, however, game specialists are considered *perestroika* professionals [3]. Business games have become a popular theme in the mass media. Television and newspapers have promoted them to such an extent that the well-known games, such as the CEO's election at the RAF minibus plant [33], the all-union summer camp at Artek, and the Baikal-Amur main railway line, are as popular among their followers as world sports events.

This article presents an overview of a newly developed type of game known as open games [11, 12]. Open games have turned out to be extremely efficient methods for solving weakly structured organizational problems. Their development is an achievement unique to the USSR, and the open-game movement has claimed the attention of scholars from all over the world. Appearing toward the end of the 1970s, this new kind of game united the activities of various scholars who represented many different disciplines. In fact, proponents of open games constitute an invisible college. When we speak of the open-game movement, we mean not only games but also various imitations and spin-offs such as open-game techniques separate from the games themselves, integrated problem-solving sessions, game-training schools, and situational-analysis sessions that use the gaming techniques. The members of the movement publish their own journal, *Kentavr* [Centaur], which declares the creation of a new variety of Homo Sapiens they call *Homo Ludens* (gaming man) after the well-known book, *Magister Ludi*, by Herman Hesse [19].

In 1989 there were more than thirty independent teams conducting such games [22, no. 1, pp. 59–70]. According to recently published reports, as many as 10,000 top-level managers, scientists, and officials took part in 136 open games during 1990. Because of the unofficial, grassroots nature of open games, the actual number of group leaders is unknown. Considering the rate of expansion of the games, the figures above have probably doubled by this writing.

Can one really explain what an open game is to someone who has never played one? The gaming specialists would unanimously answer negatively. "The only way to learn the rules of this game of games is to take the usual prescribed course, which requires many years; and none of the initiates could ever possibly have any interest in making these rules easier to learn." [19, p. 6]. To really grasp the essence of the game, it must be experienced either by participating in one or by creating one.

Nevertheless, I will try to convey a feeling for what this method is by addressing the following questions:

• How are open games different from business games and simulations?

• What are the objectives and achievements of the open-game movement?

• What are the results and products of the game?

• What are the origins of the game movement?

• What is the essential principle of an open game?

• What is involved in the organization and preparation of an open game?

• Does it have any analogues in the Western world?

• What is the social importance of open games?

Business games versus open games

Business games as such have more than half a century of history. The first business game in the USSR was conducted in 1932 at the Leningrad Institute for Engineering and Economics. The game was created to model the opening of a new typewriter manufacturing plant [7, pp. 3–6]. The first business game in the United States, "The Imitation of Top-level Management Decisions," was developed in 1956 by the American Management Association (AMA). This project laid the foundation for future business games. At present, creating a business or teaching game is a highly labor-intensive process. It requires methodological research work which ultimately results in a package of computer programs, audio and video equipment, instructions, and other game documentation [1].

The first open game was produced by members of the Moscow Methodological Seminar, headed by G.P. Schedrovitskii, in 1979. Called an organization-action game, its theme was: "New Approaches to Complex Interdisciplinary Applied Research Projects." Its purpose was to investigate the ability of scientists in areas of basic research to move towards self-organization and cooperation to solve complex problems. The organization-action game was defined as a way to reorganize the collective thinking and action of representatives of different professions and scientific disciplines.

Soon after the initial open game, others were organized, such as the innovation game [15]; the design game [21, 43]; the imitation game [24]; the practical game by A. Prigozhin [42, pp. 76–83]; the psychotechnical game [40]; and the teaching, organization-management, and organization-thinking games [22, no. 1].

Several adherents to the open-game movement differentiate open games from business games. Dudchenko [13] contrasts two types of games in the Table. Peter Schedrovitskii [38, p. 9], speaking in particular about organization-action game rules, says, "In the game promotion, a new game-search, game-improvisation emerges as a result of the rules used at the very beginning of the game." He then adds, "during the first steps of the game, the organizers are the only ones who are aware of the primary perceptions and principles used for constructing the game. They have the knowledge and the experience to organize the thought process. They also have the authority to invent new rules of the game. During the course of the game, however, individual participants and working groups take the initiative in defining the structure of the game."

Tiukov [24, pp. 50–53] claims that a game is a union of form and activity. A business game may require players only formally to fulfill

Business Games versus Open Games

Business games	Open games
There is a strict set of rules to the game.	The playing rules need not be followed strictly.
There is a closed system of rules.	The system of rules changes in the process of playing the game.
The game requires *much quantitative information*.	The game does not require any additional factual information. All the participants are *familiar with the problem*.
The game strategy is based on role playing by the participants.	The game strategy is based upon the personalities and emotional participation of the players, and on their own *self-determination*.
The solutions are *predetermined*.	The solutions are *unknown*.
The goal is to teach.	The goal is to enable participants' transformation.
The basic task is to structure patterns in standard situations.	The task is to learn how to deal with unique problem situations that have no ready solutions.

Source: Dudchenko, V. [13, p. 25].

the rules of the game and the functions and actions according to assigned roles and a predetermined game plot. In this case, "no game motifs will appear and the game will not change the player psychologically." In other words, if a participant takes part in the game, but is not totally emotionally challenged, the game will not change him or her. In traditional business games, A. Tiukov states, the substance of the work and the ways it is run stay hidden from reflexive analysis. The real game activity, according to Tiukov, arises only when the participants "shift their attention from the results and products of the thought process to the general means and logic of it."

The open-game movement, having formed virtually independently from business games, has the following origins:

• the works of the Moscow methodological seminar, which were used as a basis for open games [37, 22];

• systems analysis as the methodology of analysis and problem solving; methods of creative thinking and searching for ideas [2];

• American and Soviet experience in design ("brainstorming" [32],

"morphological analysis" [44], "synectics" [18], "functional-cost analysis" [30], the "algorithm for solving design problems" [4], the design seminar [20, 39]);
• organization development, action research [27, 28, etc.], social changes [5, 9, etc.], and organization consulting;
• classical philosophy and logic (one of the predecessors of open games, heuristic methods, derives ultimately from the Greek oracles at Delphi, through Socrates, Bacon, Descartes, and Euler);
• the total immersion technique of foreign-language learning by the Bulgarian scholar G. Lozanov [23];
• the "social innovations" movement (Tavistock Institute for Human Relations), and other types of sociopsychological techniques [25];
• and, finally, business, children's, and military games.

Within the framework of gaming practice, it has become possible, and fruitful, to unite various cultural traditions, scientific approaches, paradigms, and practical methods. Presumably, the process of assimilation of other types of sociotechnical and psychotechnical practices in gaming techniques will continue precisely because of the main qualities of the games—their *openness* and ability to bring about personal transformation.

The essential principle of open games: Personal transformation

"In an organization-action game," says Naumov [31, p. 25], "*the principle of personal transformation* is most important for players and organizers alike. An organization-action game promotes personal transformation, unlike brainstorming, synectics, or business games, which are established for solving concrete problems." According to open-game doctrine, in order for society to be transformed, scientific testing of possible transformation alternatives and strategies is absolutely necessary. In essence, "games and the gaming methodology became a way of realizing democracy, *glasnost'*, competition, and responsibility; those principles on which *perestroika* thinking is based" [3, p. 9].

Personal qualities, not usually worked on or encouraged in daily circumstances, are developed in game playing. People look for sense and direction in their activities, evaluating their past practices in the context of a certain system of values. Games are responsible for developing a program of actions aimed at changing present situations. In a game, stereotypes are rethought and dismissed, limitations that normally restrict the establishment of effective cooperation are eliminated, and responsibility is voluntarily assumed.

CEOs of large enterprises who participated in an innovation game concluded: "As a result of participating in this game we have come to the realization that we are capable of accomplishing more than we had previously thought we could" [13]. The people who took part in this game, after feeling, seeing, and "touching" the stereotypes of their work, realized that the limits for activity, initiative, and autonomy were based in their own consciousness, habits, and stereotypical reactions to typical situations. One popular stereotypical reaction that the author sees is the inclination, in critical situations, to use demagogic formulae instead of deep analysis and open discussion, to appeal to higher authorities, and to think that the solution does not depend on them personally.

Essentially, the game procedures and techniques are also the techniques of personal transformation. These major techniques are illustrated by two examples of games: the organization-action game and the innovation game. In the organization-action game, which is oriented primarily toward the development of analytical skills and thinking, the leading processes are self-determination, mutual determination, and introspective analysis. In an innovation game, the methods of organizational and sociopsychological training play the key role in the participants' development. The program includes a series of procedures and techniques directed at the creation of optimal interaction within groups. Organizational training, as described by the authors of *The Innovation Game Program* [14], consists of the intensive acquisition of experience in organizing group work. This method is based on insights and feelings that the gaming group experiences by means of the sequence "action, analysis of mistakes, search for alternatives, and action." In the framework of organizational training the following problems of skill development are posed and resolved: (a) introspective analysis, which is imperative to the understanding of organizational activity; (b) the organization of group work; and (c) contriving situations that promote self-organization and self-transformation in groups.

Sociopsychological training within the game facilitates the process of acquiring knowledge and skills in effective social behavior, helps increase competence in relationships, and cultivates the skills of self and group psychoanalysis, including collective relations, constructive resolution of conflicts, emotional and behavioral self-control, assumption of certain sociopsychological roles, and control over group sociopsychological processes.

The principle of transformation is applied not only to game participants but also to game teams. Almost every game team practices two kinds of activities: organizing the game and analyzing the process in order to make improvements to it.

Organizing and scheduling open games

An open game is a planned and purposeful whole. Its leading principle is to create and support a structure that can best promote collective thinking and problem solving. It is not intended as a device to advocate a particular decision or point of view of a game team, an expert, or anybody else. Because it is designed to be open-ended and to produce a self-generative thinking community, it is demanding of staff resources and skills.

Open games are typically organized as follows:
• The participants are brought together in an isolated community for as long as it is necessary for them to solve the problem (usually not less than five days, and sometimes as many as twenty). This temporary night-and-day community shares an understanding that the problem being addressed is really important to themselves and to other concerned people.
• The place is chosen to guarantee some degree of "social island" conditions for the participants and a maximum of freedom and comfort for face-to-face interaction.
• The working day is at least ten hours (with lunch and dinner breaks), but the participants often work literally around the clock.
• There is a game policy forbidding the participants to arrive late or leave early.
• A usual game day includes the following: group work, plenary, and club activities (free discussion, recreation).

The game structure consists of the following phases:
1. situation analysis and problem identification;
2. participants' individual and group self-definition regarding the problem under consideration, declaration of values, principles, and positions; setting of goals and objectives;

3. search for new approaches, strategies and decisions, planning;
4. programming;
5. constraints, testing against reality and original value criteria;
6. plenary introspective analysis of the game session, its personal and collective results and products.

At the beginning participants are divided into several groups. There are various techniques of dividing the players up. The most frequently used ones are:

• Thematic. At the first meeting, the participants analyze the problem by separating it into several subproblems. Afterward, each participant chooses to work on one of these subproblems, and thus thematic groups are created.

• Positional. Again, the participants themselves choose the group they want to join. This time each group represents an organization, movement, social or professional group concerned with the problem.

• Competitive. The game team distributes the participants to several groups with equal creative potential to work on the same problem, and thus produce competitive projects.

Each group has its own track in the game, with the tracks coordinated at the daily plenaries. Each plenary is devoted to an analysis of the deadlocks and bottlenecks in each phase of the game. A spokesperson for each group makes a presentation of the day's results and all participants discuss the results. No restrictions are placed on the group returning to the work of earlier phases if it is felt that they need some reworking.

By phase 3 (search for new approaches), a new community (the game community) comes into being and takes responsibility for conducting the game.

Preparing an open game

Preparing a game is a specialized professional activity. Thus, people who make up the game teams consider this work as a part of their professional occupation (such as consulting, research, etc.). The methodology of the game is not specialized by academic disciplines; in other words, it is not dependent on the content of the problem that faces each particular game. A certain game *culture* has been formed, i.e., a number of techniques, concepts, and theories that serve the game practice. Special training is needed to be a team member.

Preparation for an open game takes about two months and includes the following procedures:

• diagnosing the organizations (or regions, cities, etc.) where the game is to be conducted, as well as its spheres of activity; problem diagnosis;

• determining the major opinions about the issues under consideration, as well as the important conflicts;

• interacting with the clients: reformulating basic problems and goals and identifying expected results;

• projecting and creating a scenario for the game; preparing the game team.

The selection process of the players is determined by the type and scenario of the game. Nevertheless, several general principles can be formulated from past game experience. There are several categories of players that are typically selected for the game [42, pp. 10–11]:

• "problem bearers," representing various aspects of the issue to be resolved, including social interests, nomenclature, professional and role positions;

• researchers and experts familiar with the problem, representatives of different approaches towards its solution;

• "donors" and "catalyzers": people with socially valuable innovative experience, ideas, and programs that are close to the subject of the game;

• specialists in organization and methodology of the work processes (problem analysis, planning, programming, project management, etc.);

• specialists in organization and methodology of the game itself: technicians or facilitators, methodologists, researchers, administrators, members of the media, etc.;

• other potential implementors of the solutions proposed during the game.

Of course, a candidate who satisfies several criteria at once is highly desirable.

Game results and products

Open games are considered a means toward (a) personal and group transformation, (b) realization of people's potential, (c) management or organization consulting, (d) organizational development, (e) collective analysis, (f) communication, (g) problem solving, (h) design of new types of organizations and organizational structures, (i) the implementation of innovation, and so on. Behind the diversity of game purposes, there is a multitude of directions for the open-game movement and within the movement, a variety of game subtypes depending on their goals, methodology, technology, resources, time consumption, and finally, the desired results.

Each type of game and each game itself has its own goals, problems, and a number of expected results. Only some of these results are tangible products, and only a few typically culminate in projects or recommendations that meet professional criteria and standards. However, the essential results of the game "live" in the minds of the game participants and of all those affected by the results of the game.

In order to trace the course of game results, it is necessary to highlight the role of the game *client*. Before the game starts, the client's role includes making the decision to hold the game, organizing the participants, and paying the expenses. During the game, the client's role changes, and moreover, new persons emerge who appropriate this role as a means of self-determination. Most of the participants will begin to actively influence the course of the game and the form and content of the results. They become the true *clients* and *owners* of the results. The self-determination of the players and "appropriation" of results are not simply by-products of the game, but essential conditions for a successful game.

Thus, the central goal of open games is accomplished. Reform activities are established which, in addition to new ideas and projects, can develop the participants' skills. Nevertheless, neither the skills nor the projects can be viewed as exhaustive or complete: the construction and solution of the problem is only a specific experience, which participants will further study and develop after the game.

Experts unanimously believe that the results of the game can be very problematic. Rozin [34, p. 48] sees the problem as follows: "The broadening and changing consciousness of the game participants does not always lead to changes in their daily activities because they are influenced by the complex socio-organizational structures of industry and by colleagues who did not receive game benefits." However, the author agrees that "without changing one's consciousness or adequately broadening the understanding of one's activities, which are the desired consequences of the game, one cannot progress. Without methods learned from the game, it is undoubtedly more difficult to insure the success of innovations and improvements of organizational structures" [34, p. 49].

One way to increase implementation of projects developed during open games is to create new social roles that take effect after the game. Examples of such roles are given below in a description of the game, "The CEOs' competition."

The CEOs' competition

In January of 1987, in the RAF minibus plant in Elgava, a small town in Latvia, the first all-union competition to fill the vacancy of chief executive officer of the plant was conducted using the organization-action game [33]. The game was a practical attempt to learn about the process of democratization in the USSR by "playing out" some possible scenarios for the future. Two or three days of a game represent two or three years of real life. In this sense the game is life in condensed form.

This experiment was meant to prepare the way for economic and social reforms. The economists who were promoting the experiment considered the elections to be a way of making the plant more independent from the central administrative apparatus that often made unreasonable and harmful demands on the plant's senior management. Sociologists also stressed that election of plant managers would improve workers' attitudes by giving workers greater participation in managing the plant.

Unfortunately, the elections of enterprise managers that followed the decree of the plenum of the Central Committee of the Communist party in January 1987 brought disappointing results. Instead of real democratic elections, most elections that took place around the country were a sham. This happened because in the last fifty years in the USSR people had became accustomed to having only one candidate to choose from, and that candidate was endorsed by party officials.

The CEO's competition became a way of discovering the hidden aspects and controversies of the process of democratization of the workplace. The game was deliberately designed in a way that would facilitate the discovery of such problems in terms of ideas as well as in terms of people's actual relationships. The main task of the organizers was to make the content of conflicts the subject for special analysis, to emphasize their essential foundations, and to transform every conflict into a situation which everyone understood.

By the time the game started, there were several separate factions, each of which could be considered a client: the youth newspaper *Komsomol'skaia pravda*, the RAF enterprise, the Central Committee of the Latvian communist party, the ministry of the automobile industry, and, finally, the group of methodologists or game technicians headed by V. Popov. A critical point is that the viewpoint of the team of game technicians concerning the substance and form of the elections was not the same as that of other clients. Thus, from the very beginning an uncertain situation which was threatening to turn into a series of local organizational (technical) conflicts was not treated directly, but was intensified by self-determination of the team. In this way, the team had brought into question the traditional perceptions of the clients.

When they designed the game, the team operated according to the following premises:

1. If the new head of the enterprise is put into the old system of management, he will be ineffective. Therefore, only a radical change of the whole management system from top to bottom (that is, a system innovation) can really change the situation. Thus, during the elections a new program and strategy for plant transformation should be designed and implemented.

2. The object of the game should be not the competition of candidates, but their cooperative work on the analysis of the situation and framing the strategies to transform the plant.

According to the first proposal that was submitted by the game team, the game was to consist of two stages and last approximately fifteen days. In contrast, the clients insisted on the traditional form of the competition. This misunderstanding created a conflict between them that lasted throughout the entire game. The main argument against the game team project was that it would take workers away from their jobs for much longer than traditional elections, and, therefore, would slow down production (the plant's output was chronically below its potential by 40 percent or more).

The game proposed by the game team clearly refuted this argument. Productivity rose and the plant fulfilled its monthly quota for the first time. But, most importantly, the new perspectives of higher productivity and rationalization of the production process were established. In short, the game created certain social mechanisms that caused an increase in workers' motivation and interest in the fate of the plant. This effect is relatively close to the results that Elton Mayo observed at

Western Electric in 1929–1932, though it is very different in the way it was achieved.

In its final version, the game was conducted in two stages. The first one was a four-day organization-action game that concentrated on analysis of the situation and development of alternative strategies for plant improvement. The second stage, which lasted for three days, was conducted as an election campaign of five candidates.

The candidates became the main characters during the second stage. They enlisted the support of their co-workers who participated with them in the first stage of the game to finish the "revolution" of the plant and to involve the entire work force in a democratic discussion of the plant's future. This meant that during the first stage the candidates for the CEO position experienced major changes of attitudes and expectations, including a change in their self-definition and their objectives. In this way the five candidates were no longer competitors for the same position, but became an integrated team who were united by a common view of the situation and a shared understanding of the problems, and who possessed programs for action. This transformation then made it possible to make substantial changes in the workplace. The candidates understood that they were not part of a contest, but were, in fact, the creators of a historical precedent and model of the democratization process. The candidates who had gone through the first stage of the game began to view themselves as a "commando" group that could quickly change the situation, as well as the consciousness and everyday life of their co-workers, by using only themselves, their convictions, behavior, persuasive ability and programs as tools of influence. Afterward, one of the five candidates was elected by the plant workers based on the best program for the plant's turnaround.

The following goals were fulfilled in the game:

1. the consultants and the five candidates for the CEO position designed the options for transforming the RAF minibus plant using system analysis of the situation;

2. the game helped the candidates determine their own position in this new situation, and enabled them to set their personal goals for the game, the CEO contest, the elections, and the post-election period;

3. the game involved the workers in designing and implementing the plant's development programs;

4. during the game all the important roles of a professional manager were practiced: organizer, administrator, manager, and politician.

Soviet open games versus Western search conferences

The method in the West most comparable to Soviet open games is the search conference. This method was first designed and managed by Fred Emery and Eric Trist in 1959. It was further developed and demonstrated by Dr. Emery and his colleagues in the early 1970s at the Centre for Continuing Education at Australian National University in Canberra [16, 17].

Open games and search conferences were developed independently of each other. There are several reasons for this. First, because they are techniques of working with people, such methods appear in the scientific literature only after they have been developing for some time and have received acceptance in the scientific community. Secondly, due to their practical nature these techniques are transferred primarily by means of person-to-person training (recall Hesse's remark) and direct sharing of experience. The third and the most obvious reason is the existence of language and cultural barriers between social scientists in different countries. Publications devoted to search conferences had not been translated into Russian when open games were being developed. Over the last twenty years or so there has been a steady growth of interest in Europe, North America, and Australia in the search conference and the application of this technique to a wide variety of planning issues and situations [8, 10]. The search conference has been used by business enterprises as a participatory approach to corporate planning and by unions in analyzing organizational and policy options. It has been deployed extensively as an agent of adaptation in education systems in local government and in government departments. There has been a growing interest from clubs, credit unions, and other voluntary associations, and it has been adopted in a range of national policy issues [8, p. 3].

Open games and search conferences have in common such things as objectives and spheres of application, the principles of participant choice, organization and scheduling, and even some elements of technology.

As can be seen from the above description both methods have broad and largely overlapping spheres of use as well as similar purposes and claims.

"The core of most of the claims is that the search approach generates cooperative and purposeful activity in groups, and finds its typical expression in participatory planning. For some, the emphasis is placed on strategic or corporate planning, with the claim that searching can be used to identify strategic objectives and set priorities. Others emphasize the contribution that the search conference can make in values clarification, in problem solving, or in conflict resolution. In contrast with traditional top-down, expert-based approaches to planning, the search conference is said to be better at generating commitment to plans, and therefore at improving the prospect for implementation" [8, p. 4].

All of these purposes are equally true of open games.

The two methods are distinctly different from such other traditional techniques as business games, the Delphi technique, working committees, conferences, and seminars (see Emery and Emery [17, pp. 287–92]). The two techniques were consciously designed to allow people to escape from traditional assumptions and best guesses, from something that is the "average" or considered "expert opinion." They were created as alternatives to the "organizational dinosaur," as Emery put it so well [17, p. 259]. Both techniques create situations and an atmosphere where democracy can be effectively put into practice.

In both techniques, social values are actively involved and there is an emphasis on the organization of group thinking. "By taking the individuals participating in it out of their own narrow worlds," both techniques begin to create a shared world or shared context [17, p. 272].

With respect to choosing participants, both methods require only that the participants have shown leadership in the past by displaying an active concern about the problem under investigation. In both techniques the work is separated from the participants' regular life. Search conferences as well as open games exercise two main forums for working: small groups and the plenary session. Each small group includes a representative of the organization team (although his/her position in the group significantly differs in the two techniques). Neither method uses much technical equipment: "All that is needed is plenty of large sheets of paper on the walls, and a couple of felt pens. . ." [17, p. 272].

In general, then, search conferences and open games seem very similar. Nevertheless, there are sharp dissimilarities in terms of their background and theoretical and methodological frameworks, as well as their technologies. Open games focus on the participants' transformation, rather than on their learning, as search conferences do. Open games also focus more on processes rather than on practical immediate results such as plans and problem solutions. In order to facilitate the transformation of participants, a game includes a reflection period and a phase called "problematization" where individual values, paradigms, and self-perception are challenged. These phases, as consciously set goals, are not a part of the search technique.

Because of more challenging objectives, in open games the team members face higher expectations than in the search conferences. The team member is not only a facilitator but also plays an indispensable role in forming a new way of group work and in conducting socio- and psychotherapy training. They also, as a rule, work with a large number of participants (from 30 to 200), as opposed to fewer participants in search conferences.

Summarizing all differences, open games, from my point of view, are far more effective in situations requiring the solution of nonroutine interorganizational problems and the search for innovative solutions. They also allow for the radical intellectual and personal transformation of participants. In fact, many participants acknowledge that the intensity of events and the profound personal changes they experience in the game could be considered equal to several years of life. Some participants have asserted that, as a result of the game, they changed their philosophy of life and their own role in it, including their professional activity.

The open game as a process of personal and professional transformation can be usefully applied in the Western world, when bureaucratic organizations put people in a position of partial responsibility where they lack conditions for effective collective thinking or problem solving.

Is it the sunset of the open-game movement?

Open-game techniques continue to be popular because they complement modern social conditions. With their help, a new culture of social interaction and problem solving is emerging. This culture is typified by the openness and diversity of the foundations of open games, their interests in social subjects, and their dialogue form which allows open and honest competition of various opinions and interests. This method lets society know itself better, look at its own face, realize that there is no "unanimous opinion" (and that there should not be one in an open society), and lets it gain from having different approaches and strategies compared and openly discussed.

Open games are a means of realizing the principles of democracy, *glasnost'*, competition, and responsibility, the principles on which social transformation is based. The elections of senior executives at RAF and Baikal-Amur railroad, the design of a new city with the participation of the population, and other games are new techniques that activate thinking and personal responsibility and build up new social actors who implement social change.

The open-game movement has played an exceptional role in unfreezing the professional and personal stereotypes that had developed in totalitarian Soviet society. The organization-action game questions the values of life and in this respect is a means of political influence. It has helped people question previous experience and search for ways to organize efforts within an organization or a region, as well as in whole territories and communities. This movement was by nature innovative and opposed to official ideology.

A methodology has been created for solving complex, weakly structured problems involving specialists, management and, most importantly, all interested or concerned people. This methodology ensures high motivation and integration of efforts in resolving common problems. To this end open games can be used in other countries. However, the open-game movement itself is having serious difficulties. Despite its popularity between 1979 and 1989, the movement remained uninstitutionalized. Now, in the conditions of the collapsing administrative-command system, the movement has received an opportunity to institutionalize itself and form its own organizational structure. As of the late 1980s, this process had begun. In my opinion, this attempt to structure the open-game movement is one of the main causes of the slowdown of the movement, which is by nature spontaneous, innovative, and unstructured in its organization.

Another concern is the nature of social problems that need to be addressed. The necessity of joint constructive efforts is evident today in light of the break-up of the Soviet state. Open games have shown themselves to be an effective tool for problem solving and unfreezing, but they hardly can serve as a developer of constructive skills. Whether they will continue to be effective in the new conditions, time will tell.

References

1. Abt, C.C., *Serious Games*. Lanham: University Press of America, 1987, 176 pp.
2. Ackoff, R.L. *Creating the Corporate Future. Plan or Be Planned For.* New York: John Wiley & Sons, 1981, 297 pp.

3. Afanas'ev, A. *Vybor* [Choice]. Moscow: Sovetskaia Rossiia, 1988, 100 pp.

4. Al'tshuller, G.S., Zlotin, V.L., and Filotov, V.I. *Professiia—poisk novogo: funktsional'no-stoimostnoi analiz i teoriia resheniia izobretatel'skikh zadach kak sistema vyiavlenia rezervov ekonomii* [Profession—a search for the new: a functional cost analysis and a theory of inventions for improving efficiency]. Kishinev: Kartia moldoveniaske, 1985, 196 pp.

5. Bennis, W. *Changing Organizations*. New York: McGraw-Hill, 1966, 223 pp.

6. Bennis, W., Benne, K., and Chin, R. *The Planning of Change*. New York: Holt, Rinehart and Winston, 1985, 487 pp.

7. Birshtein, M.M., Zhukov, R.P., and Timofeevskaia, T.P. "Vozniknovenie i sostoianie sovetskikh i zarubezhnykh delovykh igr" [The emergence and status of Soviet and foreign business games]. In *Aktivnye metody obucheniia i delovye igry* [Active methods of teaching and business games]. Novosibirsk: Institut ekonomiki i promyshlennogo proizvodstva, 1981, pp. 3–6.

8. Crombie, A. "The Nature and Types of Search Conferences," *International Journal of Lifelong Education*, Vol. 4, No. 1 (1985), pp. 3–33.

9. Chin, R., and Benne, K. "Change Strategies in Human Systems." Paper presented at Conference on the Planning of Changes. Seattle, Washington: University of Washington, July 1990.

10. De Nitish, R. "Search Conference and Conscientization Process in Building Institutions." In R. De Nitish, ed., *Alternative Designs of Human Organizations*. New Delhi: Sage Publications, 1981, 243 pp.

11. Dondurei, D., and Zhezhko, I., eds. *Proryv k real'nosti: Sotsial'noe proektirovanie v sfere kultury* [Breakthrough into reality. Social design in the cultural sphere]. Moscow: Nauchno-issledovatel'skii institut kultury, 1990, 426 pp.

12. Dudchenko, V.S. "Igrovye metody v sotsiologii" [Game methods in sociology], *Sotsiologicheskie issledovaniia*, 1990, no. 12, pp. 103–112.

13. Dudchenko, V.S. "Innovatsionnye igry: metodologiia i metodika" [Innovation games: methodology and method]. In I. Zhezhko, ed., *Igrovye metody. Sotsial'noe proektirovanie v sfere kultury* [Game methods. Social design in the cultural sphere]. Moscow: Nauchno-issledovatel'skii institut kultury, 1987, pp. 22–42.

14. Dudchenko, V.S., ed. *Programma innovatsionnoi igry* [The innovation game program]. Yaroslavl: Institut povysheniia kvalifikatsii rabotnikov ministerstva nefti i gaza, 1987, 107 pp.

15. Dudchenko, V.S. "Innovatsionnaia igra kak metod issledovaniia i razvitiia organizatsii" [The innovation game as a method of research and organizational development]. In B. Sazonov, ed., *Novovvedeniia v organizatsii* [Innovations in Organization]. Moscow: Institut systemnykh issledovanii, 1984, pp. 54–69.

16. Emery, M. *Searching: For New Directions, in New Ways, for New Times*. Canberra: Centre for Continuing Education, Australian National University, 1982, 414 pp.

17. Emery, M., and Emery, F. "Searching: For New Directions, in New Ways. . . For New Times." In J.W. Sutherland and A. Legasto, eds., *Management Handbook for Public Administrators*. New York: Van Nostrand, 1978, pp. 257–301.

18. Gordon, W.J.J. *Synectics: The Development of Creative Capacity*. New York: Harper & Row, 1961, 180 pp.

19. Hesse, H. *Magister Ludi: The Glass Bead Game*. New York: Bantam Book, 1969, 520 pp.

20. Jones, J.C. *Design Methods: Seeds of Human Futures*. New York: John Wiley & Sons, 1982, 100 pp.

21. Kazarnovsky, A.S. *Khoziaistvennyi mekhanizm i sovershenstvovanie upravleniia proizvodstvom* [Economic mechanism and the development of manufacturing management]. Kiev: Znanie, 1984, 48 pp..

22. *Kentavr* [Centaur]. 1990, Nos. 1 and 2.

23. Kitaigorodskaia, G.A. *Metodika intensivnogo obucheniia inostrannym iazykam* [A methodology of intensive learning for foreign languages]. Moscow: Vysshaia shkola, 1986, 103 pp.

24. Ladenko, I., ed. *Igrovoe modelirovanie: metodologiia i praktika* [Game modeling: methodology and practice]. Novosibirsk: Nauka, 1987, 231 pp.

25. Lawrence, W.G., ed. *Exploring Individual and Organizational Boundaries: A Tavistock Open-Systems Approach*. Chichester, New York: Wiley, 1979, 256 pp.

26. Lippit, R., Watson, J., and Westley, B. *The Dynamics of Planned Change: A Comparative Study of Principles and Techniques*. New York: Harcourt Brace, 1958, 312 pp.

27. Lewin, K. "Action Research and Minority Problems," *Journal of Social Issues*, Vol. 4, No. 2 (1947), pp. 34–36.

28. Lewin, K. "Frontiers in Group Dynamics: Part II, Social Planning and Action Research," *Human Relations*, 1947, no.1, pp. 143–153.

29. Lewin, K. "The Research Center for Group Dynamics at Massachusetts Institute of Technology," *Sociometry*, 1945, no. 2, pp. 126–136.

30. Miles, L.D. *Techniques of Value Analysis and Engineering*. 3d ed.: E.M. Walker, 1989. 366 pp.

31. Naumov, V. "Organizatsionno-deiatel'nostnye igry" [Organization-action games], *Priroda*, 1987, no. 4, pp. 24–33.

32. Osborn, A.F. *Applied Imagination: Principles and Procedures of Creative Problem Solving*. 3d rev. ed. New York: Scribner's, Charles, Sons, 1979, 417 pp.

33. Popov, S.V., and Schedrovitskii, P.G. *Konkurs rukovoditelei. Vsesoiuznyi konkurs na dolzhnost' direktora mikroavtobusov RAF: analiz sluchaia* [The CEO's competition. The all-union competition for CEO at the RAF minibus plant: A case study]. Moscow: Prometei, Moskovskii pedagogicheskii institut, 1989, 94 pp.

34. Rozin, V. "Metodologicheskii analiz delovoi igry kak novoi oblasti nauchno-tekhnicheskoi deiatel'nosti" [A methodological analysis of busines games as a new area for scientific-and-technological activity], *Voprosy psikhologii*, 1986, no. 6, pp. 46–58.

35. Schedrovitskii, G.P. "Skhema mysledeiatel'nosti: systemno-structurnoe stroenie, smysl i soderzhanie" [Mental activity scheme: systems structure, meaning, and contents]. In D. Gvishiani, ed., *Sistemnye issledovaniia: Metodologicheskie problemy* [Systems research: Methodological problems]. Yearbook. Moscow: Nauka, 1986, pp. 124–146.

36. Schedrovitskii, G.P. "Organizatsionno-deiatel′nostnaia igra kak novaia forma organizatsii kollektivnoi mysledeiatel′nosti" [The organization-action game as a new method of team thinking]. In V. Chairov and P. Baranov, eds., *Metody issledovaniia, diagnostiki i razvitiia mezhdunarodnykh kollektivov* [Research, diagnosis, and development methods for international work teams]. Moscow: Mezhdunarodnyi institut problem upravleniia, 1983, pp. 153–178.

37. Schedrovitskii, G.P. "Organizatsionno-deiatel′nostnaia igra kak novaia forma organizatsii i metod razvitiia kollektivnoi mysledeiatel′nosti" [The organization-action game as a new form of organization of team thinking and activity]. In B. Sazonov, ed., *Novovvedeniia v organizatsii* [Innovations in organizations]. Moscow: Vsesoiuznyi institut systemnykh issledovanii, 1983, pp. 153–178.

38. Schedrovitskii, P. *K analizu topiki ODI* [An analysis of organization-action games]. Puschino: Nauchny tsentr biologicheskikh issledovanii, 1987, 43 pp.

39. Sidorenko, V., ed. *Metod proektnogo seminara* [The design seminar method]. Moscow: Vsesoiuznyi institut technicheskoi estetiki, 1989, 100 pp.

40. Tszen, N.V., and Pachomov, J.V. *Psychotekhnicheskie igry v sporte* [Psycho-technical games in sport]. Moscow: Fizkultyra i sport, 1985, 151 pp.

41. Zhezhko, I. "Igry otkrytogo tipa kak metod razvitiia i aktivizatsii" [Open type games as a method of development and motivation]. In I. Besedin, ed., *Filosofskie i sotsiologicheskie aspecty aktivizatsii chelovecheskogo faktora: Issledovaniia sovetskikh uchenykh* [Philosophical and sociological issues of human factor development and motivation: Research by Soviet scholars]. Moscow: Institut nauchnoi informatsii po obschestvennym naukam, 1988, pp. 94–115.

42. Zhezhko, I., ed. *Igrovye metody* [Game Methods]. Moscow: Nauchno-issledovatelskii institut kultury, 1987, 178 pp.

43. Zhezhko, I. "Proektnaia igra: Dosug v gorode" [The design game: Leisure in a city]. In V. Glazychev, ed., *Kultura goroda: Problemy kachestva gorodskoi sredy* [City culture: Problems of a city's environmental quality]. Moscow: Nauchno-issledovatelskii institut kultury, 1986, pp. 186–196.

44. Zwicky, F. "The Morphological Approach to Discovery, Invention, Research, and Construction." In F. Zwicky and A.G. Wilson, eds., *New Methods of Thought and Procedure*. New York: Springer-Verlag New York Inc., 1967, pp. 273–297.

12

The American MBA Program: A Russian Student's View

Stanislav V. Shekshnia

"And for this I left my home, an almost completed dissertation, a position in the department, and a recently created company?" My disillusionment knew no bounds. It was my first class in an American business school—Economics—and I felt like I had been transported many years back, to my very first lecture in my very first year at Moscow University. It wasn't just that the professor was talking about things with which I had long been thoroughly familiar; rather, it was that the students around me were taking in his words as practically a revelation, as if it were they and not I who had come from far-off Russia, where no one had ever heard of microeconomics. It seemed like everything was new to them, and the simplest problems threw them for a loop. I was saddened—what could they possibly teach me here? I felt like getting on an airplane bound for Moscow.

Quite a bit of time has passed since that first class; I have completed the Economics course and many others besides. Has my opinion changed? It has become vaster and many-sided and by no means as unequivocal as it was then.

* * *

The very titles of business school courses put romantics from the former Soviet Union in quest of the market economy into a state border-

Russian text © 1991 by Stanislav V. Shekshnia. No Russian title. This unpublished manuscript is translated and printed here with the permission of the author.

ing on ecstasy—Marketing, Entrepreneurship, Strategic Management, Accounting (not bookkeeping, as they taught us in the former USSR—Accounting!), Operations Management, and so on. What more could be desired by a future captain of Soviet economy who was brought up under conditions of directive central planning?

However, after careful examination, it turns out that 90 percent of this accounting is made up of our own bookkeeping and the subject that is taught in Soviet economic higher educational institutions under the long and intriguing title, "Analysis of an Enterprise's Economic Activity." There are quite a few examples of this kind of coincidence. Strange as it seems (strange only at first glance; in reality, it is to be expected), the problems relating to an enterprise's internal activities—production itself, the administration of technological processes, and intraproduction inventory—seem to be approximately the same here and in the former USSR.

However, when it comes down to the external function of the enterprise and its management—that is, the market itself—all parallels disappear. The Marketing course astonished me, in particular by the way the manager thinks under conditions of the market, by the logic of making decisions. This course and others similar to it teach you to take a totally different view of everything that takes place in the economy and, in particular, how this economy functions and why: it functions for the consumer—indeed, in order to please the consumer, for it is he, the consumer, who calls the tune in this celebration of life. And if you want him to call your tune another time, you had better try to please him in everything.

The Marketing course opened up to me a whole world, hitherto unknown, that was magnetic and mysterious. The very first timid steps into that world were difficult and required the concentration of all my knowledge (so scanty in this sphere) and all my life experience (even more scanty) with respect to the market economy, whereas my American classmates were as much in their element as a fish in water. Can you imagine how wild it is for our shortage-tormented souls to have a two-hour discussion about what is the best packaging for deodorized socks—two or four to the package?! But here that's a reality; that's what business is all about.

In general, reality is present literally everywhere in the school of business. It is life, practicality that carries the day, relegating "pure science" to the role of assistant. The goals of management education (in English there is a very precise definition of what goes on in business school—professional training) are spelled out precisely and even rigidly. The goal is to train managers to run companies appropriate to the first half of the 1990s. Anyone who comes to the school with other goals is not likely to be happy in this program, because everything is subordinated to the main purpose and there is practically no space or time for anything abstract.

The required courses—and two-thirds of them here are required—are another surprise for the graduate of a Soviet higher educational institution who fought during his student years for the freedom to choose the subjects to be studied. These courses are selected so that, in the aggregate, they cover the basic aspects of the practice of management and provide a fundamental understanding of the economic system of society. Having learned them, the graduate of a business school who has had no prior economics education (and the majority of them here are like that—recall my astonishment in that first class) is capable of effectively carrying out a variety of managerial functions, although he is still far from having a theoretical understanding of what he is doing and what is taking place in the economy. Actually, he never gives much thought to it, considering the intensity of his work.

Elective courses make it possible to specialize in functional sectors of management—finance, accounting, marketing, management information systems, and small businesses. But this specialization is also of a purely applied character, inasmuch as it provides students not so much with general knowledge about the topic as it does practical skills and techniques of working in the particular profession.

In general, the business school is a rather rigidly structured institution that does not encourage deviations from the norm, philosophizing, and abstract discussions about the meaning of human existence. It is a micromodel of big business, in which, according to the way things are viewed here, everything is quite rational and manageable; all it takes is a mastery of a particular set of tools and techniques, which is exactly what is taught in business school. The actual MBA program does not require any exceptional abilities—quite the opposite, in fact, for it is designed for the ordinary person who does not have special training. It is by no means the case, however, that anyone who wants to can actually get the MBA degree; not everyone is capable of doing the amount of work that the program demands. An eighty-hour work week is hardly an exaggeration, and the courses are structured in such a manner that the student has to make a constant effort. To miss a class in business school is a real tragedy; it is frequently impossible to make up for lost time—not because the material is difficult, but because days are only twenty-four hours long and it is very difficult to find the time to go over what was done.

If you recall that in the former USSR "between classes students live it up," you will understand clearly the surprise that awaits graduates of Soviet higher educational institutions as they start out in the MBA program.

Another unexpected thing is the professors—or, to be precise, their method of teaching and style of behavior. You will practically never hear lengthy and detailed lectures in business school, nor seminars in which students give answers lasting up to ten or fifteen minutes, with lengthy debate and commentaries by the instructor. The class is very concrete; its purpose is to teach every student what is required and to give him the opportunity—sometimes to force him—to show that he has learned it, has mastered the specific skill and is capable of using it on his own.

A particular method of teaching management, the spice of it, is the case study. As he explores the case the student comes up against a real problem of management that he must solve on his own (without any coaching). The case, which frequently is no more than ten pages long, contains a mass of information that needs to be gone over and interpreted, but a lot more information is not accessible, so it has to be substituted with reasonable assumptions that proceed logically from what is given in the case or is known from other sources. In effect, the case simulates a real-life situation in which the manager is forced to make a decision without possessing all the information required to do so.

Nevertheless, the case is still a teaching aid, a kind of game, and the extent to which the students believe in the reality of what is described largely depends on the instructor. Teaching cases is quite an art, and not everyone is equally proficient at it. Some genuine virtuosos are able to keep the class in suspense all 120 minutes and force the students literally to "live through" the case, but other instructors prefer the calmer, traditional methods of teaching.

Another thing that graduates of Soviet higher educational institutions find unusual at first are the relations between students and instructors, which are devoid of any formality and outwardly seem almost friendly; they call one another by their first names, pat each other on the shoulder, and get together for a few beers. Behind this purely outward appearance, however, each side soon gains a precise realization of his rights and duties, his place and role in the training process.

Mildness and proper treatment of everyone constitute the basis of the instructor's comportment. However, this mildness and friendliness must never cross unseen but very strict boundaries—everyone knows how to keep his distance and not become dependent on the other.

As for grades, a matter that is of such great importance to all students, their objectivity is perhaps the most sensitive aspect, not so much for those who receive them as for those who give them. God forbid that any instructor should be accused of lack of objectivity; for him this would be tantamount to being accused of professional incompetence. This is why the system of grading has been worked out so meticulously, why the instructor spends so much time explaining the system to the students, and why the actual process of giving grades is so important. In order to emphasize objectivity, the general evaluation is made up of several components—participation in class work, several papers, a project (frequently a group project), and a written exam (which might not be given). To people like us who are used to having everything decided by an end-of-semester examination, this simply boggles the mind, but for management education it is probably to be expected—the world of business demands constant effort and is always giving grades.

The abundance of papers to be written in business school is astonishing at first, but then it becomes clear—the instructor has to ensure the objectivity of his grades to the maximum in order to ensure himself against any possible misunderstandings due to students' dissatisfaction. In this case, however, the objectivity is quite dubious—everything is so overly formalized, and quite often you can't see behind the written lines the person who wrote them.

No matter how great the differences in the system of instruction in the United States and the former USSR, school is school, and successful studies require approximately the same qualities—imagination, assiduousness, the ability to work independently, communicativeness, and, of course, industriousness. For this reason, getting into the training process was not that painful for me and it went rather quickly. By the middle of the second academic quarter I felt quite confident, and at times it even seemed as if I had spent my whole life going to school here.

Much more difficult was the process of getting adjusted to American life—cultural adaptation, including what takes place in business school outside of the educational process.

A short time after I arrived here, in fact, it became obvious that a myth that was popular in Russia—namely that Russians and Americans are very much alike, practically twin nations (a myth in which I, incidentally, also took part in spreading after I returned from my first trip to the United States in 1987)—proved to be nothing more than a myth, just another attempt to pass off a wish as reality.

The Americans, or at least those with whom I go to school (let us avoid generalizations in order not to make another gaffe), are not at all like us, nor are they anything like we imagine them to be. We and they have very different systems of life values, concepts of what is good or bad, attitudes toward work, tastes, traditions, and even general education.

Some of my classmates don't even know that Alaska is separated from the contiguous territory of the United States by Canada and are genuinely surprised when they find out that just a century ago Alaska was part of Russia. On the other hand they are able to contrive things on a computer that in our country only a magician can do. In Russia, if you were to ask your classmate to lend you a three-ruble note until the next day, that's perfectly natural; here, they simply wouldn't understand it.

There are some other, more serious things that need to be kept in mind both by those who intend to come to American business schools from the former USSR and those who will be hosting these people. In particular, there is the individualism of Americans, something that is totally uncharacteristic of our culture, a trait that is manifested literally in everything—behavior in classes, communication, daily life, and so on. Reliance on one's own powers, the basic motto in American life, is very hard for people who have been brought up in a society that has long and firmly established collectivist traditions.

Another thing that is very difficult for us to grasp in relations between people is that here, everyone is friendly but there are practically no friends in our understanding of that word. People do not get involved in your personal life and do not allow anyone to get involved in theirs. The ability to keep one's distance, an ability that we hardly possess, is a very important aspect of life here.

And when it comes to relations between students, it's virtually a closed book. Whereas in the former USSR students constitute a unified force standing up collectively against the instructor in the struggle for good grades, here it's every man for himself—in fact, each one is first a competitor in the struggle for a higher grade, and only then a comrade-in-arms.

Overall, then, how shall I evaluate my first year of experience of attending an American school of business? Were my first impressions correct, in that Economics class, when I was thinking about catching the first plane back to Moscow?

Probably I was wrong after all. Business school has already given me a great deal. In particular it has taught me to work systematically in ways that, formerly, I used only occasionally. In addition, I have found out through my own experience how complicated and variegated the modern world is, how important it is to understand cultural differences and to know how to adapt in order to get ahead in this world.

Of course, I have acquired certain professional skills and have made progress toward becoming an American-trained manager. How well these skills will serve me in Russia is another matter. And, in general, do we really need an American education? Is it worthwhile to take our best specialists away from their homes and jobs and send them to American business schools for two years? Unquestionably this is a good thing for "developing friendship between peoples, for cooperation and mutual understanding," but to what extent is it justified economically?

If we undertake to answer this question in a purely utilitarian manner, from the standpoint of today, the answer has to be in the negative. What is being taught here is just as remote from our own economic practice as our economy is remote from the American. The Soviet graduate of an American business school might become an odious figure in our disorderly economy, and any attempt he makes to work according to the rules learned in the United States could be cause for derision.

The central problem in our economy is that no matter what we produce, people immediately snatch it up, whereas here the basic problem is how to sell things, how to get customers. What we continue to be most in need of are specialists in the opposite of marketing—namely, finding resources, something that people here can hardly even imagine.

However, if we look ahead and think about transforming our economy into a more civilized one, then a Western managerial education is simply essential. It is necessary, however, to see to it that a well-thought-out system replaces the primitive approach that prevails today. Obviously it will be necessary to change the principles governing the selection of those who are to go to school in the United States. At present the basic criterion is knowledge of the English language and an idea about the American economic system. As a result, most of the people who go there are graduate students in economics institutes or even people who already have graduate degrees (candidates of science)—that is, people who are more oriented toward research and teaching work than toward practical managerial activity. We ought to be sending engineers, applied economists, and managers from enterprises. And there is no need to be afraid because they don't know anything about the American economy; that way they won't suffer disappointments of the kind I suffered in my first classes.

The training of Soviet specialists in American business schools can have a real impact on our economy only when it takes on substantial proportions. Students at the present time—who are so few in number—simply disappear in the uncurbed disorder of the post-Soviet economy; instead of being the bearers of managerial culture they become merely oddballs. If the national economy were to get a yearly infusion of hundreds of holders of the MBA degree (more than 700 business schools in the United States graduate 80,000 MBAs every year, so this is completely feasible), progress in management education and development would become a reality.

One more conduit to management development in our economy would be the training of teachers for Soviet business schools in the United States. However, it is probably not advisable to send them to take two-year MBA programs; life is brief, specialization is very important in today's world, and a professor of organizational behavior is by no means obligated to have a thorough knowledge of finance. What is most important is to give him the opportunity to get a sense of the spirit of American education, to understand its style and methods—that is, to become immersed in the atmosphere of the business school. To do this, it is probably sufficient to take specialized four- to ten-month programs offered by many American business schools.

As far as the prestige of getting an MBA is concerned, not more than one-thousandth of a percent of the population in the former USSR has even the vaguest idea of what it is.

* * *

Was it worth it to abandon everything to go and attend business school? Taking a glance backward one more time, I think that it probably was worth it after all. But had I known in advance about everything that I would come up against there, a year ago, I wouldn't have gone; it was too unlike my American dream.

Part III

TRAINING PROGRAMS FOR SOVIET MANAGERS IN THE UNITED STATES

Introduction

In Parts I and II we learned how management training and development programs are being conducted in the former USSR. We now turn to an examination of another option that has been provided to an elite cadre of several hundred Soviet senior executives. These individuals have had the opportunity to learn about the market economy firsthand by coming to the United States to study in business schools and do internships in companies.

Management education is a critical factor in the successful transition to the market, and it is important that it begin at the top of the organization. When the chief executive officer (CEO) undergoes training in the theory and methods of market-based management, there are two major benefits. First, the CEO has the authority to make significant changes in the organization based on his or her newly acquired knowledge. Second, the CEO's willingness to be trained in this new domain is a clear signal to others in the organization that change is inevitable and that they too must learn how to work under new conditions.

Since the late 1980s enterprises in the former Soviet Union have been faced with the unprecedented challenge of transforming themselves into market-oriented competitors. Until that time Soviet managers functioned in a centrally planned economic system in which they carried out plans and orders received from the State Planning Agency (Gosplan) and officials in their industrial ministry. Suppliers and customers were also allocated to the enterprise by central agencies.

Under these conditions Soviet managers had no need for, and therefore had no experience in, such market-based fields as strategic planning, marketing, and finance. In addition to mastering this subject matter in their management programs in the United States, the senior executives faced an even greater challenge, namely, developing a new managerial mindset of risk taking, accountability, and decisiveness.

Overview

Part III consists of descriptions of management development programs for senior executives from the former USSR developed by four American academic institutions. Although the programs differed with respect to program length and type of clientele, the general format and objectives were quite similar. A major outcome of all the programs was that participation was a source of satisfaction and learning for not only the Soviet executives but for the Americans involved. Recognizing the historic import of having Soviet managers attend their business schools, in all cases the program directors provided opportunities for individuals in the university, business, and civic communities to interact with the Soviet visitors.

In chapter 13, "Developing a Program for Soviet Managers at Northeastern University," McCarthy underscores the need for new managerial knowledge and skills by comparing the management function as it existed in most Soviet enterprises before *perestroika* with the requirements of managing in a market-based economic system. He then describes the fourteen-week management program at Northeastern University for sixteen executives from the Ministry of the Aviation Industry. The program, begun in the fall of 1989, consisted of three components: English language instruction, seminars in business subjects, and internships in American corporations.

A similar program for a second group of executives from the Ministry of the Aviation Industry was conducted simultaneously at California State University at Hayward. In chapter 14, " 'Sedpro': Three Soviet Executive Development Programs at California State University at Hayward," Wiley, Kamath, and MacNab describe their experience with the aviation ministry executives as well as two subsequent programs. One was a one-month program for twenty-five senior- and middle-level managers employed in a diverse array of industries in the agricultural sector in the republic of Uzbekistan. The third offering was a nine-week program for sixteen managers from Izhorskii Zavod, a St. Petersburg steel plant that employs 26,000 people.

In chapter 15, "A Training Program for Russian Bankers at Middlesex Community College," I report on a three-week program for fifteen presidents and vice-presidents of banks from the Russian republic. The program was run by Middlesex in collaboration with the School of Management at Suffolk University. Like their counterparts in the aviation industry who had attended the programs described in chapters 13 and 14, these banking executives were particularly impressed with what they saw and learned in the banking institutions they visited. This experience gave them the opportunity to put their classroom learning into a practical context.

The program that I describe in chapter 16, "The Fuqua School of Business Program for Soviet Executives," differs from the others presented here in its inception and scope. The program came about as a result of the philanthropy of Mr. J.B. Fuqua who decided to donate $4 million to the Fuqua School of Business to train Soviet senior executives in the workings of the market economy. The one-month program has been offered three times to executives from a cross-section of industrial and service sectors. Excerpts from interviews with some of the graduates in late 1991 indicate that the program is already having a significant impact on the way they are managing their enterprises.

The future of Western involvement in management education in the former USSR

The programs described here are pioneering efforts on the part of American business schools to address the acute need for managers in the former USSR to become versed in the market economy. Because the demand for retraining Soviet managers is so great and the need so pressing, it is likely that there will be a growing involvement of American and other Western business schools in this training effort. Collaboration may take various forms in addition to the models presented here. This is important because, in spite of the benefits, sending Soviet managers abroad is expensive, time-consuming, and disruptive, and some critics question whether such an approach provides sufficient linkage with conditions in the former USSR to make application of knowledge possible.

Although the United States lags behind Europe in developing collaborative relationships with management institutions in the former USSR,[1] there are signs that American involvement is increasing. For example, numerous federal agencies, foundations, and international education exchange programs offer funding or other support for research, educational exchanges, technical assistance and training programs related to Soviet business and management education.[2] Another promising approach is that of establishing consortia of business schools to conduct collaborative training programs. A notable example is the one developed by five leading business schools—Harvard, MIT, Northwestern, Stanford, and Wharton.[3] Through their Central and Eastern European Teachers Program, in 1992 and 1993 they intend to retrain over one hundred business faculty, including a number from the former USSR.

Given the increasing number of American business schools involved in training management educators and managers in the former USSR, it is important to consider the major issues in designing and delivering training programs for these specialized groups. Based on the experience of the four institutions described in Part III, the issues include the following:

• designing a program that satisfies the specific needs of a diverse clientele of managers studying in the same training program (participants usually come from different industries and enterprises of different sizes and capabilities);

• analyzing executives' needs for career development and considering ways of addressing these needs;

• course content (balancing the theory and practice of management in a market economy; tailoring the courses to the specific business, political, social, and cultural conditions in the Soviet republics);

• coordination of training with Soviet management development institutions before and after training in the United States (to facilitate practical implementation of knowledge and to foster executives' career development);

• language of instruction (knowledge of English as a prerequisite versus simultaneous translation);

• internships in U.S. companies (locating partner companies, formalizing and structuring the internship, integrating classroom instruction and management practice experienced in the internship);

• design of cultural programs to learn about American social and business customs and practices;

• program evaluation (mechanisms for evaluating the effectiveness of the programs, comparison with other forms of management training);

• follow-up assistance to program graduates;

• future forms of U.S. involvement in management education in the former USSR.

Notes

1. See Burton Bollag, "American Colleges Told They Are Missing Opportunity for Collaboration With East European Institutions," *The Chronicle of Higher Education*, September 5, 1990, pp. A39, A41.

2. See "Guide to Eastern European and Soviet Trade, Research, Exchange and Training," *Business and Management Education Funding Alert*, vol. 3, no. 11 (Lexington, KY: University of Kentucky and American Assembly of Collegiate Schools of Business, January 1992), pp. 4–11.

3. See *Central and Eastern European Teachers Program* (Harvard Business School, unpublished, September 1991).

13

Developing a Program for Soviet Managers at Northeastern University

Daniel J. McCarthy

Changes in the USSR under Mikhail Gorbachev's *perestroika* have moved the Soviet economy toward a demand system and away from the previous command system of a centrally planned economy (CPE). As a result, the job of Soviet managers is changing from one that traditionally was centered on fulfilling the plan passed down to them from the designated ministry. The new requirements for managers allow and require more flexibility, creativity, knowledge, and responsibility for decision making.[1] However, during this transition in the Soviet economy and its enterprises, most managers are ill-equipped to deal with the numerous changes and problems. These are in the economic and competitive as well as the political, social, and technological environments. They are inherent, also, in the structure of Soviet industry, the fundamental purposes of Soviet enterprises, and in the Soviet workforce. A prevailing atmosphere of uncertainty and concern is undeniable.

This situation has created pressing needs for Soviet managers, who must adapt to the requirements of the developing market economy, uncertain though the future may be. These needs can be determined by comparing the management job in most Soviet enterprises before *per-*

This article originally appeared under the title, "Developing a Programme for Soviet Managers," *Journal of Management Development*, vol. 10, no. 5 (1991), pp. 26–31. Reprinted with permission from MCB University Press.

estroika with the requirements of managing in a market-based economic system. This article will discuss briefly the major differences. It will also discuss the management program developed and offered for Soviet managers by the College of Business Administration at Northeastern University during early 1990.

Reality of the USSR's centrally planned economy

In the socialist philosophy of the USSR, the means of production belonged to the state, as did the decisions regarding the use of that property. Accordingly, planning for the entire economy was centralized in a government agency, Gosplan, which coordinated the planning of all ministries responsible for the various segments of the Soviet economy. Such centralization of authority, it was reasoned, allowed for the most efficient and equitable allocation of resources within the economy to meet the needs of the Soviet people. The problems of CPEs, however, have proved to be numerous, and seem to have far exceeded the benefits in all Eastern European countries.[2] Illustrations of the problems plaguing the Soviet economy are waste, shortages, a low standard of living, a high level of national debt, major pollution problems, nonconvertible currency, and an inability to export, except petroleum and minerals. The economy, in essence, has virtually collapsed. Also, the advantages of job security and price stability of some products, when available, continue to influence many Soviets so that they resist the changes of perestroika.

A CPE such as the Soviet Union does not embrace the concept of the economic man. It is fundamentally antithetical to the dogma of Marxist socialism. Yet, for perestroika to work, the economic man will have to be created. This calls for a demand economy rather than a command economy, and requires the abolition of Gosplan and its central planning function.[3] A market for raising capital must emerge, as well as a freer market for a realistic allocation of labor.

Managing in a centrally planned economy

The job of Soviet managers was to fulfill the plan established for their enterprises by the responsible ministries under the centralized direction of Gosplan's five-year plan. Each enterprise functioned under the jurisdiction of a ministry which provided the funds as well as the final plan for the operation of the enterprise. Managers could request funds for research and development and equipment to carry out their assigned plan, but new equipment has been expensive and rare, with the average age in most enterprises approaching twenty-five years. Enterprises associated with ministries having the very scarce hard currency fared better than others, which may have allowed more efficient production or even some improvement in quality as a result of purchasing Western equipment or technology. Some industrial enterprises also produced consumer goods, almost exclusively for the Eastern European market, though the hope existed for exporting to the West. Exporting to the West for hard currency, however, is hardly realistic under current circumstances.

After visiting numerous factories in the Soviet Union in 1989, the CEO of an American company observed that the conditions were generally disorganized, dirty, and showed little regard for safety precautions; equipment was old and obsolete and the productivity was extremely low relative to Western standards. There were, however, pockets of excellence such as aircraft factories. Managers of the factories he visited were "ambitious to develop their factories to world-class status, but few of them had any understanding of what this entails."[4] This CEO has since established an operating joint venture with Soviet and Swiss partners.

Decades of meeting the plan have produced managers who function and are motivated only by increasing units of production. The quality, cost, timeliness, and true need for their products have not been very important criteria. And the production itself has been hampered by chronic shortages of raw materials and by obsolete technology and equipment, as well as by the desperate lack of motivation within the Soviet workforce. In this environment, managers have not been able to develop the skills needed in a competitive worldwide economy. Marketing and finance have not even been in the lexicon of these managers. Making deals to obtain the needed raw materials is standard, and most production figures are reputed to be false. An outstanding authority of Soviet management noted in addressing these weaknesses that "it follows that the choice facing Soviet leadership is either to abandon central planning in favor of a decentralized economic mechanism, or to accept the prospect that those features of management behavior that have endured for the past forty years are likely to endure as long as central planning is preserved."[5] Finally, key decisions have been heavily influenced by the union representative and the Communist Party representative in the enterprise. And it goes without saying that many managers owed their positions to the fact that they were members of the Party.

Perestroika

The major roles for enterprises and managers under *perestroika* are contained in the Law on the State Enterprise adopted in June 1987. Enterprises are expected to become self-sufficient and self-financing—in short, profitable. Furthermore, they are expected to pay their debts on time. These requirements should, it seems, focus managerial attention on the need for cost-consciousness as well as the required measurement techniques.

With regard to product decisions, the Enterprise Law called for more autonomy for managers. Markets for enterprise products were to be researched and some advertising was encouraged. Direct relations between enterprise and customers were now permitted under some circumstances. And, for the first time in their careers, these managers would have the authority to negotiate directly with foreign firms regarding imports, exports, and joint ventures.

With the new autonomy comes an increase in the importance of human relations in the managerial job. Aganbegian, a leading advocate of the changes toward a market-based system, believes that the attitudes of the Soviet workforce may be the most difficult challenge for Soviet managers. "In my view, the most difficult question in reshaping the economic mechanism is how to give the workers a sense of involvement in the end result of the labor."[6] And a second Soviet authority adds, "in the Soviet Union, a manager rises to a position of responsibility without any idea of human relations. . . .They don't even get a one hour lecture on the subject."[7]

It is clear that *perestroika* has brought substantial change to the jobs of Soviet managers. They are now expected to manage in a far more market-oriented economic system. Yet they are ill-prepared to do so after a lifetime in the demand system of the Soviet CPE. One American authority with long experience in the USSR has concluded, "The biggest obstacle to Soviet economic reform is not political ideology or government bureaucracy. Rather, it is the Soviet managers' lack of experience in such areas as market planning, production management, international finance, and organizational development."[8]

The Northeastern program for Soviet managers

With the background described above, what type of educational program could realistically benefit these managers, virtually all of whom have had only technical education and experience? And, contrary to the experience of technically trained managers in the Western world and Far East, the Soviet managers have not experienced the competitive realities of an open-market–based economic system.

The Northeastern faculty members selected for this program decided upon a three-phase approach: English, market-oriented business subjects, and an experience with a U.S. company. This approach, undertaken after consulting with the Soviet Ministry officials, is quite similar to those used by other American universities such as Wake Forest's Babcock School of Management, Duke's Fuqua School of Business, and Eastern Washington University.[9]

English component

Since few Soviet managers speak English, it was decided at an early stage to expose the Soviets to a month-long immersion in English, oriented to business and economic topics. They discussed short-case situations, worked as groups in English, and made presentations in English. Although this phase improved their English substantially, the majority did not move to a high level of speaking and listening comprehension before the second phase of their program. Needless to say, it is critical to assess in advance the level of ability of any group before proceeding with a program of this type.

Business subjects

The business content of the program was designed to address directly the needs of these managers, created by *perestroika* and described earlier in this article. In summary, they were exposed to a mini-MBA program, emphasizing the role of each topic in a market-based competitive economic system. This point cannot be overstated, because, although these managers were very senior and intelligent, their previous experience had been in a completely different environment. Thus a basic macroeconomic segment covered the realities of a demand economy in a worldwide setting. Marketing was a critical component of their program with strong emphasis on the marketing function in a demand economy, basic perhaps, but essential for these managers. Operations stressed the roles of technology, logistics, quality, supplier alliances, just-in-time, and similar topics, completely alien from this audience. A brief coverage of cost accounting, likewise, was new ground for managers for whom output, and not cost, has been the driving motivation.

Finance, sources of funds, cost of capital, and capital markets were important topics for these managers if they were to gain an understanding of operating in an open economy. One of the key requirements facing them is to understand the financial realities of market economies. Profit as a motivation and goal, after all, has been despised in the socialist doctrine of the USSR. The basic function of profit is explained and understood only with difficulty in settings such as this program. The challenge for us, as instructors, was to explain the most fundamental concepts without seeming to patronize or sell our ideas.

Human resources management was high on the agenda of these managers, particularly methods of incentive and motivation. Given the years of disincentive and lack of motivation in the USSR, every idea and method was of extreme interest. Strategy formation was completely new but intriguing to managers, who in their careers had seldom had the opportunity to look ahead, analyze, and develop a direction for their operations. They did, however, identify more with implementation of strategy, having spent careers carrying out plans passed down from ministries and Gosplan. In these areas of human resources, management and strategy, we labored to explain the basic premises, objectives and methods which we judged valuable in a setting of worldwide competition among nations with market-based economies.

It must have seemed overwhelming to these managers. The English was new, but these concepts were as foreign as the language they were seeking to master. No doubt, the language would be the easiest of their dual challenges but, if *perestroika*-type reforms are to succeed, this type of management education is an indispensable requirement.

Methodology, also, must be planned carefully and executed with patience. Oral and visual presentations were used. Overhead transparencies helped more than in a normal program, the visuals reinforcing the oral communication. Use of models, short cases, numerous company examples, and reference to European and Japanese, as well as North American, companies proved beneficial to the learning of these men.

Clear objectives, stated at the start of each session and repeated after, set the context so necessary to support the communication of new and confusing concepts. Instructors were encouraged to speak very slowly, to emphasize and repeat key words, and even to use several synonyms to ensure understanding. We avoided colloquialisms and slang and learned to use fewer words to express an idea or concept. Fewer words are far easier to follow and understand in a new language. Frequent pauses also helped our manager-students, who were spending full days and weeks in a classroom setting. We asked often, "Is that clear? Do you understand?" All such techniques facilitated communication and aided in understanding, our group reported to us. It was a new and even trying experience for many instructors used to moving at a much faster pace and at a more advanced level.

Company experience

Experience-based education is a taproot of Northeastern's educational philosophy. Thus it was a natural response to have these managers spend time in a company during their program. And it was clearly a highlight for them. They wanted desperately to observe a U.S. company and its management in operation. Each of these Soviets spent a month in one or two companies, mostly listening and observing, but asking countless questions as well. They were treated extremely well, and a large group of companies and managers devoted substantial time to making the experience highly valuable. Without such an opportunity to compare the classroom theory with business realities, our program would have been far less beneficial to these particular managers. Recall again their need to visualize and understand the operations of an enterprise in a competitive market-based economy. Their success was greatly enhanced by the opportunity to observe and discuss with practicing managers who spend every day doing what these Soviet managers will be expected to do. We, and they, considered the experience to be indispensable to this type of program.

   At the conclusion of their three months with us, the Soviet managers were joined by company representatives in a panel session to discuss the total program experience. This was meant to be a final attempt to link theory and practice in the minds of our Soviet participants. This linkage must be established to validate the classroom learning which centered on concepts entirely new to them, but which they will be expected to implement over the coming years in the USSR.

Conclusion

At first glance, the needs of Soviet managers might appear to be similar to those of technically trained North American managers. In one sense this is so; they must be exposed to the same range of business subjects. The difference derives from the vastly different needs created by the new demands of *perestroika*, after a career spent managing in a centrally planned economy. Every concept of every subject is new, as is the basic context of a market-based economic system which must be the prevailing theme of every topic. This context is understood and accepted by Western managers and those from the Far East. It has, however, been antithetical to the socialist doctrine of the USSR and the CPE which emanated from it. This reality, coupled with a language barrier, places new demands upon the management development programs and processes we might offer. But the changes and new approaches are crucial if the needs of Soviet managers are to be addressed effectively.

References

1. Aganbegian, A.G. "What *Perestroika* Means for Soviet Enterprises," *International Labor Review*, vol. 128, no. 1 (1987), pp. 87–89.

2. Winiecki, J. *The Distorted World of Soviet Type Economies* (Pittsburgh: University of Pittsburgh Press, 1988), p. 4.

3. Gumble, P. "Plan to Overhaul Soviet Economy is Unveiled, Throwing Premier's Political Future into Doubt," *Wall Street Journal*, September 4, 1990.

4. Lankton, G.B. "Trip to the Soviet Union: September 16–29, 1989," Nypro Inc. Company document, 1989, pp. 5–8.

5. Berliner, J.S. "Soviet Management from Stalin to Gorbachev: A Comparison of the Harvard Project and SIP Interviews," in: *Soviet Industry from Stalin to Gorbachev: Essays on Management and Innovation* (Ithaca: Cornell University Press, 1989), p. 34.

6. Aganbegian, p. 89.

7. Brown, D. "Welcome, Comrades, to Marketing 101," *Management Review*, vol. 79, no. 3 (1990), pp. 30–32.

8. Naylor, T.H. "The Reeducation of Soviet Management," *Across the Board*, February 1988, p. 30.

9. Brown, pp. 30–31.

14

"Sedpro": Three Soviet Executive Development Programs at California State University at Hayward

Donna L. Wiley, Shyam J. Kamath, and Bruce MacNab

The purpose of this chapter is to describe three Soviet management development programs conducted by the Institute for Business Research and Development and the faculty of the School of Business and Economics at California State University at Hayward. The first group, organized by the Soviet Ministry of Aviation Industries, was comprised of fifteen top managers from aviation enterprises throughout the Soviet Union. The second group was organized by the Academy of National Economy of the Council of Ministers of the USSR in Moscow. (This Academy conducts training for top managers from all of the ministries.) This group was made up of twenty-five top managers from agricultural enterprises and financial institutions in the Republic of Uzbekistan, a central Asian republic. The third group, which is in residence as this article is being written, consists of sixteen top managers of a single enterprise, Izhorskii Zavod, a large steel production company on the outskirts of St. Petersburg. All three programs were financed by the respective ministries or enterprise in hard currency, paid in installments before, during and after each program's completion. This article will present an overview of these three programs and will examine some of the similarities and differences among the three groups of managers and the programs which were developed to meet each group's specific needs.

Sedpro I: USSR Ministry of Aviation Industry

Background of the program

The California State University at Hayward (CSUH) experience with Soviet management development began in 1989. After reviewing proposals from seventeen U.S. universities, representatives from the Ministry of Aviation Industries selected CSUH as one of three training sites. The other two universities selected were Northeastern University and Oklahoma City University. (Because the Northeastern program is discussed extensively in McCarthy's article in this volume, only a brief overview will be presented here.) One of the main reasons for the selection of CSUH was that our Institute of Research and Business Development (IRBD) had previously developed a very similar curriculum model for a group of managers from the People's Republic of China, whose trip had been canceled because of events surrounding Tienanmen Square. This model was readily adaptable to meet the needs of the Ministry of Aviation Industries. It was also helpful that the Director of the Institute, Dr. Bruce MacNab, could speak Russian. The location of CSUH was a second factor in the selection decision. Because of our close proximity to Silicon Valley and the greater San Francisco Bay Area, plant visits could be easily arranged for the Soviet managers to observe state-of-the-art manufacturing technology and management techniques. In addition, the business and economics faculty has strong ties to the local, state, national and international business community and has extensive experience in international marketing. Finally, one of the management faculty is a Russian émigré who could help with the language barrier. Our university also has a very strong American Language Program which could be used to develop these managers' English skills.

Design of the program

The fourteen-week course was designed to introduce the Soviet managers to the essential aspects of the American business system. The curriculum was divided into the following eight general categories: overview of American business, economics, finance, accounting, management, marketing, human resource management, and quantitative business methods. The faculty attempted to show how these concepts could be applied in the Soviet system. This proved to be difficult, as no one was (or is yet) sure what this system will be.

The integrative mechanism was the playing of BRANDMAPS,[1] a sophisticated, competitive, computer-simulated marketing strategy game, which allowed the trainees to practice many of the market-economy concepts they were learning in the classroom. They were able to experience the workings of a free-market economy and, since the group was divided into competing teams, the operations of a company in a competitive environment. They were able to witness the effects of their own strategic decisions as well as the effects of external factors, such as natural disasters. The faculty grasped the basic level at which we should be operating after the lab instructor presented his introduction to the programming aspect of the game. When the instructor told the participants to put the cost of the product in a certain column, one of the group members raised his hand and asked "What is a cost?" Members of this group also had very little previous computer experience, so the computer aspects of the game presented a problem initially, though the members learned quickly.

The first four weeks of the program were spent primarily in an American Language Program. It had been the goal of the Soviet program leaders that this language instruction, together with the participants' previous English background, would enable the class members to participate in the business classes in English. It was quickly apparent that this was not the case. Instead, the class process followed a different route, with the professor presenting small chunks of information to the two or three participants who were fluent in English and who would then translate the information to the rest of the group. Frequently, heated discussions in Russian would ensue, after which the translator would turn to the instructor and say simply, "Okay." This was quite disconcerting, as the instructor was never quite sure what was being translated or what the nature of the reaction was.

In addition to the classroom instruction, another important component of the program was visits to American businesses. Approximately twenty-six Bay Area companies hosted tours of their facilities. These tours lasted from half-day to full-day visits and were attended by the entire group. The Soviet managers were able to get a first-hand look at an oil refinery at Chevron, an electronics manufacturing process at Hewlett-Packard, U.S. banking operations at Bank of America, a computer center at Pacific Bell, and the food distribution center at Lucky Stores. Because of their connection to the aviation industry, the Soviet managers were particularly interested in the tour of United Airlines' western maintenance terminal at the

San Francisco Airport. Another highlight of the plant visits was a tour of the Anchor Steam brewery in San Francisco. A second purpose of the company visits was to provide the opportunity to make business contacts which might lead to the formation of joint ventures.

A final important objective of the program was to provide the Soviet managers with some understanding of American culture. The breaking down of communication barriers between the two countries was allowing both sides to gain insights into the others' culture. This was illustrated very dramatically in the first program, as the participants arrived in November 1989, on the same day as the fall of the Berlin wall. The welcoming banquet held to introduce the Soviet managers to their American professors was very tense at first, as we had all grown up with so many stereotypes and mistaken assumptions about each other. But as soon as we began to talk about our families, our interests in music and sports, and our mutual concerns about world peace, we discovered that we were really very much alike.

Results of the program

Overall, both the Soviet managers and the faculty of the program considered the program to be very successful. At the conclusion of the program, we held a feedback session in which the Soviet managers gave the program glowing praise. They also gave several good suggestions as to how the program could be improved for future groups. These suggestions have been incorporated into our subsequent programs, which will be discussed later. We have also maintained contact with several of the participants in the two years since the program. Several have received promotions in their respective companies, and even though their companies are now struggling because of the hard economic times, they feel that they personally are able to survive because of their experience in our program.

Sedpro II: Uzbekistan Ministry of Agricultural Industries

Background of the program

Uzbekistan, with a population of twenty million people and an area about the size of California, is the agricultural greenhouse of Central Asia. The fifth largest republic in size and the third most populous in the erstwhile Soviet Union, Uzbekistan produces about two-thirds of the USSR's cotton and a variety of agricultural and animal products such as citrus and other varieties of fruit, almonds, nuts, vegetables, rice, tobacco, hides, etc.

Based on the success of the first Soviet Executive Development Program, the Moscow-based Academy of the National Economy of the USSR Council of Ministers approached the Institute of Research and Business Development (IRBD) at CSUH about the possibility of offering short-duration management programs for Soviet managers on a contract basis. The renowned Soviet economist, Abel Aganbegian, who was a close adviser to Gorbachev and one of the architects of *perestroika*, is the Rector of the Academy and has twice visited the CSUH campus. The Vice-Rector and Dean of the Academy, Dr. Leonid Evenko, also visited the Hayward campus and met with Dean Tontz and Dr. Bruce MacNab, the Director of the IRBD, to work out a cooperation agreement and representative training contract. Subsequently, Director MacNab visited the Academy in Moscow in late 1990 to sign a formal agreement of cooperation and to finalize the details for the visit of a Sedpro group to be sent to Hayward.

The Uzbek group that subsequently visited Hayward, and which was formally designated as Sedpro II, was both unique in its conception and in its constitution. Following the early evolution of *perestroika* in the Soviet Union, an agricultural trade association called *Uzagropromservis* (UzAPS) was set up in Uzbekistan to coordinate agricultural exports to and the import of machinery, equipment and technology from all over the world; to execute barter deals and compensation trade deals; and to find partners for the creation of joint ventures in the fields of agriculture and related areas. It consists of all the apex agricultural and agro-industrial groups and cooperatives in Uzbekistan. It is a branch of the Association for Business Cooperation with Foreign Countries (ABC), formed in 1989 to represent the interests of 116 organizations in Uzbekistan. A primary objective of UzAPS is to supply the processing branches of the Uzbek agricultural industry with equipment, high technology and know-how.

UzAPS approached the Academy of the National Economy to help train its top agricultural managers and chief executives in the latest techniques of agricultural management and to help it establish contacts with leading agricultural equipment and related technology firms in the world. Given California's comparative advantage in agriculture and the fine management institutions and universities located there, the

Academy asked CSUH to design a one-month management development program (MDP) for senior- and middle-level agricultural managers.

The design of Sedpro II

The design and execution of Sedpro II proved to be a challenging and complicated task. Twenty-five agricultural executives and related staff (the twenty-sixth member was the leader and coordinator of the program on the Soviet side from the Moscow-based Academy) from backgrounds as diverse as banking, computer services, cotton cultivation, data processing, dairy farming, environmental rehabilitation, fruit cultivation and processing, machinery procurement and servicing, meat processing, sericulture, vegetable cultivation and wine growing had to be provided a fast-track education in capitalist, free-market agricultural business methods. A conventional functional integrative program was precluded because of the diversity of the membership of the group and the short time horizon of the program. The need for intensive and extensive field visits in the contract also dictated a multidimensional approach to the design of the program.

The composition of the group presented some interesting problems for program design in addition to the problems of diversity of product and functional design discussed above. The group included top-level executives and officials such as the Chairman of Uzbekistan's first private commercial bank, the CEO of UzAPS, the CEO of a Soviet-German joint venture, the Chairman of the republic's Textile and Light Machinery conglomerate and the Deputy Chairman of the Council of Ministers of the Karakalpakistan Republic on the one hand, and middle- to senior-level functional and product managers from the constituent parts of UzAPS on the other. This created a problem of multiple interests, with the top-level managers interested in strategic and high-level tactical issues and the middle- and senior-level managers interested in operational issues. Care was taken to meet the special needs of both levels of executives by adopting a modular design for the program.

While the objectives of Sedpro II were similar to those of Sedpro I, they were adjusted to meet this group's unique needs. Four key goals were identified at the outset. The first was to impart the basic principles and procedures of doing agribusiness in a free-market economy. A second goal was to introduce the participants to a wide variety of leading U.S. agricultural operations to provide them with first-hand knowledge and experience of U.S. agricultural practices and management techniques and systems. A third goal was to teach the participants about joint ventures and provide them with opportunities to establish joint ventures with American companies and other business organizations. A final goal was to introduce the visiting Uzbeks to American culture, particularly to those elements associated with agricultural communities.

The program package that evolved out of this set of objectives was a complex matrix of task, functional and product/process components. Care was taken specifically to link classroom examples and content to the field visits and experience-based learning. Instructors developed agricultural examples and course materials and emphasized topics that were thought to have special application to Soviet agriculture and to changing the Soviet agri-management system. Lecture modules were interspersed with field visits, with attention being paid to the development of participant skills and knowledge in major functional areas of management pertaining to what had been seen and experienced during the visits. Specific task skills such as computer-based management techniques, joint-venture management, marketing and advertising, pricing techniques, distribution management and a variety of financial, accounting and human relations skills were included in order to meet the specific needs of the group.

One of the main barriers encountered during Sedpro I involved problems of translating classroom lectures. The month of English language classes was understandably insufficient preparation for comprehending technical lectures. And even though they performed admirably, the most fluent members of the group were not trained translators. This problem was solved quite effectively in Sedpro II. The Institute purchased simultaneous translation equipment and the Uzbek group brought two official translators.

The field visits were integrated with the regular instructional curriculum. The economics and finance components of the program were coordinated with visits to a cattle exchange, the stock exchange and the options trading exchange. Visits to a large cotton marketing and distribution organization, the almond growers' and walnut growers' marketing associations and visits to wholesale and retail grain and food distribution outlets were made a part of the marketing component. Production and operations management components were integrated with visits to major livestock breeding, milk production, wine production and vegetable- and fruit-canning operations. An intensive set of sessions were also included on crop research, water distribution and management and other aspects of agricultural resource and research management.

The execution of Sedpro II

Given the logistical and academic difficulties presented by the Uzbekistan program, Sedpro II was executed quite differently from the program developed for the aviation industry managers. All field visits were made midweek, when traffic problems in traveling to remote locations in California's Central Valley were minimized by avoiding the weekend traffic rush out of the San Francisco Bay Area. Such an arrangement was also ideal from the standpoint of personnel availability at the sites visited. This format also permitted the matching of field visits to the subject matter taught in the classroom during the week.

Professors stressed agricultural examples and applications in the classroom. Classroom instruction in economics stressed the role of private property rights in U.S. agriculture with a comparative analysis of productivity and efficiency in market-oriented and Soviet-style economies. The role of market prices and profit incentives was emphasized in the production and distribution of agricultural products. The module was integrated with a visit to the Stockton Cattle Exchange, where the role of the auctioneer and free-market prices was demonstrated to the participants. The owner of the exchange, Brian Fitzgerald, provided a half-day lecture tour of the operations. He defined his role both as a specialist and a market maker. The integration of computers with the livestock exchange operations was a source of great interest to the Uzbek executives. A day at the Salinas Rodeo also turned out to be a lesson in market economics as a world-champion cowboy, Jack Roddy, explained the intricacies of cattle pricing and distribution and rodeo management, and then demonstrated, in competition, the technical aspects of calf roping, bronco riding and other rodeo activities.

The finance component of the program included an overview of agricultural financing and options trading in agricultural commodities. A visit to the agricultural farm banks system fell through because of logistical difficulties, but the group was given a thorough grounding in agricultural financing through lectures by the chief financial officers and executives of Calcot (the country's largest cotton marketing cooperative) and Tri-valley Growers (one of the country's largest fruit-growing cooperatives), and by visits to banks serving agricultural markets. The highlight of this component was a visit to the Pacific Stock Exchange and the Options Trading Exchange. The floor activity at the latter exchange generated a lengthy discussion on the role of financial markets and market prices in producing wealth for a nation.

The accounting instructor developed his module with a model of a firm producing and selling *kvas*, a traditional nonalcoholic Russian drink. Another accounting and tax instructor focused on joint ventures and taxation in the Soviet Union and compared it to the situation in the United States. Another instructor focused on environmental concerns in agriculture and the solutions that were adopted in the United States

The production component covered the area of operations and logistics management with agricultural examples. The group visited the wine-producing operations of Robert Mondavi and Sterling in the Napa Valley; the world's largest, completely automated cannery at Tri-valley's Plant No. 7 in Modesto, California; the cotton-growing operation at the Cotton Research Station in Shafter, California; and a number of other growing and production facilities such Blue Diamond Almonds, Sun Diamond Walnuts, Ace Tomato, Maddox Dairy, the Harris Ranch (for beef cattle) and Farmers' Rice Cooperative in Sacramento, California. Logistics management was highlighted with a visit to the Project Operations Center of the California Board of Land Reclamation, where the logistics of pricing and distributing water through centralized management was explained. At this facility, Sedpro II participants expressed skepticism regarding the efficiency of such a system even though they were quite impressed with both the hardware and software of the Center. A visit to the Port of Sacramento and a tour of its operations also demonstrated the role of market-driven logistics management. The group was then received in the Office of the Governor of the State of California, where a Russian-speaking guide led them on a tour of the state capitol.

In order to meet the third objective, opportunities were provided for the visiting Uzbeks to meet with American entrepreneurs who were involved in agribusiness. Formal instruction was also provided about joint venture creation and management. The Sedpro codirectors arranged for visits with governmental agencies such as the Small Business Administration, the Extension Services of the California

Department of Agriculture, leading banks in the Financial District in San Francisco and a number of Bay Area agribusiness firms.

The entrepreneurial spirit and trading instincts of the Uzbek executives proved to be formidable. Every evening and weekend when the Sedpro group was in town, the hotel where they were housed was full of American businessmen and other individuals discussing business deals. By the end of their stay, the members of the group had negotiated correspondent relationships with U.S. banks, computer deals with Silicon Valley firms, contracts for the purchase of machinery required to modernize Uzbek agriculture, and a number of other collaborations with Bay Area firms. The leaders of the group stayed for an additional two weeks in the United States to negotiate a number agreements with other U.S. organizations.

A significant distinguishing feature of the Sedpro II group was their propensity to learn about and practice business upon their arrival in the United States. They took detailed notes, asked hundreds of questions and talked about implementing the lessons learned in their respective organizations. Morale was very high despite the deteriorating conditions at home, as reflected in the daily news.

The fourth objective of the program, cultural enrichment, was met by creating opportunities for interaction between the members of the Sedpro group and Californians. A number of social events were held. These included an opening banquet at which Uzbek and American dances were performed, an outdoor barbecue arranged by the Alameda Cattlewomen's Association, and other get-togethers arranged by the Salinas Cattlewomen's Association, the local mosque and Islamic associations, and individual families. Another highlight of the program was a banquet that the visiting Uzbeks prepared and hosted for the university community. On another occasion, the Asian Studies Program at CSUH arranged a special Asian evening with over a hundred guests invited from all over the Bay Area for an Asian food banquet, followed by a moonlit concert of Indian classical flute. The Sedpro II program concluded with a banquet attended by the senior administrative officers of the university, the Uzbek graduates and Sedpro faculty.

The lessons of Sedpro II

Sedpro II was one of the most complex and fast-paced executive development programs that the School of Business and Economics has ever conducted. The diverse interests and backgrounds of the students and the logistical difficulties of conducting field trips to distant places in the Central Valley of California made the execution of the program particularly challenging.

The outcomes were generally positive. All the major objectives of the program were met. A formal closing evaluation of the program was conducted on the day of departure. The Uzbek executives were highly appreciative of the classroom instruction they received and were generally pleased with the field trip component of the program. However, the Uzbek executives would have liked lectures on the organization and financing of agricultural research and the links and interrelations between research laboratories and business corporations. They also regretted not being able to visit a cotton ginnery. (This had not been possible because Sedpro II took place during the off-season.)

A number of lessons were learned from Sedpro II. The first was the necessity to limit group size from fifteen to twenty people from a pedagogical, logistical and organizational point of view. It is also necessary to limit the group to a narrower range of backgrounds and interests. Both of these issues were also mentioned by the visiting Uzbeks in their formal written evaluation. A second lesson was that the simultaneous translation is a preferable alternative to instruction in English when the group's language skills are limited. Third, the fast-paced, overly concentrated content of the program caused considerable fatigue to the participants and logistical difficulties for the coordinators. Consequently, future programs need to be more evenly paced with fewer field visits.

Fourth, the care taken to understand and cater to the ethnic and religious needs of people from Central Asia reiterates the truth of the maxim that "the customer always comes first." The special arrangements made for the occasion of *Id*, the care taken to prepare a "kosher" menu for a predominantly Moslem group and the arrangement of suitable contacts in the local Moslem community was important for the success of the program.

A positive outcome of the program was the signing of a protocol to facilitate a series of general and specialized training programs for future groups of Uzbek agricultural managers, a Bank Executive Training Program for commercial bankers and the training of Uzbek managers in special Executive MBA programs of nine months to one-year duration. In addition, the leaders of the Uzbek delegation wanted to send undergraduate students for training in business and other disciplines on an ongoing basis. It is envisioned that the next group of Uzbek managers will be sent for training to CSUH in early 1992, unless this is delayed by the current upheavals in the USSR and Uzbekistan.

The leaders of the Uzbek delegation also desired that CSUH set up a joint venture with UzAPS to open a business school in Tashkent, the capital of Uzbekistan. After discussion, this was modified to CSUH's designing and helping UzAPS set up a business school in Tashkent, to be called the Uzbekistan School of Business and Economics (USOBE), to provide Management Development Programs (MDPs) for retraining and upgrading the skills of practicing Uzbek managers and to offer undergraduate and MBA programs. It is expected that the protocol will be implemented in 1992.

Sedpro III: Izhorskii Zavod

Background of the program

In the spring of 1991, the CSUH's Institute of Research and Business Development (IRBD) was contacted by Bechtel International, Inc., a San Francisco–based international engineering and construction company. Bechtel was then engaged in a consulting project to assist a large Soviet steel manufacturing company, Izhorskii Zavod (IZ), with new product development. Two of IZ's top executives, Mr. Leonid Karliukov, Deputy General Director, and Mr. Sergei Filimonov, Chief of the Department of Foreign Affairs of IZ's foreign trade firm "Izhora," were visiting in the Bay Area and were interested in pursuing the possibility of establishing a management development program. As Bechtel was familiar with CSUH's two previous programs, they arranged for the IZ representatives to visit the campus. They met with many of the faculty who had instructed past programs and received an overview of those programs. It was interesting that the first topic they asked about was human resource management. They saw HRM as one of the key issues at their facility.

As a result of this meeting, Dr. Jay Tontz, Dean of the School of Business and Economics, Dr. Bruce MacNab, Director of the IRBD, Dr. Vladimir Ozernoy, professor of quantitative business methods and a Russian native, and Dr. Donna Wiley, professor of human resource management, were invited to Leningrad (now St. Petersburg) to meet with their management group and to sign an agreement to provide business education and company visits to sixteen of their "shop" managers. These "shops" may have several thousand workers in them. The company is a vertically integrated steel production facility, founded in 1722 by Peter the Great to build the Russian Navy. Employment today exceeds 26,000 people.

IZ is a very large complex of facilities located in Kolpino, a suburb of St. Petersburg. There are more than 120 kilometers of railroad track and 16 kilometers of roads and service lanes within the plant. More than 500 freight vans service the enterprise, and more than 100 leave and arrive daily. The plant produces steel and alloy products ranging from table silverware to heavy excavation equipment to nuclear reactor pressure vessels. Because of safety and environmental concerns about nuclear power plants following the Chernobyl' disaster, orders for these vessels have fallen dramatically (although the management of IZ was very quick to point out that their products were not involved in Chernobyl', and that their technology is much safer and of much higher quality). When we toured the factory, we saw a huge vessel on the shop floor that was part of a large order recently canceled by Germany. One of this company's biggest challenges is to convert their manufacturing process to the production of more consumer-oriented goods, but this is difficult because of the enormous size of their current technology. The plant has historically been state-owned and subsidized.

About twelve years ago, a new General Director, Vladimir Vasilev, was appointed at IZ. The new General Director was well educated and well read in Western literature. Upon noticing a lack of interest in quality and a lack of personal motivation among workers, he recognized the need for creating new ways of doing business. He filled key management positions with younger managers who were more flexible and adaptable to new approaches. He knew that these managers needed knowledge of Western business practices, but there was no source of such knowledge. In 1985, before *glasnost'* and *perestroika*, he created a new center for management education. To do this, he needed the permission of two ministries. This request was considered radical and the management of IZ was considered "strange" by the central planners. Nonetheless, permission was granted.

The next stage in the process was the attempt to gain independence from the Ministry of Steel Industries. Three years ago, they essentially declared themselves independent and broke away as an independent enterprise. They sought to implement the principles of a market economy, but no such economy existed. In addition, the central government still had power over their access to resources and raw materials.

IZ is also facing many internal challenges. An increase of employees from diverse ethnic backgrounds has created some internal conflicts. There is worker unrest, as people are uncertain about the results of the proposed economic changes in the Soviet Union. Rampant inflation is resulting in demands for higher salaries. Because legislation has not yet created the mechanisms for a market economy, there is the increasing threat that IZ's most talented management will leave the organization and look for opportunities to start businesses on their own, where there are fewer governmental regulations than in the steel industry and more opportunities to make money.

In spite of all of these problems, there is great pride at IZ. The company has no debt, no strikes, and no stoppages of production. It is one of the only companies whose production has not diminished significantly during this difficult period. The company is striving to operate on three basic principles: "to produce the best quality; to take professional responsibility for our work; and to take the initiative as professionals and create change." The company is decentralizing its organizational structure and passing authority for decision making down the line. It was in this context that IZ decided to send sixteen of their key managers for training at CSUH. The top management's ultimate goal is to spin their large divisions off into relatively autonomous profit centers, giving each division's manager more control over his own business. Needless to say, our group was tremendously impressed with the courage of these managers and all that they have been able to accomplish, given their political and economic situation.

The design of the program

IZ conducted a very competitive selection process to choose the participants for the program. According to Deputy General Director Karliukov, the key selection criteria was "creativity." The group of sixteen managers who were finally chosen included department chiefs of metallurgy, machine shops, maintenance, chief of economics, foreign trade and computers. They are quite young, considering their high-level positions, with ages ranging from twenty-eight to fifty. The group arrived on November 10, 1991 for a nine-week program consisting of approximately 230 hours of classroom instruction and about sixteen days of company tours.

English skills continue to be one of the main considerations (and problems) in conducting the in-class instruction. IZ's top management was very committed to having the participants develop their English-speaking skills. However, because of cost considerations they elected to conduct language instruction at their facility prior to the program and to conduct the CSUH classes in English without a "professional" translator. Several of the participants had made astonishing progress since our visit in June, while others still speak very little English. Fortunately, two of the participants are quite fluent, and have done an excellent job of translating in class. However, those with limited language skills are very limited in how much they can participate, both in and outside of the classroom.

This is the first program we have conducted in which all of the participants are from the same organization. This homogeneous group composition has several advantages compared to the diverse mix of participants in the two previous programs. First, since the participants knew each other prior to the program, they had already developed a high degree of group cohesion and trust. Second, since they are from the same company, they share a common frame of business reference in terms of industry, product, and culture. In addition, they have very similar interests and concerns, making it much easier to address their specific needs during the class lectures and to arrange appropriate plant visits. This also provides us with the opportunity to develop a critical mass of trained managers who can return to their company with a consistent body of knowledge and skills. Such a critical mass should generate sufficient support to make it easier for them to put what they have learned into practice than it has been for members of the two previous groups, despite the difficult external situation to which the current group will be returning. In contrast, each member of the first group was the sole representative from his enterprise, and the enterprises were spread throughout the Soviet Union. The ability of the current group to implement their learning should also be aided by the high level of support they will receive from top management.

In addition to the objectives cited for the two previous programs, i.e., to acquaint the participants with the principles of a market economy, to provide exposure to how these principles are practiced in U.S. firms, to familiarize them with the mechanisms of forming joint ventures, and to introduce them to American culture, this program had several unique objectives. As discussed earlier, one of the charges given to the program designers by IZ's General Director, Mr. Vladimir Vasilev, was to develop a team of individuals who would be capable of directing their divisions, referred to as "shops," as relatively autonomous profit centers upon their return. Thus, our main goal is to provide them with in-depth coverage of the knowledge and skills required to manage an enterprise. Much classroom attention is being paid to the processes of strategic planning and strategic marketing, as well as to the financial aspects of running a business. A second unique objective of this program is to foster the participants' skills in new product development. Therefore, a classroom session on innovation was added. Thirdly, because of the firm's goal to privatize in the near future, a classroom session on the privatization of firms in socialist systems was conducted. The effective utilization of human resources was also one of this company's key concerns. Therefore, the current program contains sixteen hours of classroom instruction on human resource management along with eight hours of instruction on topics related to organizational behavior and eight hours on general management theory.

Several aspects of HRM are of particular relevance to this group of Soviet managers as well as to managers in all Soviet enterprises. Employee motivation is one of these key areas. A common criticism of the socialist system is its failure to provide individual incentives for high levels of productivity. Therefore, the question most frequently asked by these managers is: "How do you motivate your employees?" In our classes, we examined various theories of motivation and mechanisms utilized by U.S. companies and by companies in other countries to put motivation theories into practice. We discussed various approaches to job design as a means of providing intrinsic rewards to employees. One approach of particular interest was the use of autonomous work teams. According to one manager, this approach is currently being implemented in his division. It was interesting for the instructor to discover that Soviet managers are as reluctant to relinquish their power and authority as are their American counterparts. We discussed at length the changing role of the manager as decision making is delegated to employees.

We also spent a great deal of class time discussing the design of compensation systems. Two specific compensation issues were of most interest. First was the issue of internal pay equity and the process of job evaluation. One of the problems facing their and other Soviet firms is the lack of adequate pay differentials between various jobs and hierarchical levels. These managers reported that their employees were reluctant to be promoted into management because of the increased level of job demands and the lack of commensurate increases in financial rewards. The instructor explained the point method of job evaluation, and then used one of the participant's jobs, along with one of his employee's jobs, to demonstrate how pay differentials among jobs are established.

The second compensation issue of particular relevance to this group is that of pay for performance. Although IZ technically has a pay for performance system, the managers agree that the extent of the differential separating the excellent employees from the poor employees is not sufficient enough to provide a true performance incentive (which is a criticism also frequently made about merit pay systems in U.S. companies). In addition to individual incentive plans, we also discussed other alternatives of rewarding employees for their contributions, such as bonuses, employee recognition programs, suggestion rewards, gain sharing, and profit sharing. However, the Soviet managers are very pessimistic about their ability to institute new compensation systems because of the current economic situation.

Another HR area of interest to these managers (because of its future importance to Soviet managers) is that of employee recruitment and selection. In the past, many employees, particularly graduates of technical institutes, received their job assignments from the central government, giving neither the company nor the individual much latitude in the selection process. This system is no longer in place. Therefore, these managers are very interested in how American companies select their employees, and so we discussed a variety of recruiting and selection methods.

As in Sedpro I, the playing of BRANDMAPS, the strategic marketing game, is one of the key components of Sedpro III. The game has been even more successful in the current program because of the participants' initial level of sophistication, in terms of both their previous exposure to Western business concepts and their level of computer skills. (IZ has already implemented considerable computer technology throughout the company, though not at the levels desired by top management, and conducts computer training for its employees). Although we are only midway through our program, they have already played several sessions of the game. Competition between the teams is fierce, and one team made the observation that the team which is performing best so far is the one which has made the fewest changes in their marketing strategy, allowing their customers to become familiar with their product. One marketing concept which is still foreign to them is advertising. They dislike the advertisements on U.S. commercial television networks and stated that good products should sell themselves!

We are currently in the process of conducting the company tour component of Sedpro III. One of the structural differences between the current program and the two previous programs is the placement of the plant visits. It was decided that the majority of the classroom component would be completed before the plant visits began. This provides the participants with as much knowledge about U.S. business practices as possible so that they can better understand what they are seeing on the tours. This was not possible during Sedpro II because of the short duration of the program and the distances involved in travelling to remote agricultural sites. The group will visit a variety of companies in the high technology industry, including Varian, Hewlett-Packard, Raychem, and Novasensor, as well as the Pacific Stock Exchange, Bechtel, and Pacific Bell.

One of the highlights of the plant visits so far was a trip to New United Motors Manufacturing, Incorporated (NUMMI), a GM-Toyota joint venture in Fremont, California. Since NUMMI has only recently opened its doors to visitors from the general public, our group was one of the first to receive a guided tour of NUMMI's state-of-the-art manufacturing facility, which is serving as a model for other GM factories. (NUMMI will not be affected by the layoffs announced by GM in December 1991.) The group also learned from company officials about how NUMMI has incorporated Toyota's production concepts and management philosophies and about NUMMI's goal of building the highest quality vehicles possible at the most competitive price. Two of the most important concepts applied at NUMMI are *kaizen*, the continuous pursuit of improvement, and *jidoka*, the quality principle. They also learned about NUMMI's just-in-time inventory control process, which they had discussed in class.

While the participants have been most impressed by the manufacturing facilities and technologies they have observed, the most frequently asked questions for company representatives continue to pertain to human resource management issues. Invariably, they ask how the companies motivate and compensate their employees. At NUMMI, they saw first hand the concepts of autonomous work teams and employee involvement in practice, and were able to observe the outstanding results NUMMI attributes to its employees' commitment and participation.

As in Sedpro I and II, one of the most important aspects of Sedpro III is the opportunity for cultural exchanges. We have already had several such occasions, including spending Thanksgiving in professors' homes, attending a party hosted by a Bay Area entrepreneur in their honor, and attending the annual faculty Christmas party held in the home of the Dean of the School of Business and Economics. From our Russian guests we have learned about the importance of music in the Russian culture, as they play and sing Russian folk songs for us at these various social events.

Although it is too early to judge the success of Sedpro III, we have already received most favorable comments from the participants about their experience at CSUH. They have found the lectures interesting and informative and constantly comment on the friendliness and warmth of the American people. From the instructors' perspective, we find the courage and dedication of these men remarkable, considering the daily news of the virtual dissolution of the country they left only one month ago.

Conclusions

Several conclusions and recommendations can be drawn from the CSUH experience with Soviet management education. First, any program should be tailored as closely as possible to the needs of the particular participants. It was extremely helpful for several of our faculty to have the opportunity to visit the IZ facility and to hear directly from top management their goals for the program. Second, language continues to be an issue and a barrier to the effectiveness of any program. The optimal solution is to have participants who are fluent in English. If this is not feasible, another solution is to have as much of the class material as possible, particularly overhead transparencies and handout materials, translated into Russian. If possible, send the participants such materials in advance. In addition, several books on U.S. business practices are already translated into Russian. If participants have read these materials in advance, their understanding and class participation can be increased. Also, if a translator is to be used, make sure that this person has familiarity with business terminology. Third, group composition is another key consideration. The current experience demonstrates the advantages of having groups comprised of managers from the same company. If this is not possible, make sure that as much is known about each individual participant as possible. Fourth, such experiences can be extremely physically and emotionally draining for these managers. It is sometimes difficult for people who are used to being very active (and in charge) to adjust to the student role and to sit in class for long periods of time. Opportunities for frequent physical activity should be provided. Program designers and instructors should also be sensitive to any political, social, cultural and philosophical issues which may arise. It must be recognized that not only is the economic system changing in the Soviet Union but an entire way of life is changing also. Participants are struggling with complex questions such as what the appropriate levels of social support mechanisms are in a society and whose responsibility it is to provide such support. Fifth, it should be noted that all of the participants in these three programs (with the exception of one translator in Sedpro II) have been men. We have attempted to have women participants included, but attitudes toward gender roles both at work and at home are very different in the Soviet Union (see the article by Komarov in this volume). The final, and most important conclusion, is that the participants have not been the only ones to benefit from these programs. Conducting these three Soviet management development programs has been an extremely rewarding and enriching experience, not only for the faculty who have participated, but for the entire university community.

Now that the new Commonwealth of Independent States has come into formal existence on January 1, 1992 and the Soviet Union as we have known it ceases to exist, this region will continue to face tremendous difficulties and challenges. It is our hope that U.S. academic institutions such as ours can continue to train managers who can provide leadership to their various enterprises as they move towards a market economy.

Note

1. Chapman, R.G. (1991). *BRANDMAPS*. Englewood Cliffs, NJ: Prentice-Hall.

15

A Training Program for Russian Bankers at Middlesex Community College

Sheila M. Puffer

In 1991 Middlesex Community College, located in suburban Boston, conducted two three-week training programs for presidents and vice-presidents of banks in the Russian republic. The programs were tailored to the banking industry, with the goal of providing Russian banking executives with knowledge of western banking and financial practices to enable them to begin transforming their banks into full-service market-oriented organizations. The programs were also in line with Middlesex Community College's goal of developing an international perspective by providing opportunities for faculty, students, and staff to learn about events around the world and to study and teach abroad. This chapter describes the origin of the program, its structure and content, the participants, evaluation of the results, and prospects for the future.

The origin of the program

Middlesex Community College, with campuses in Lowell and Bedford, Massachusetts, is the largest community college in the state, with 4,500 students in the day division, and more than 20,000 students in

---

Note: This chapter is based on an interview with Carole A. Cowan, President of Middlesex Community College, and David M. Kalivas, Director of the Center for International Studies at the College, conducted on December 23, 1991.

day and evening credit and noncredit programs. The College never expressly intended to specialize in training Russian bankers when it began its international initiatives in the late 1980s. As often happens in dealing with Russians, the opportunity arose rather serendipitously through a series of informal contacts.

In the fall of 1989 President Cowan, then dean of administration and finance, went to the USSR on a higher education study tour sponsored by the Center for U.S.–USSR Initiatives. During her visit she signed an exchange agreement with Moscow State Pedagogical Institute. Shortly thereafter Middlesex hosted a group of students from the institute on a cultural exchange. In 1990 two faculty members from Middlesex went to the USSR to explore the possibility of exchanges for faculty and students. During that visit a colleague at the Pedagogical Institute introduced one of the visiting Middlesex faculty members, David Kalivas, to Aleksandr M. Varekha, who was involved in creating the International Business School that was soon to open at Moscow Friendship University (formerly Patrice Lumumba University). Dr. Kalivas initiated negotiations with Dr. Varekha to conduct a training program in the United States for Russian bankers.

Program structure and content

The banking program was developed through a partnership of three institutions. The International Business School at Moscow Friendship University and Middlesex Community College had compatible philosophies in that both believed in practical, "hands-on" training. However, being a two-year community college, Middlesex did not have any faculty members who specialized in upper level courses in banking and finance. Therefore, they turned to their colleagues at the School of Management at Suffolk University, headed by Dean Jack Brennan. Suffolk had strong ties with Middlesex and had experience in conducting training programs for Soviet managers.

The program was financed in U.S. dollars by the newly created Commercial Banking Association of Russia, and was paid for in advance. In addition to the training program, the fee paid by the Association covered administration, accommodations in a first-class hotel, meals, transportation in the United States, internships, and cultural activities.

The three-week program, preceded by an orientation at the International Business School in Moscow, consisted of two weeks of seminars and a four-day internship in a variety of U.S. banking institutions located in the greater Boston area. The seminars were taught in English by four or five faculty from the School of Management at Suffolk University as well as two or three practitioners from the banking industry. The lectures were interpreted into Russian. Seminars were conducted on the following topics: financial markets, monetary policy, banking structure, government regulations, strategy and planning, and customer service.

The four-day internships were made possible by the largesse of Greater Boston banking institutions who provided, free of charge, information, expertise, and access to their organizations in exchange for establishing contacts with these influential Russian bankers with whom they might eventually form partnerships. The program director arranged to give the bankers exposure to a full array of banking experience by having them visit different types of banking operations. The bankers were split into two groups (eight in one, seven in the other) and were sent for two days to each of two banking organizations. The companies that participated in the two programs were Bank of Boston, BayBank, Enterprise Bank, Washington Savings Bank, and the Northern Massachusetts Telephone Workers Credit Union.

The format of the internships consisted of three activities: a tour of the bank, in-house seminars, and "hands on" experience. The series of seminars were conducted by the principals in charge of each department, typically a vice-president or managing director. The principal would explain the operation of the department and describe in detail the use of documents and forms. The participants were then given the documentation for their own use.

The Russian bankers were also given an opportunity to experience first hand some banking operations. For example, at the Northern Massachusetts Telephone Workers Credit Union they stood behind the tellers as they interacted with customers. The participants were given a step-by-step explanation of the transaction as it occurred. Another highlight at the credit union was the opportunity to experience voice recognition technology. Customers were able to do their banking by telephone by having the computer recognize their voice and match it to their account. The Russian bankers were also impressed by the great deal of money, effort, and attention devoted to customer service. They commented that the banks had a cheerful atmosphere which was reflected in the decorating scheme, the advertising, and the attitudes of the staff.

The organizers encouraged the bankers to discuss in the evenings what they had learned that day in order to clarify their understanding. The organizers also suggested that the bankers continue to maintain contact with one another upon their return to Russia. By forming an on-going network, the bankers were thought to stand a better chance of implementing their knowledge.

The participants

There were fifteen participants in each of the two programs, as well as two interpreters. All the participants were presidents and vice-presidents of banking institutions from many different cities in Russia, including Moscow, Irkutsk, Ufa, Sverdlovsk, and Volgograd. Most of them did not know each other prior to the program. They ranged in age from thirty to sixty-four, with the average age about fifty. They were highly experienced and knowledgeable in their field, but their responsibilities had been restricted mainly to managing and distributing funds allocated from the central banking authority. As a result, they were eager to learn about Western banking practices, which were entirely new to them. The oldest participant, who was beyond retirement age (which is sixty for men, and fifty-five for women), was particularly energetic and receptive to new ideas. There were four women in each of the two groups.

Evaluation of the program

The training program for Russian bankers can be evaluated from the perspective of the participants as well as the organizers. The participants expressed satisfaction with the program and were particularly impressed with the practical, "nitty gritty" information they learned in the internships. In fact, they said they would have preferred to have spent all their time on internships. However, this is probably short-sighted, in that information about the principles of banking in a market economy are probably conveyed more efficiently in a classroom setting. This information can then serve as the basis for getting the most benefit from the internships.

The faculty and administrators at Middlesex Community College, Suffolk University, and the Commercial Banking Association of Russia were also satisfied with the two programs they have conducted for the Russian bankers. In planning for the next group, they are working on refining the program to better meet participants' needs. They recognize that each group is different. In light of this, the Middlesex administrators want to learn more about the participants' experience and expectations in advance in order to work with them in tailoring the program to their specific needs. The administration also plans to refine the seminars into a more cohesive package, and to expand the internships to five or six days.

Prospects for the future

The banking program for Russian managers has been rated a success by all those involved and the program will continue with a third group next year. The administrators are proud that they have been able to accomplish so much with a small budget and staff. They operated on a "shoestring," used no state funds, and realized a modest profit. They recognize that the success of the program is due to the commitment and dedication of people that goes far beyond the requirements of a nine-to-five job.

A critical factor for the success of such an international program is the ability and commitment of the program director. As Middlesex's President Cowan articulated, the director needs to have special qualities: energy, directiveness, and an ability to gain the Russians' trust. President Cowan is pleased that the program director, David Kalivas, possesses these qualities, yet she is sensitive to finding a way to continue the program without exhausting him or "burning him out."

President Cowan stated that the program for Russian bankers was a rewarding experience for everyone who has been involved. Faculty, students, and staff have become exposed to a much larger world, and the program has taken on a life of its own. For President Cowan, the extra effort had the personal benefit of making her job more rewarding: "There is always something new in a job that sparks you. It is these new initiatives that provide that spark beyond the routine of the job." Professor Kalivas noted that managing the program was a personal growth experience for him: "I was once content to stay in the classroom and teach my courses, but I am not content to do that any longer. There is a whole world out there that I am seeing in a different light."

The Russian bankers' program and other international initiatives also provide rewards for Middlesex Community College as an institution. President Cowan noted: "I see people being able to identify internationally like they have never been able to before. Before, Middlesex was known as a quiet community college in the suburbs. We are now the largest community college in the state. We are a 'second chance' or 'only chance' institution for so many, and now we are opening doors for them. If we can give these people access to the whole world, we are not exposing them just to Boston, but the globe, and we want to help them feel successful in that environment. Our student government association set aside $15,000 in student activity money to fund international education programs for students. We are also planning to send some of our faculty members to Russia on the small profits earned from the Russian bankers' program."

The College is also strengthening its ties with the high technology companies located nearby, and hopes to provide training for companies planning to do business in Russia. The program director, Professor David Kalivas, is also planning to head a trade mission to Russia for American bankers next year.

President Cowan recognizes that there are trade-offs in managing international programs such as the one for the Russian bankers. She says: "The program has worked only because the faculty have opened up their homes and their hearts to the Russians. They have become committed on a personal level, and from there we can build. I only wish that more people at the College could get involved. Other concerns are that there is a creeping isolationism in the country, and our faculty have not had a salary increase in four years. But if we take the position that we cannot afford to work with the Russians, we will become stagnant and fail to grow. Therein lies the challenge and the potential rewards."

16

The Fuqua School of Business Program for Soviet Executives

Sheila M. Puffer

The program for training Soviet senior executives at the Fuqua School of Business (FSB) came into being as the result of the personal initiative of Mr. J.B. Fuqua, chairman of Fuqua Capital Corporation. In the late 1980s Mr. Fuqua began to contemplate retiring from business and wanted to engage in some type of philanthropic activity in his retirement. He had read for many years about the declining economic and business conditions in the Soviet Union and wanted to help improve the situation in some way. Mr. Fuqua decided that giving Soviet managers access to American management education was the best way he could contribute. To that end in 1989 he provided a grant of $4 million to the Fuqua School of Business at Duke University in Durham, North Carolina. The Fuqua family had been generous supporters of the School for many years, and therefore the Fuqua School was a natural site for the project. The goal of the program was to give Soviet senior executives the know-how to change their enterprises in order for the businesses to function according to the principles of a market economy.

Administration of the program

The program is managed by a full-time director at the Fuqua School who works in collaboration with staff members at a Soviet partner

Note: This chapter is based on an interview with J.B. Fuqua conducted on December 20, 1991. I am grateful to Mr. Fuqua for giving me permission to include material from the notes prepared for him by Thomas F. Remington concerning their trip to Moscow and St. Petersburg in November 1991.

institution. The partner for the first three groups was the Academy of the National Economy. The Fuqua staff decided to diversify its relationships and selected the fourth group in collaboration with the Russian Academy of Entrepreneurship, a newly created organization that promotes free-market management education and is similar to the Young Presidents' Group in the United States.

The financing of the program is done entirely through the Fuqua grant, with the Soviet participants paying only for their transportation to New York. The Fuqua grant covers training costs, meals, lodging, transportation in the United States, and cultural activities. Expenses incurred on the internships in U.S. firms are usually paid for by the host companies. The Fuqua program, which is purely philanthropic and nonprofit, incurs $7,000 to $8,000 in expenses for each participant.

The participants

Mr. Fuqua stipulated that the participants be at the most senior level, equivalent to chief executive officers, in order to ensure they had sufficient authority to use their knowledge from the program to make significant changes in their organizations. He also wanted the participants to constitute a heterogeneous group, representing a variety of industries and regions of the USSR. Since the program was initiated in 1990, four groups of thirty executives have received training at the Fuqua School. They have come from industries such as energy, cigarette production, food processing, glass manufacturing, and automobile manufacturing. Knowledge of English is not a requirement.

The thirty participants in each group are selected from one hundred applications provided by the Soviet partner institution. The Fuqua program director chooses fifty of these to be interviewed, and the thirty who are considered most suitable are admitted to the program. The Fuqua staff make sure they have the final say about who attends the program rather than leaving the decision to the Soviet partner institution. Mr. Fuqua says, "We told the Soviets that we knew they were like Americans. If we let them make the decision, they would select their brothers, nephews, and uncles."

Structure of the program

The program, which is preceded by three months of training at the partner institution in Moscow, consists of three weeks of classroom instruction and one week of internships in American companies. The program was designed specifically for the Soviets by the faculty at the Fuqua School of Business, and is taught by the faculty as well as outside experts from other institutions. Courses are taught in English with simultaneous interpretation into Russian provided through headphones. The topics are similar to those covered in MBA programs and include marketing, human resources management, cost accounting, economics, business plans and entrepreneurship, and employee stock ownership plans (ESOPs). Two days are devoted to a computer game in which the participants compete with each other in a simulation of real-world business conditions. During the classroom instruction phase the participants study ten hours a day. In addition, they spend their evenings doing homework or engaging in cultural or social activities with members of the community and social and business organizations.

Numerous American corporations recognize the potential commercial benefit of making contacts with senior-level Soviet executives and have willingly provided internships for the participants. Most companies host two executives simultaneously for a week. The most effective internships are those that are formally structured, have a planned program of activities, and are in the same industry as the Soviet executive's enterprise. For example, Mr. Fuqua personally arranged for three participants to visit several large companies in Atlanta that had been started by entrepreneurs. He structured the program hour by hour in order to expose the Soviets to different aspects of developing a business, including new product development and equipment design. Other successful internships included a cigarette factory executive's visit to the Camel cigarette factory, and a vodka producer's visit to Pepsi Cola, which imports Russian vodka to the United States in exchange for soft drink distribution in the USSR.

Evaluation of the program

In November 1991 Mr. Fuqua spent ten days in Moscow and St. Petersburg and had the opportunity to interview some of the graduates of the three programs that have been conducted to date. He found that these executives are hard at work managing the transition of their enterprises from the state planning system to the market economy. The task is fraught with uncertainty due to the unstable political, economic, and legal environment. Nevertheless, the managers are taking steps toward making their enterprises more productive and competitive by privatizing them and offering new incentives to their work force.

One of the graduates, Vladimir Gurov, is CEO of the Bolshevichka Menswear Factory in Moscow. He reported that his enterprise is doing well, having annual sales of 162 million rubles and a profit of 22 million rubles. His assessment of the Fuqua program included the following:

> "The most beneficial result of the Fuqua program is that now I grasp how sophisticated a system the market economy is. It needs a different mentality from what we are used to. I used to think of myself as individualistic, closer to American culture. But now I see how collectivistic my mindset really is. It takes a long time to change the mindset of an entire country. For example, the Israelites had to wander in the desert forty years to get the mentality of slavery out of their systems. We need time to acquire new experience.
>
> "At the FSB I got a good understanding of what the market is, but I can't use this knowledge here. The environment is not stable. We use our money to buy large stocks of supplies, which is counter to good business practices. But we fear severe price increases in the near future. What cost us 50 rubles two months ago now costs 200 rubles. Our best suit cost 250 rubles last year, and is now selling for 3,000 rubles. The inflation process has to be managed."

On a practical level, Mr. Gurov has begun to make some changes in his clothing factory as a result of his experience in the Fuqua program. He learned about the importance of accounting and made his chief accountant his first deputy. This is an important deviation from the organizational structure found in traditional Soviet manufacturing enterprises. Typically the position of first deputy is held by the chief engineer who is the head of production operations.

Mr. Gurov has also implemented a new incentive system and is experiencing good results:

> "We have 2,000 employees in total at two factories in Moscow, plus two in Kaluga. We have piece rates plus bonuses for meeting quality goals. We pay for quality, not productivity, because productivity follows quality. We are unusual in the attention we give to quality. Partly our quality is a result of our incentive system, but it is also due to the use of good equipment, good materials, and good labor relations. We want to enter the European market using foreign materials and selling production abroad. I believe we are able to compete with Western manu-

facturers, but we need a half-year's training time. We can do it. We have a good team here, and that is our main asset. Our quality level is steady."

Another graduate of the Fuqua program, Vladimir Chelnokov, is director of the investment department at Avtovaz Bank. Founded in 1988 as one of the first commercial banks, it is the bank formed by the Avtovaz firm, which manufactures Lada and Zhiguli cars, and the Kamaz truck plant. It is a joint-stock bank founded to service the commercial banking needs of the two organizations. With offices throughout the USSR, it currently has 700 employees, capital of 750 million rubles, and total assets of approximately 3 billion rubles. It makes loans to the auto industry, aerospace industry, new commercial structures, and consumer loans to private citizens to purchase cars.

Mr. Chelnokov has found much of what he learned in the Fuqua program to be useful. He frequently refers to the materials on finance, business start-ups, privatization, and marketing. For example, he has had to estimate the market price of stock, judge the market potential of an enterprise, and conduct market research. He uses the material from FSB to train financial and loan officers in the securities and investment department and the credit and loan department. They use a checklist from the FSB program to analyze clients applying for a loan, and require clients to submit a financial statement and their current contracts. The bank is also trying to use its new knowledge of privatization to help state firms go private. The bank wants to become a shareholder of the firms. However, the bank is proceeding cautiously because, as Mr. Chelnokov notes, privatization is in "legal limbo. It is unclear who in fact owns the buildings at present. We are afraid of losing our investment. This is a typical attitude of many banks, although some banks are more accepting of risk."

Aleksandr Somov is general director of Interstroi, the Soviet–American–Turkish joint venture involved in construction engineering projects. He is also the general director of Stroika, formerly the foreign trade organization of the State Construction Administration, and now a private firm. He assessed the Fuqua program as follows:

"In April 1991, when I came back, it was hard to put the material from the course into effect. We had learned the classical theories and methods of the market system, and we tried to grasp and assimilate them. But when we got back, we saw that we couldn't use them as such. Now, a half-year later, the situation is radically different. The next group that goes over won't face such sharp dissonance between the program and the reality here."

A concrete result of Mr. Somov's participation in the Fuqua program is the prospect of a joint venture with Fluor-Daniel Corporation, the company in which he spent his internship, to build the extraction and refining site for the Chevron Tengiz oil project.

Sergei Akulov is CEO of the Uritskii Tobacco Factory in St. Petersburg. The plant employs 1,500 workers in the manufacture of cigarettes and "papirosy" (unfiltered paper tubes packed with a small amount of tobacco). The plant has been leased from the state since January 1, 1991. It is no longer required to manufacture standard brands of cigarettes according to the state plan. Instead, it is now taking out patents on brand names. Mr. Akulov articulated the lessons he learned from the Fuqua program as follows:

> "The most important benefit of the FSB program is the philosophy that we learned that the results of a firm's performance depend on the effort of its people. Each person must consider himself responsible for the performance of the whole operation. This idea represents a 180-degree turnaround from the idea we had here in the past. For example, the very idea that some Western organizations grant their employees paid leaves— that they care about them that much—came as a revelation to us."

Mr. Akulov has applied his knowledge of worker incentives and employee stock ownership plans. Unlike traditional Soviet enterprises, the firm does not have a bonus system. However, there is no limit on the amount that workers can earn. The average wage is 1,800 rubles a month, compared to the average wage in the city of 450 to 500 rubles. The plant provides other incentives through its retail outlet that sells food, cigarettes, and consumer goods to employees. The company sells videocassette recorders and Zhiguli cars to employees at the state price. (The state price of a Zhiguli is 16,000 rubles, as opposed to 100,000 to 120,000 rubles on the black market). Mr. Akulov has also instituted a profit-sharing plan. By agreement with the city, which owns the factory, they determine the firm's income. Each employee, including Mr. Akulov, gets a part of the firm's profit proportional to his or her pay, with another portion of the profit invested in plant operations. The incentive system is working well. Productivity is 80 percent higher than last year. There are no discipline problems. Profit is four times greater than last year, while prices have doubled.

The company is preparing to go private. The work force will buy out the firm over a period of six months, starting in January 1992. To finance the buyout they will use their profits, bank credits, and the shares of each worker. Since Mr. Akulov is deputy chairman of a bank which was founded by the plant, the company has ready access to bank credit to buy the firm. Because of the legal restrictions on private property, the company will consist of 25 percent private capital, 25 percent worker shares (equivalent to an ESOP), and 45 to 49 percent stock, which will be owned by investors, including foreign investors.

Prospects for the future

By all accounts, the Fuqua program for Soviet senior executives has been highly successful. When he initiated the program, Mr. Fuqua said that he would be happy if 15 to 20 percent of the graduates were to apply their knowledge and make a difference in their country. He was delighted and somewhat surprised to learn on his latest trip to Moscow and St. Petersburg that the executives were applying more about the market system than he had thought, and that some executives said that the program changed their lives. The program is also having a positive impact on the faculty at the Fuqua School of Business. They made a special effort to design the custom program and were enthusiastic in implementing it. The members of the community and the corporations who participated also found the program to be a rewarding experience.

The program will continue with the same format, but will evolve as refinements are made to better meet the participants' needs. In particular, the internships will be more structured. They are the weakest part of the program but have the potential to be an invaluable hands-on learning experience. The groups will be expanded from thirty to forty executives. The grant provides three or four programs per year for the next four years with the present level of funding.

One disappointment for Mr. Fuqua is the dearth of programs of this type in the United States. Mr. Fuqua had hoped that his grant would serve as a catalyst for other business schools to develop similar programs for Soviet managers. So far, no other philanthropists or academic institutions have followed his example. It is clear that programs of this type, while expensive to administer, have the potential to make a positive impact on the economic situation in the former Soviet republics. If they can be implemented on a larger scale, the rate of change can be greatly accelerated.

Part IV

MANAGEMENT EDUCATION ISSUES IN JOINT VENTURES

Introduction

In 1987 the USSR joint venture law made it possible for Soviet enterprises to form joint ventures with foreign firms. Since then the number of joint ventures that have been registered has grown substantially. In 1987 there were 23, in 1988—168, in 1989—1,083, and at the beginning of 1991—2,905. With 375, the United States had the second largest number of registered joint ventures, after Germany which had 394. Of the total, however, only 1,027 (35 percent) were in operation in January 1991, including 839 (29 percent) that were actually producing goods or offering services.[1]

Joint ventures have been viewed by many government officials and enterprise managers in the former USSR as a quick way to launch Soviet enterprises into the market economy. The idea was that the foreign partner would supply technology and know-how in exchange for access to the vast Soviet market. As the statistics presented above attest, putting a joint venture into operation is a daunting and difficult task. This should not be surprising since joint ventures are one of the most complex business alliances.[2] Another setback is that too many joint ventures in the former USSR simply sell products imported from abroad. The partners in such operations are viewed as taking advantage of the shortage of consumer goods to make their personal fortunes without regard for job creation and long-term benefits to the economy.[3]

Creating a joint venture with the intention of building a strong operating base for growth and development in goods and services requires

235

detailed planning and painstaking effort. The four joint ventures presented in Part IV all exemplify this philosophy. None is in it for the "quick buck." One of the major investments that these joint ventures are making is in recruiting, training, and motivating personnel, including at the management level. Since they cannot afford to wait for people to graduate from the new business schools, they have opted to send their Soviet employees to company training programs abroad as well as to invest large amounts of time training them on the job. The executives interviewed in these chapters acknowledge that a primary reason for the success of their joint ventures has been the high caliber of people they have been able to attract. In spite of the many differences that Westerners and Soviets have in work style, the willingness of both parties to work out new ways of doing things together is a gratifying, albeit challenging, experience.

Overview

Part IV opens with chapter 17, "Managing a Plastics Extrusion Operation in Moscow." Gordon Lankton, President of Nypro Corporation, describes how his philosophy of worldwide expansion of his company and his longtime personal interest in the USSR led him to seek out opportunities in Moscow. Lankton was aware that a competitive advantage in the plastics extrusion industry consists of locating plants in close proximity to the customer and that the USSR was a vast potential market. However, he also realized that the complexities of establishing a joint venture in the USSR would put a strain on his firm. He decided, therefore, to join an existing joint venture between a Russian firm and a Swiss firm called Rotel-Mikma. In his account of the early operations of the venture, Lankton relates examples of how the partners learned to trust one another and make decisions together.

In chapter 18, "Manufacturing Spectrometers in St. Petersburg," Jack Medzorian, Vice-President and General Manager of Baird Corporation, discusses his company's joint venture with the Leningrad Optical Mechanical Company, the largest optical instrument manufacturer in the former USSR. The Russian firm approached Baird with the proposal for the joint venture to manufacture spectrometers in the USSR. Although Baird would have preferred to continue exporting to the USSR rather than set up manufacturing operations there, Baird realized that it was in his company's long-term interests to begin manufacturing rather than leave the opportunity to competitors. Medzorian recounts how the partners of Baird-Lomo dealt with their conflicting objectives, such as their opposing views on exporting production. He also describes the company's efforts in training their Russian managers to take responsibility for decisions and to think creatively. Already the joint venture is seeing positive results from this effort.

Chapter 19, "Manufacturing Cameras in Moscow," is the story of Polaroid Corporation's joint venture, Svetozor, as related by USSR country manager Peter Hemingway. The alliance came about as the result of relationships that Polaroid's previous chairman of the board, William McCune, had made at the USSR Academy of Sciences. Svetozor has a small staff that assembles cameras and sells cameras and film at a retail outlet in Moscow. To earn hard currency to pay for the imported materials, Svetozor contracts with its joint venture partner to manufacture printed circuit boards and plastic moldings for Western customers at its facilities in Obninsk outside Moscow. Hemingway discusses the three sets of goals that had to be reconciled—those of Polaroid, the joint venture partner, and the Russian employees. This chapter also provides rich detail about the ways in which the business objectives and human resources philosophy of Polaroid were transformed into practice to bring out the potential of the Russian staff members. For example, the Russian general director embraced Polaroid's philosophy of broad job descriptions to foster personal initiative, responsibility, and creativity. Hemingway describes the case of an employee who responded to the challenge and benefited the joint venture in a substantial way. The reward system is also described with emphasis on the importance of understanding that Russians need to be compensated for taking the risk of leaving the state sector where job security and medical, food, and cultural benefits were the norm.

Finally, chapter 20, " 'Doing It All For You' at Moscow McDonald's," presents an inside look at what is probably the most famous joint venture in the former USSR. Approximately 50,000 customers file through the 700-seat restaurant in Pushkin Square every day. The joint venture with the Moscow Restaurant Trust resulted after fourteen years of negotiations initiated by George Cohan, the president and CEO of McDonald's of Canada. In this chapter Moscow restaurant manager Glen Steeves describes the intensive selection process that he and his managers conducted to hire the first 600 employees. In response to a single advertisement in a Moscow newspaper, they received more than 30,000 applications. Of these they personally interviewed 5,000. Steeves goes on to describe the various training programs provided to Russian managers and crew members. While the training programs and quality standards are identical to those at McDonald's worldwide operations, the company is sensitive to the unique characteristics of the Russian work force and pays close attention to the types of rewards that will best motivate these individuals.

Future educational needs of joint ventures

As the political and economic conditions in the former Soviet republics become more aligned with those in the West, a greater number of Western firms will be attracted by the prospect of joint ventures. However, past experience shows that early failure awaits most of them. The seeds of failure are often found in issues of control, conflict, and goals.[4] One way of preventing failure is for joint venture partners to invest heavily in training both their Soviet and Western personnel. This training should include an understanding of each other's goals and expectations, the development of interpersonal skills to manage conflict and foster collaboration and trust, and the mastery of sound business practices in all functional areas adapted to the environment of the former Soviet republics. The training should include formal programs as well as on-the-job training and coaching. As the chapters in Part IV show, training of such broad scope is expensive in terms of time and money, but it lays the groundwork for long-term success and growth.

Notes

1. *Vestnik statistiki*, 1991, no. 6, p. 10.
2. O. Shenkar and Y. Zeira, "International Joint Ventures: Implications for Organizational Development," *Personnel Review*, vol. 16, no. 1 (1987), pp. 30–37.
3. Boris Alexeyev, "Joint Ventures: Is the Formula Right?" *Soviet Life*, October 1991, p. 41.
4. Randall S. Schuler, Susan E. Jackson, Peter J. Dowling, and Denice E. Welch, "The Formation of an International Joint Venture: Davidson Instrument Panel," in M. Mendenhall and G. Oddou, *Readings and Cases in International Human Resource Management* (Boston: PWS-KENT, 1991), pp. 83–96.

17

Managing a Plastics Extrusion
Operation in Moscow

*An Interview with
Gordon Lankton, Nypro, Inc.,
by Sheila M. Puffer*

Sheila M. Puffer: What kind of business is Nypro Incorporated in?
Gordon Lankton: Nypro, which originally stood for Nylon Products,
is a manufacturer of plastic components using a process of injecting
plastic into molds. We are a contract manufacturer that produces products for a wide variety of uses according to our customers' specifica-
tions. Our biggest customers are in the health care industry for whom
we produce plastic parts for use in intravenous sets, blood analysis,
blood separation, toothbrush handles, and disposable contact lenses.
We also manufacture parts for fire extinguishers, carburetors for lawn
mowers, plastic enclosures for floppy computer disks, and plastic price
tags for clothing. We are headquartered in Clinton, Massachusetts and
have locations worldwide, including Ireland, Singapore, Puerto Rico,
and Hong Kong. Our annual sales are $100 million.

How did you get involved in your Moscow joint venture?
I went to the Soviet Union in 1976 just because I wanted to see it. I
travel all over, all of the time, and at that time I hadn't yet seen the Soviet
Union. So I went from Japan through the Soviet Union, including Siberia.
And that was an awakening to me. I realized back then that they weren't
going to conquer the world, that their system was lousy, and that they
really weren't going to make it. Prior to going there I thought that with

---

This interview was conducted on June 1, 1991.

their sputniks and all of their space exploration they were really going to be successful, but after seeing the country I knew they weren't.

So for fifteen years or so I lost contact with what was going on over there, although I am always interested in foreign affairs. One day I was going through my mail, and I had gotten an invitation to go on a trip down the Volga River to discuss joint ventures. There was a new joint venture law that was passed in 1987. Americans were being asked to participate in this, and the Russians wanted to tell us about it. My wife and I went on this Volga trip with mostly Fortune 500 CEOs, but also with a few people from small companies. I became very intrigued by the idea of a joint venture with the Soviet Union primarily because of the need and the fact that I could see some real value coming out the United States' and the USSR's cooperating with each other as opposed to being at each others' throats for forty years. So basically, I was looking for an opportunity to participate. We talked on the boat about all the formalities, legalities, and complications. It seemed insurmountable, but that didn't discourage me. I said, "I know Nypro can't do this on its own. Let's try some other approach." In my conversations, I had heard about a joint venture between Rotel, a Swiss Company, and a Russian firm. I had never heard of Rotel, but we have Swiss partners who told me that it is a very well-respected Swiss company that makes kitchen appliances. I ended up calling the president of Rotel, and, after we got together in Boston and again in Europe, he took me to Moscow. In April 1990 we were able to join into an existing joint venture with ownership at 20 percent. And that is how we got started. The partners are Rotel, also at 20 percent, and Mikro-Mashina, a seventy-year-old Russian company that makes appliances such as electric razors and clippers for barber shops, coffee grinders and coffee makers. They make them in a very crude fashion. Their products would never be accepted in the United States. because they resemble products that were made here in the 1930s.

What is the name of the joint venture?

The name, Rotel-Mikma, was established before Nypro joined it. We call it "Miro" for short.

Why did Nypro decide to enter into a joint venture in the Soviet Union?

We recognize that the short-term profits cannot realistically be the motivation. Since even the most optimistic economists believe that the ruble will not be convertible with Western currencies for at least three to five years, it is doubtful that Nypro will see any hard-currency return from this venture during that time. Nypro's motivation in establishing this joint venture stems from the fact that Nypro intends to be part of the global business scene, wherever that takes us—even, in some cases, when there is a risk that profit objectives cannot be met in the foreseeable future.

Our model is McDonald's. They spent fourteen years planning their Moscow restaurant.[1] Can you imagine how foolish this idea must have seemed fourteen years ago—irrespective of the potential risks that still exist? McDonald's establishes clean, cost-effective, efficient operations all over the world that are the same everywhere. This is what Nypro is intending to do with its custom-injection molding business. So far, Nypro is in twelve locations around the world. Moscow is our thirteenth. These plants are clean, cost-effective, efficient and, hopefully, unique.

American businessmen, in general, are taking a "wait and see" attitude in the USSR. Speculation about Gorbachev's demise persists. For the risk averse, this "wait and see" attitude makes a lot of sense. However, because short-term profit-oriented American companies are not willing to take risks, the Germans and the Japanese are moving in to take over the lead position in a world economy that was once spearheaded by Americans. Although Nypro is not a large public company, we feel a compulsion to play a role in the rapidly changing world environment. To sit back and watch is one thing—to be part of it is much more exhilarating. Yes, there are risks—but we are willing to take some reasonable risks in order to be a player in the rapidly changing world business environment.

What is your role in the joint venture?

I am a director. We meet quite frequently, every three to six months, either in Switzerland, the United States, or Moscow. My area of expertise, obviously, is plastics. They want to build up their capabilities with respect to plastics because most of these appliances have small electric motors, a little bit of electronics, and a lot of plastics. When they modernize and introduce new products they want to do it with high quality plastics. My technical area is to bring them the latest technology in plastics. The joint venture decided that the first thing to concentrate on would be tool building, which is the smart way to do it. Until you have good molds for plastic items you really cannot develop a business. I have always said over the years that plastic molding is 70 percent tooling. If you get the tooling right, you have only 30 percent more to worry about. Rightfully so, they chose among themselves to concentrate on that. They are buying the best equipment in the world— EDM equipment out of Switzerland. I supported this. When the idea came up at a board meeting, I confirmed that this was absolutely the right thing to do. They're building the foundation first. With time they're going to add really sophisticated molding equipment. At the moment they have thirty-eight plastic machines, but these machines are from the dark ages. They are awful. Their technology is terrible. There are wires hanging all over the place, which is typical of Russian industry, except in the aircraft and aerospace industries.

What kind of operation do you have in Moscow?

We are a joint venture associated with a large Soviet company. The unique thing about these joint ventures is that they don't have to adhere to all of the Soviet laws, which are very restrictive about what exclusively Soviet-owned enterprises can do. In the latter you have to pay people practically the same salaries regardless of the position. The plant manager might make 600 rubles a month, and the person operating a machine on a routine basis might make 400 rubles a month. The salaries are almost comparable regardless of position, and this is part of the communist philosophy. This has created very little incentive for anyone who wants to get ahead. If they do get ahead they really don't make any more money and receive no personal gain. So you could be managing a factory with 20,000 workers and still be making just a little more than the lowest worker in the factory. The joint ventures don't have to adhere to these rules. When the joint venture law was passed in 1987, these ventures were set up like Western businesses with a board of directors and ownership by partners from different countries. They are also operated in the same fashion. We can pay people what we want to pay them. As a result, we are getting very, very good people to join our company. They are leaving the old state-owned companies.

As far as equipment is concerned, we can use our Soviet parent company's equipment. The parent company is like a factory in that we can rent equipment by the week or by the day. If we get an order for a product, for example, Swiss-designed coffee makers, we will have access to molds, assembly people, and whatever else we need. We can go over to the Soviet parent company and say, "Okay, Mikro-Mashina, we want to borrow your molding machines for a month to make components for this product." We would then go over to the stamping department of Mikro-Mashina and would actually rent out time from our parent company. This is a short-term arrangement. The long-term objective is for us to install really sophisticated equipment of our own and start manufacturing ourselves. We are trying to do this on a gradual basis. We currently have three full-time employees in the joint venture—the general manager, the administrative manager, and the accountant.

Are your operations primarily for exporting products out of the Soviet Union for the European market, or are they for internal consumption in the USSR?

The general rule is eighty–twenty. We are targeting to have eventually 80 percent of our products stay within the Soviet Union and 20 percent exported. The reasoning behind this is that, as everybody already knows, the consumer products in the Soviet Union are awful. Terrible. There are not enough of them. The people are unhappy. There is chaos throughout the society not only because of the lack of quantity, but also because of the poor quality of consumer products. I think the government has recognized this. This factory, by the way, is part of the aircraft ministry. The government told the aircraft industry that there is such a need for consumer products that thirty percent of their production will not be in airplanes but will be in consumer products. We are part of the aircraft ministry that is making these kinds of consumer products.

Our joint venture is currently producing only for export. We are exporting 30,000 hair clippers a year to Europe. We buy products from our Soviet parent and make such modifications as changing the wiring. We currently have a barter deal with Yugoslavia in which we trade hair clippers, razors and coffee grinders for electric saws.

What kinds of things struck you as being different in working with the Soviets? What kinds of management practices did you find were different and what did you have to adjust to?

I don't know if it is unique with our joint venture partner, but I have been extremely impressed with their work ethic and with their talent— their engineering ability and everything else. I have worked with people from all around the world. We have joint ventures in Japan and all over. These people with whom we are associated are very hard working, very dedicated. I will get off a plane in Moscow at four o'clock in the afternoon, and I'll go directly to the factory without checking into the hotel. I'll still be there at ten o'clock at night, and I will already be deep into some kind of engineering problem with them. That's the kind of drive they have. I don't know what motivates them, because the communist society has not developed that kind of initiative in the past. It seems to be developing now from this joint venture.

One person who particularly impresses me is the chief engineer from our Soviet parent, Mikro-Mashina. He is the driving force of the joint venture. It would not be much of an exaggeration to say that the whole thing would die if he weren't there. He's dynamic and has an ability to develop talented young people who are loyal to him. At our board meetings, which are ten-hour marathons, the chief engineer keeps everyone's attention. He has pages of minutes prepared and makes lists of what he wants people to do. He himself is motivated by the desire to do a good job, to make better products and to sell them abroad. Perks such as a dacha [country house] or foreign travel are not his main interest. He demonstrated this during a visit to the United States when I took five Russian colleagues on tours of several manufacturing companies. The chief engineer was very excited about a molding plant we had just visited. After the tour, while the others went shopping, the chief engineer spent two hours at that plant, and then spent an additional five hours that Saturday afternoon "hammering" the technical person about costs, machine capabilities, and the like. He was awake all night thinking about how and where he could build the same plant in Moscow. He has even picked out the land for the plant site.

Have you observed any differences in communication practices between the Soviets and yourselves? Can you give examples of breakdowns in communication or misunderstandings due to cultural differences?

Well, the Russians don't understand the use of capital whatsoever. Accounting is almost impossible to discuss with them because they don't understand banks, interest rates, depreciation, or any of the common terminology we use in business situations in the West. When you get into a conversation about issues such as "Are you profitable?" or

"How did you price this product?" there is absolutely no comprehension between the parties, and these are very intelligent people.

How do you handle it?

We are struggling with it. We brought in Arthur Andersen, the financial consulting firm, to help us set up financial statements because we can't read their statements, and they can't read ours. We don't know whether they are making money or not. The Russians think they are making money. What it really comes down to is how much is in the till at any particular time. As far as they are concerned, as long as there is money to be spent, they are making money. But concerning depreciation, there is no understanding how this kind of system works. So the differences in financial and accounting practices have probably been the most interesting thing.

Can you give an example of a case where there were different points of view between the partners? What kinds of interpersonal issues arose?

Well, the hottest issue we've had so far is whether we should bring in a fourth partner. There is a leading company in the hair clipper business located in the midwestern United States. That company has made some indication that they would like to become partners. They have been to Moscow a couple of times and we have been out to see them. They are a very different company. I'd say they are very provincial. I came from the Midwest, so I can say that. They really have not figured out how to operate out in the world, especially in Moscow. We are trying to bring them in because they have some technology that could help us with our corporation. This company wants to be in the joint venture because we can produce some of their products to sell in Europe. There exists all the reasons in the world to bring them in, but they are extremely difficult with respect to lawyers and legal documents, signing this, and using their technology, and all of those kinds of things. Overly so, as far as I am concerned. They just want absolute, complete protection—hundreds of pages of legal documents protecting everything that goes on. It's a constant problem and it's very frustrating that nothing ever comes out of this.

Business is a matter of trust. You know, we went into this joint venture with trust, and very little else. I hadn't even read all the documents at the time we went and invested our money into the Soviet Union. The documents were only in Russian and German, and not in English at that time. I have since gotten them translated, but we went in because we thought it was the thing to do, and we trusted the people. This firm in the Midwest won't do that.

What were some of the indicators that told you that you could trust these Soviet partners?

I guess you have to do that by working with them, and seeing how they operate and how they talk. I think everyone has ways of judging character. You work with people for a while and you know how they think, how they operate. That's why I enjoy joint ventures. It gives you the opportunity to do that. You form your opinions as to whether they can be trusted or not.

Are there specific instances that come to mind?

Yes. Our general manager does a lot of deals, especially barter deals. For example, he's trading our razors to Yugoslavia for electric saws. In trading these products, we don't understand the economics of it because the accounting system is so different. You wonder what's going on from the sidelines. The Soviet general manager appointed a person to his staff who then made a large number of deals, but the deals were on the borderline of being legitimate. The general manager fired this guy even though he was making a lot of good business deals because he was too close to the borderline, and the laws are not very clear about that. The laws allow some ambiguity to occur, but you have to be careful as to how you interpret them. I came to the conclusion that our Soviet general manager is a good person and a good entrepreneur. He knows how to make these kinds of transactions. I am convinced that he is very straight and that he is not going to get us, or anyone else, in any kind of trouble.

How have you resolved decision-making issues?

The same as we do everywhere else in the world. We sit down and talk about it for quite a while, battle it back and forth, and finally come to a consensus. I think it's a mutual thing. I mean, I love working with these people. They are marvelous to talk to and to work with. I thoroughly respect them. They are good, honest people. We just keep talking to work things out and finally come to a mutually agreed-upon solution.

For example, on one occasion I needed to have five of the Russian managers sign documents agreeing to have the Midwestern company become a fourth joint-venture partner. I strongly suggested to them not to change anything in the documents because the prospective partner wouldn't understand and the negotiations would become more difficult. I spent two or three days discussing these documents and explaining the legal implications to my Russian colleagues. They listened very carefully and ended up not changing a word. I was very pleased at how they responded to reasoning.

Training is critical issue in having an effective joint venture. How have you handled it in your venture?

We ran a three-week training program in the United States for three Soviet engineers. They learned about computer-aided design (CAD), and we gave them CAD software. In addition to the technical training, the engineers were impressed by the informal relations among people in the company and the supportive management style.

What are some of the areas that you think are most critical for Americans and Soviets to know about each other to work well together?

They have to realize that we are very much alike. I am amazed in my dealings with the Russians to find out how much like Americans they are. I have tried to figure out why that is the case. I think it is because they come from a diverse background like we do. In the United States we have people from all kinds of races and backgrounds, immigrants from all over the world. Our society is very complex, and so is theirs. They have Moslems from Central Asia and Asians from the east. With these different ethnic groups they have somehow managed to put it all together in society. I think it is their background, the size of their country, and the open spaces. They are unlike the Japanese, who are not too much like us, really. We deal with the Japanese all the time, and quite successfully, but they aren't very much like us. They are confined to a crowded little island and space has always been a problem to them. All sorts of things have transformed them into what they are. Russians end up being very much like us. They are fun loving. Just good people to be with.

Note

1. An interview with the operations supervisor of Moscow McDonald's appears in Chapter 20 of this volume.

18

Manufacturing Spectrometers in St. Petersburg

An Interview with Jack Medzorian, Baird Corporation, by Sheila M. Puffer

Sheila M. Puffer: Mr. Medzorian, please give us an overview of Baird Corporation.

Jack Medzorian: Baird Corporation was established in 1936. In 1987 we were acquired by IMO Industries Inc. of New Jersey, which averages about $1 billion in sales annually. Our products are analytical instruments in the field of spectroscopy that perform trace element analysis of materials, mostly metals, chemicals, water, petroleum, agricultural products, pharmaceuticals, geochemical and other types of materials, for assuring quality control and identifying hazardous elements in the environment. The other part of our business is in optical systems, which involves military and security products in the field of night vision, laser warning, and hazardous chemical detection. All of this is related to the general field of electro-optics.

We have 600 employees and are headquartered in Bedford, Massachusetts, with foreign subsidiaries located in Holland, China, Brazil, and Russia. More than 60 percent of our sales are from exports.

What are the characteristics of your Russian joint venture, Baird-Lomo?

We established the joint venture (JV) in 1990 following about two

---

This interview was conducted on November 8, 1991.

years of discussions with the firm Lomo, which stands for Leningrad Optical Mechanical Company and is the largest optical instrument manufacturer in the Soviet Union. The equity is split fifty-fifty between the two partners. The joint venture involves a technology transfer of four of our spectrometer models. The term of the agreement is ten years. We are located in St. Petersburg. The territory of the joint venture is primarily the USSR, but the JV can also export through Baird Corporation.

What are the objectives of the joint venture partners?
A lot of the objectives of the two partners coincide, but there are also some differences. For example, Baird would have preferred exporting into the USSR rather than manufacturing there. But we were also realistic and understood that someday somebody would manufacture our type of spectrometers in the USSR, and we decided that it might as well be us. In our case the initiative was taken by the Soviet partner who approached us with a proposal for a joint venture. We quickly gave them a positive answer, and two years of discussions and negotiations followed. In December 1990 we kicked it off.

In the case of the Soviets, they had low interest in importing and had a preference to produce locally. They wished to export out of the USSR, but that was not Baird's primary objective in establishing the joint venture. So exporting became a rather tough negotiating point.

We both wanted our profits in hard currency, so that was not a problem. As far as Soviet technology is concerned, we had a high regard for it and felt it was one of the justifications for the joint venture—to have a base in the USSR to tap Soviet technology. The Soviets, on the other hand, had a much higher regard for our technology. I suppose the complete solution would be to have a combination of both.

The Soviets were definitely interested in our management expertise. We thought that was fine, at least in the initial period. However, we felt we needed to have Soviet managers even though they lacked the necessary training. Our goal is ultimately to rely on them.

We asked ourselves why we should have a joint venture with a Soviet company. One of the reasons was to protect our existing market in the USSR, where we had already been selling, as well as to expand our market share. We also felt it would be easier to have access to Soviet technology if we had a base of operations there. Another factor was our desire to gain a competitive edge. If we did not create a joint venture, we could see that eventually our competition would do it. Then we would have a reduced market share and could be forced to exit the market.

What is the structure of Baird-Lomo and what were the contributions of each party?

The joint venture is a limited liability company. Baird Corporation contributed technology, know-how, hard currency, and management assistance and training. In addition, quality control and marketing were two areas where Lomo felt they needed help from us. Lomo provided the factory and office premises, the utilities, infrastructure, ruble currency, and locally available equipment.

Which primary human resources issues in the Soviet Union are relevant to your joint venture?

Normally a trade union is required. The pay for Soviet employees has to be in rubles, not in hard currency. Incentives are provided. One way to give incentives is to allow the Soviets to order goods available for hard currency from a catalog. This is offered at the end of the year if they meet their goals.

Common perquisites in large Soviet enterprises include health care and schooling. Lomo, which is a large enterprise with 27,000 employees, even has a farm where food is produced for their cafeterias as well as for purchase by their employees. This way Lomo employees can avoid waiting in long lines in state stores.

As you can see, the Soviet companies tend to be quite paternalistic. In a joint venture employees tend to lose all that. They also have less job security. You have to make that up to them somehow, usually with higher pay. So, typically, employees in a joint venture receive a higher rate of pay. It might be double or triple that of a typical Soviet enterprise.

What type of accounting system do you use?

Accounting must be done according to the official Soviet system. It is quite different from Western practices, although it is currently being revised to be more similar to the West. For example, in the Soviet system the books do not reflect a sale until payment is actually made. In the West you record the sale at the time the order is shipped, and show it as a receivable. Other aspects of the Soviet accounting system include an annual audit which must be performed by the USSR audit agency. There is a tax holiday of two years following the first year the enterprise becomes profitable, and capital reserves can be deducted for tax purposes.

What are some of the critical issues facing the joint venture?

One critical issue is the nonconvertible currency. Recently enacted legislation now permits the joint venture to countertrade in products other than its own. So that policy has been liberalized. In our case we will be selling our product partly in hard currency and partly in rubles.

The difficulty of obtaining raw materials or parts is another critical issue. Suppliers are uncertain, and deliveries are not met. The pricing is quite difficult to ascertain. In places where there are shortages, some enterprises, typically cooperatives, have begun to demand payment in hard currency.

Another critical issue is export. Lomo wishes to export, whereas Baird has its own export organization and is already exporting into areas that the Soviet partner wants to enter.

What other kinds of problems are you encountering?

I would summarize them as being in the following areas: bureaucracy, quality control, marketing, pricing, uncertainty about costs, decentralization of authority, valuation of real estate, and, of course, the political risk.

What are the opportunities associated with your joint venture in the USSR?

First, there is a large unfilled demand from a population of 280 million, so early market penetration is important. The Soviet customers prefer to buy from a local source if they perceive that Western technology and quality are used. There is a loyal and well-educated work force. Decentralization of decision making and authority has begun. And, finally, there is the opportunity to gain access to Soviet technology.

The main topic of our discussion is the ways that Soviet and American managers can learn from each other how to work most effectively together. Mr. Medzorian, please tell us what differences you found and how you worked together with your Soviet partners to find common ways of doing these things. Let us start with the decision to create your joint venture. Did your Soviet partners come with different perspectives, and did they have a different vision of what was to be achieved?

I think we have pretty common ground in terms of understanding our objectives. There are some areas where we had a divergence of goals, but I think those are classical for all JVs and I understand them.

They felt a great need to manufacture within the Soviet Union optical emission spectrometers (OES), which are essential for the development of the economy. They perceived a need for quality control, so they considered OES as key to the attainment of quality products. From our point of view, manufacturing in the USSR was not something we particularly wanted to do, but we quickly decided that better they do it with us than with somebody else. It was a decision we made with little hesitation. So we had no real difficulties on this point.

Although the Soviets would really prefer to export the product and you didn't have that objective, you didn't see it as a stumbling block, did you?

No. Once in one of our discussions the issue of export came up. I remember this particular discussion when a young financial individual who was trying to assert himself said: "Well, Baird should agree to export 50 percent of the production of our JV." Of course, there was no way we could make that commitment.

My answer to that young man was that, first and foremost, the JV must prove that it can build quality products in the Soviet Union and satisfy its customers. Once we have earned that reputation we can go around the world and say: We are Baird-Lomo, we have great quality, and you can verify this by contacting our many satisfied customers. But simply to say we must export 50 percent of our products doesn't make it happen. We have to first earn the "right" to export. That was my speech to the young man. I am not sure he understood, but I think he did.

It seems that it is important to explain to your partner the step-by-step process that the JV has to go through. That, perhaps, suggests a lack of sufficient knowledge on the part of the Soviet partner?

I would say it suggests immaturity. I suppose it is because, first of all, he was a young man and he just didn't have the experience. I could understand his wishes and his desires for the JV to export in order to generate hard currency, but exporting does not just happen the way he thought.

Your joint venture is one of the few that is planning actual production already, and now you have a track record of day-to-day decision making. What are some examples of what the decision-making process is like?

We have been operating since February 1991 and our track record is really not that long at all. But in that period of time we have trained our people. We've sent them to our Dutch subsidiary and have trained them in how to sell and service our products. I think they took this training quite well; they were very responsive to it.

We've also talked about our business plan for 1992. We were given a plan by our Managing Director, who is Russian. The plan sounded okay in terms of objectives. But we found in there some proposals which we didn't like. These had to do with getting into some businesses that we really don't have expertise in. And I was curious as to why he put them on our agenda. I know that feeling, the opportunistic attitude, which prevails throughout the Soviet Union. People are trying to latch onto almost any opportunity which comes along to make a buck or ruble without regard to the question of who and what we are and what our goals are. You might satisfy an objective of making money, but on the other hand you might diverge from your goal of being the dominant spectrometer manufacturer in the Soviet market. If you don't keep your eyes on that target, somebody else will come and take your business opportunity away. That's exactly what could happen to our JV. So we had a discussion with our Managing Director to explain to him that his proposals do not meet our business goals, even though it might be a great opportunity. We could probably make a couple of hundred thousand rubles if we did that, but if we put our resources into our main business, imagine how much more successful we could be. I think he understood that.

Another problem I see inherent with Soviet managers is that they seem to be unwilling to make a decision. Maybe it's the fear of being punished for making a wrong decision. Maybe seventy years of the communist system has taught the people to be very cautious. On the other hand, our Western style demands that management make decisions with some sense of expediency, so that the opportunity doesn't get lost. I am sure we have to work on improving the Soviet response time, but only gradually, because it's so ingrained in the culture.

Do you find that your Soviet partners hold back at all in terms of keeping unpleasant news from you? Is it part of their way of making decisions?

I didn't see that at all.

What are some implications for you as a Western manager that decisions are not being made at the local level, in St. Petersburg?

It just slows down our timing.

What are the critical types of decisions you want to be involved in?

For instance, I felt that one of the high priority actions was to begin the set up of satellite organizations in the key industrial areas in the Soviet Union. It could be as simple as one individual who would be our contact in that area, and who would be knowledgeable about our products. These individuals would have to be trained but would possess some experience in spectroscopy and generally know the needs of the potential customers for our equipment.

I mentioned to our Managing Director that this action should be top priority. I explained that these people from key locations in the Soviet Union would act as our "bird dogs" looking for prospects. The last thing we would want to happen is for someone to buy a competitive spectrometer because we wouldn't know about the demand. We can assure that we would always compete for spectrometer purchases by having our people in the field in constant touch with prospective spectrometer customers. I think he understood that. We also started to talk about where some of these key areas are. Fortunately, our partner, Lomo, has offices in Moscow, the Urals, Kiev, and St. Petersburg. But when I say key areas, besides those places, I mean Novosibirsk in Siberia, Kharkov in Ukraine, and Kazakhstan, a rich republic where we have quite a few installations. These are areas into which we need to branch out.

I thought that by making your point to your Russian managers it was clear that they would fulfill the objective, but it didn't happen as quickly as you thought.

It hasn't happened yet. What I told you about occurred only four or five weeks ago. I didn't expect that they would do it by now. But I did emphasize that it is a high priority action for the next twelve months. I will have to wait to see whether the message has gotten through.

What are some key means that you can use to keep decision making on track, in order to have your Soviet colleagues take responsibility?

I would like to see monthly reports. We do have a plan for 1992 and we have asked for monthly reports to measure performance against the plan. I think this forces people to focus on the plan. It doesn't have to be a rigid Soviet plan, where you have to produce 5,000 of something that should be the color green and a particular shape. We live in a dynamic world, so the plan can change; but at least once we've decided on a plan that is worthwhile to pursue, we should measure our performance against it. And one way to measure progress is via monthly reports.

What do you think is the most effective managerial style in working with your Soviet colleagues—an autocratic style or a more participative one?

I'd say participative, because our colleagues are bright people and they have a good knowledge of Soviet customs, the people and their preferences in terms of equipment. You know, there are some unique characteristics in any market—the customer and his buying reasons, his motivation for buying. Some are unique to the situation in the Soviet Union. For instance, there is an organization that deals with the reclamation of scrap. And they have been selling scrap to Western customers in bulk, unsorted. When they get a price, it is kind of a general price. Because the customer doesn't know what he's getting, they offer a low price. Our people convinced this organization that if they were able to sort the scrap, they might find the scrap is worth maybe ten times what the average price is. For that they needed a spectrometer and knowledge of spectroscopic methods.

So our colleagues were creative. They offered to write a procedure for this organization on how to sort scrap, for which they will get paid in rubles, and then they will sell them one of our spectrometers.

You said that you've trained your Soviet sales and service staff in Baird methods. You sent them to Holland for three weeks. Were there any surprises on either side with regard to the knowledge they gained? Was it difficult for the Soviets to assimilate the knowledge about the way that Baird does business?

I don't think so. I thought they enjoyed it very much and they fit in nicely. It was not so much teaching them general selling methods, but mostly getting them to understand our equipment, how to sell it, how to compete against our competitors' equipment, what their features are—that type of education as opposed to generally how to sell. I think we still have to decide how to sell in the USSR.

It is generally known that for the Soviet Union the whole concept of marketing is very underdeveloped. So, probably everything these people learned was quite new for them, wasn't it?

Yes, and some of that came out when we took on the project of translating sales literature into Russian. We found some interesting nuances which came out of the translation. We reviewed the translation because we didn't want our JV people to commit us to something we could not or would not want to do. We found that they made some gross claims and some very vague statements in other instances. We discussed this matter with them and stressed the danger of our company making misrepresentations. Our Soviet colleagues finally agreed with us. I forget the concrete examples, but I'd say they wanted to be much more aggressive in their claims about the performance of our equipment.

Overpromising, perhaps?

Yes, that type of thing. And we didn't want to invite problems.

So you have to be careful. And that may be a good lesson in the sense that if you make a statement you really have to stand behind it. There are some legal implications and it could compromise your business reputation.

I wouldn't say this is a general problem. It could just be a problem with us. I would recommend that it is worth carefully editing the promotional literature which is translated into Russian to ensure that there are not any statements included which could be misleading or damaging.

The Soviets have zero experience in marketing because they have never had to do it before. I'm not sure, but I suppose in the communist system there was an allocation of goods where you had to sign up for products you needed. And I'm not even sure that you had a choice of what size, model or shape. Whatever happened to be available was what you got, based on the Gosplan.

Now it's quite different. You have to go to the customer and convince him that he should buy your equipment. You should be careful what kind of representation you make to the customer. If you exaggerate, he may take you seriously. Then when the product is delivered, suddenly he is unhappy. But he might have been perfectly satisfied if you had stated exactly what you could do. So you needlessly created an unhappy customer who might have been perfectly happy if you had made an honest representation.

That is a very good example of the emerging marketing issues in the Soviet Union.

In closing, Mr. Medzorian, what comments do you have in regard to the kinds of programs that would be most useful to train Soviet and American managers to work well together?

There are all kinds of programs. There are the academic ones, such as what you have at Northeastern University. And that's great. Your MBA program, which is attended by Soviet students, is a good example of what and how it can be done.

In the case of our joint venture we can't wait until the academic programs have their effect. We have to do it kind of on the fly. For us it means a sort of exchange program—Soviet workers and managers coming here or to Holland, where we have our European subsidiary, and spending time there, two or three months, working there, seeing how we operate in the Western style and then for the converse, to have people from our side go over to the USSR and spend time with the joint venture to learn how to deal with the Soviet customers.

We have decided that in order to keep everything on track we will probably put a Western individual in the JV to work in the Soviet Union on a more or less steady basis until things start to take off. He will, first of all, coordinate our activities. And you need to communicate. The language barrier is a problem. English is, at best, a second language, if it exists at all among our colleagues there. You need to ensure that even people who can speak English understand your communication. You need to verify by saying: "I know what you said, but what do you mean by that?" Then you need to train, educate, and monitor. For that we need to have one of our own people there. We will do that.

It sounds as though you are preparing yourselves for a long-term effort, and I wish you much success.

19

Manufacturing Cameras in Moscow

An Interview with
Peter Hemingway, Polaroid Corporation,
by Sheila M. Puffer

Sheila M. Puffer: Would you please give us some background on how the joint venture came about?

Peter Hemingway: Sure. Polaroid has been operating in the Soviet Union for approximately twenty years selling directly. During that period our most successful products have been those that deal with the scientific and the medical industry where hard currency had been allocated from the central budget on a regular basis. When we sell equipment we have to guarantee a supply of film for the next year and the years after. When hard currency was allocated, that was okay. But when you talk about the consumer market, success was sporadic. We would sell cameras one year when hard currency was allocated, but you couldn't guarantee that money would be allocated in the following years for consumer products. So the consumer was saddled with the dilemma that, if they purchased the camera one year, they would not necessarily be guaranteed a supply of film the next year. So we focused more on technical and industrial films in those twenty years.

In 1987 the Soviet joint venture law was passed which allowed foreign firms to enter into joint ventures with Soviet enterprises. We saw this as an opportunity to control our own destiny regarding consumer products, as well as to expand our industrial products. In addition, our chairman of the board at that time, Mr. William McCune, had

This interview was conducted on November 26, 1991.

had long relationships with the Academy of Sciences in the Soviet Union, in particular, one academician, Mr. Velikov, who was an adviser to Gorbachev. Through that relationship we became introduced to the Ministry of Atomic Energy. We looked at that ministry and found that they had a lot of manufacturing operations and design institutes. A lot of those technologies supplemented what Polaroid already knows about plastic molding, machining, and electronic assembly. So in addition to the relationship there was also some synergy present. We could take basic technologies, enhance them with Polaroid know-how, and create a joint venture that had some energy in it.

In 1988 we started serious negotiations, and in 1989 we signed a joint venture agreement. In September 1989 we began manufacturing cameras in the Soviet Union and started selling them in December. We opened our retail store in May 1990. In our joint venture headquarters there are thirty people. They manufacture cameras and film, sell in the retail store, and perform financial, inventory control, quality control, and administrative operations. We also have a facility that produces printed electronic circuit boards.

Our joint venture is one of the most sound joint ventures ever created under the joint venture law. It's not that others are not viable, and certainly others may be more profitable than ours. But ours has tried to incorporate all of the principles that the people who created the joint venture law were looking for. The heart of the joint venture law is that the joint venture must be self-sustaining financially. It cannot rely on general Soviet funds. It must generate its own hard currency to sustain itself. In order to do that, we had to export. However, we did not want to export our own cameras or film because we have plenty of capacity in the West. So we had to find new products to export.

We decided to focus on the technologies of electronic assembly and plastic molding. We created operations that manufacture products for Western customers in those two technologies. Today we assemble electronic printed circuit boards and produce plastic moldings for customers in the West as a contract manufacturer. We sell these products for hard currency which we then bring into the joint venture. We purchase parts from Polaroid to assemble cameras and film. We sell those cameras for rubles and then try to find more products to manufacture for rubles and expand the joint venture in that manner.

Basically, we are dealing in two currencies: hard currency and rubles. We create our own conversion rate within the joint venture. It has been working successfully for the last two years. It's getting a little bit interesting now because of the ruble exchange rate that's exploding. When we created the joint venture there was only one exchange rate of 0.6 rubles to the dollar. Today there are three exchange rates.[1] Two of them are very close, around 1.6 rubles to the dollar. Then the tourist rate was introduced a year and a half ago. It started out at a rate of 6 rubles to the dollar, and most recently it's up to 47 rubles. Also during that period they created a currency exchange. Today that exchange is trading rubles at a rate of about 100 to 1. So the environment for the financial part of the joint venture has become much more challenging. However, within our little joint venture, as long as our ruble and dollar exchange rates can be matched, we can survive.

We've brought in a lot of high-tech Western equipment for electronic assembly and for molding. We brought in management and, we hope, good management practices, which we taught to the Soviets. We've trained the Soviets in the West. We are self-sustaining. We are creating markets in the West for Soviet products. So, I think that this joint venture has met just about all of the criteria the joint venture law had been hoping for, namely: (1) to provide high-tech modern equipment and technology; (2) to create Soviet manufactured products for export; (3) to create Western markets for those products; (4) to bring Western management techniques and practices to the joint venture; and (5) to train Soviet managers and workers in Western management.

It's not a very large joint venture, which would be a deficiency from the Soviet side. It's a $6 million investment, which is relatively small compared with some of the oil companies and some of the big industrial manufacturers that have invested in the Soviet Union.

How did you go about selecting people for the joint venture, starting with the top management?

It was probably the most difficult task I personally had to deal with over there. That's because it's qualitative, not quantitative. The general director of the joint venture was selected by the Soviet partners. His nomination was presented to Polaroid essentially as: "He's either acceptable or not acceptable." He was selected from acquaintances of the partners. He worked in the ministry, but was not employed by the Soviet partners specifically. He became involved very early on. He was a very good administrator, a solid person, very honest, a person of high integrity, who was very interested in making the joint venture successful.

The other employees were hired by the general director and myself. In a small joint venture of twenty people it's fairly easy to find qualified workers. Generally you know twenty or fifty individuals with whom you feel totally comfortable in terms of job qualifications, attitude, chemistry. You can select from that group. So for a small enterprise, finding qualified candidates was not a major problem. As the enterprise grows, hiring gets much more difficult. In fact, you can be misled about the general population because your initial workers are selected from the best possible candidates.

We described what the jobs would be and selected the people who we thought had the basic backgrounds for those jobs. Training became very important after that. We selected people on the basis of acquaintanceship because we couldn't find a personnel placement firm in the Soviet Union. That was the first step. Then the management people we hired repeated the process to select the next tier. We made sure that the general director and myself approved all employees. It put a structure around the type of employees we wanted in terms of integrity and compatibility with the rest of the organization.

Does that mean that you personally interviewed all the candidates?
Yes.

What were some of the characteristics you were looking for?
The most important one was honesty, which is difficult to evaluate in an interview. There had been many concerns raised, not only by the Western partner but also on the part of the Soviet general director, that the work ethic of many Soviet employees consisted of taking advantage of the enterprise. Honesty was viewed a little differently there than we might view it here. A Soviet worker got paid low wages, and therefore felt he was entitled to "privileges" which we would call dishonest. In the retail sector this resulted not so much in stealing money, but in putting goods under the counter either for sale at a higher price or for their friends. So a concern for honesty was the first thing.

Then there was the general work ethic. The general director or whoever was doing the hiring knew the work ethic of the person and would make a recommendation. My questions in the interview focused more on the persons themselves. What hobbies did they have? Were they interested in teamwork or were they more individualistic? Did they have the right attitude and experience to work in a team atmosphere or did they work best in an individual activity? What was their level of knowledge of the primary skill we were seeking, and how much training was going to be necessary?

So people's technical skills were basically a given, because they had been screened.

Yes, the basic aptitudes were there. We knew we had to train everybody in Western practices to meet Polaroid's goals. It was important to understand each others' goals in the joint venture, and not necessarily just what we thought were the right goals, because both sides have different objectives and neither one is particularly wrong in selecting the ones they want.

Goals are a starting point. What expectations did you have and how were they similar and, perhaps, different from what the Soviet partners had?

First was awakening to the fact that, since we were self-financed, we did not have enough hard currency to produce a product for the general population. If we opened the door to the general population, we would have a line as long as Leninskii Prospekt. So Polaroid's goal was to determine how to get the product to a wide segment of the population. The company didn't want to appear to be exploiting the Soviet citizen. You can charge a very high price for a Western good and get it. But we were concerned because those types of products typically went to the same people—the top tier of the political or academic hierarchy, the privileged class. We wanted to reach the average consumer in the Soviet Union. So if we were to price the camera as high as the market would allow in a market economy, we would screen out the average consumer.

We decided to create a salon type of sale, which is common in the Soviet Union and perhaps in Europe. We have similar clubs in the United States where you are allowed to purchase if you join this club. In the Soviet Union usually the employees' union of the enterprise represents the employees by sending a letter to the joint venture. We sell directly to the employees, but the enterprise serves as a spokesperson for the employees. We generated a waiting list and categorized it into market segments: manufacturing enterprises, government operations, institutes, schools, charity groups (such as veterans' organizations), and children's organizations that normally wouldn't have an opportunity to buy the camera. We agreed among the joint venture management on what percentage of our cameras we would sell to each of these segments. We were then able to keep the price low because we were inviting the people in and could control the number of cameras they bought. This made large-scale black market sales difficult, if not impossible. All we had to do was be sure that the price would enable us to meet our exchange rates because we were making the product for rubles and selling it for rubles.

The other danger faced by Western companies in the Soviet Union is transshipping. If you set too low a price in rubles, customers can transship them to markets in other parts of the world. We avoided this problem by selling only one camera and a relatively small amount of film to each individual. We have been operating under that scheme for about eighteen months. We've sold a fair number of cameras that way. In April 1991 we started experimenting with prices based on ruble-to-dollar market rates to determine if and how much product we could expect to sell at true market prices. We figured we could sell the cameras at a much higher price. The way the value of the ruble is going, we will probably be doing that a lot more in the future. That's one goal.

And the Soviets had a different concept of how to sell the cameras and some of their business objectives were different from yours?

I didn't think the Soviets were as interested in helping their average citizen as they were in having the joint venture as an entity be successful financially. The employees were also interested in getting a good personal reward simply for being employed in the joint venture and not because of their individual performance. The employees did have to sacrifice quite a bit to come to the joint venture. They had to take a risk. When you're in a state organization you've got job security. You also have some assurance that food will be provided. There is often a commissary where you can buy food. You get a hot meal every day. There are medical clinics and day care centers for the employees. In a small joint venture we don't have the kitchens to provide a hot meal every day. We can't guarantee a commissary. You give up job security. All these things are given up when you leave a big enterprise. So when Soviets come to the joint venture they are taking a lot of risk and they expect a greater reward for that risk, just as we would. Employees were more concerned about their own financial rewards than about reaching the average Soviet citizen and allowing the Soviet citizen to see a new product. In this way the goals were a little bit different for the two groups in the joint venture.

The third group that had goals were the three Soviet partners. Two were manufacturing operations and one was a design institute. I think all three had expectations that the joint venture would utilize their resources, provide them with access to Western markets, enhance the technology of their manufacturing or design capabilities, and bring in Western equipment. In the two or three years we have been operating, only one of those partners has had the satisfaction of reaching his goal. We still have a lot of work to do with the other two as far as finding Western opportunities for them. They can claim ownership to some of the profits, but at the present time we are reinvesting all of the profits. For the other two, so far we haven't found any product to manufacture or any mechanism to use their skills in the Western market.

That's the three sets of goals we had: the employees, the partners, and Polaroid. Polaroid, I think, is meeting its goal of reaching the population and learning the market characteristics. I think we need to do more as far as publicity goes, although we have received some publicity in the last nine months on the success of the joint venture, which is good. We also need to do more with regard to pacing the expansion of our operations.

You said that, when you made the decision to hire your staff, you sat down with the general director and developed some job descriptions. What was the reaction of the prospective employees to the types of functions you were proposing to them? Was this something that they were used to, looking at a set of well-defined set of responsibilities?

This was a very enlightening process and also a very pleasant process, because the one thing the Soviet general director insisted on (and it is a philosophy that a lot of Western companies, including Polaroid, are following) was that he did not want the employees to think they had a specific set of tasks to do and that there was a boundary to their job. The employees could be asked to do any chore in the joint venture. They had a primary function, but in addition they might be asked to lug trash out, to drive a vehicle, to assemble cameras, or to sell cameras. Every employee we hired welcomed this opportunity. They said they would like to have more responsibility and to experience different parts of the operation. The job description was something they were used to. They had in their old jobs a list of tasks they were supposed to do every day. It wasn't that the tasks were much different in our operation, but the fact that they could do more, that they had more responsibility. It was a good process and a surprise to me that not only was the general director so insistent on it, but that the employees welcomed it so much.

That's interesting in that the general director is a Russian himself. That's a different way of thinking from what we have heard in the press that the average Soviet worker is not used to accepting responsibility.

I'd just mention again that, when you are dealing with such a relatively small group of thirty employees in the joint venture headquarters, the selection process can be very tight. In addition, you are generally selecting people you know. You know their qualities, their chemistry, what they want out of life. You know what you're getting. It's not like interviewing people off the street. You can't construe this as typical of all Soviet workers, nor of all American workers.

You mentioned that the Soviet workers incurred a lot of risk in coming to the joint venture. How did you address those concerns, and what kinds of rewards did you provide them?

My feeling was that it was worth a 50 percent increase in pay plus bonuses. The 50 percent consisted of 20 percent for the extra risk, 20 percent for hiring the cream of the crop, and 10 percent for another factor. So I figured they should get a 50 percent increase in pay just for coming to the joint venture. In addition, they would participate in the bonus system, and it is very lucrative in the joint venture. They could almost double their pay in rubles by coming to the joint venture.

Was that for both the professionals and the workers, that is, 50 percent more than they would typically earn in a Soviet operation?

Yes, although some were hired at more than 50 percent, and some a bit less. The other part of this was creating a job structure and pay system. The part that was new to them was that within a job description there is a range of pay as opposed to *a* pay. People with the same job could be paid differently based on how well they performed the job or how far they were along the learning curve in that job. That took a long time for them to understand.

How was the bonus system developed?

The other part that was difficult to implement was the bonus system. This particular Soviet management group based the bonus on whether the enterprise met its goals in the production and sales of Polaroid cameras and film. If the enterprise did that, then everybody got a bonus, and basically got the same bonus, the same percentage of their salary, unless they really messed up. It was a rather negative incentive system. It was not the type of bonus system I thought we were putting into place. In the wording of the bonus system people could be paid from 0 to 50 or 100 percent of their pay in bonuses. The idea was to review that on a quarterly basis. There was an annual bonus as well, which depended on how well the joint venture performed.

In practice what happened was that everybody got a 50 percent bonus as long as we produced and sold the cameras and film. So if an accountant wasn't performing very well, as long as the production people and the sales people did their jobs, he got his bonus. In the two years that we have been operating we have had a learning period, a discussion period, and a correction period. In the last year we've been trying to correct the system so that each individual gets rewarded based on goals they set for their own particular job as opposed to the goals of the enterprise. This is a case where I did not appreciate the necessity of explaining the bonus system in the beginning. If the Soviet enterprise makes its goals, then everyone shares in the bonus equally. In the Western system people share in the bonus based on their own contribution. We are trying to incorporate a system like that into the joint venture now. The employees are participating in the design of it and I am coaching them on the formats that we would use. The employees I have talked to in the joint venture would prefer it that way. My guess, based on the characteristics of this select group, is that all the employees would want to be rewarded on their contribution. I think the when people don't want to be rewarded on contribution it is because they don't want to contribute a lot. They want to share in the fruits of what the others produced.

What type of performance appraisal system are you using?

It's not a very complicated system, but at least it's a start: What do you reward people for, how do you measure it, how do you give feedback to them, how do you guide them in their career. It was surprising to me that, at least in this group, they had no experience in career counselling or feedback on their performance. It was truly at ground zero. You may say things to the Soviet employees that you assume are at least basic knowledge of performance. Yet there was total incredulity that they would ever get any feedback from their manager. Again, I emphasize that this is true for this group, but I make no claims about the Soviet work force in general.

Are you essentially using a standard Polaroid performance appraisal instrument and adapting it for Soviet use?

Polaroid is going through a different system to reward for breadth of the job. It's a very complicated system to administer. I am not introducing it at Svetozor. Instead I am introducing the old system which is more quantitative. You take a list of criteria for job performance such as job proficiency, dependability, quality of work, accuracy of work, and you measure the level of performance within the job. You tell employees how well they are doing and then have a discussion around career issues. You talk about where they are headed and what they should be doing for on-the-job training. It's a very straightforward system, more quantitative than qualitative. It doesn't fit as well with the philosophy of breadth of the job, that is, doing all kinds of jobs, but it certainly can be adapted to that.

Setting goals can be a rather sensitive process when you have input from the employees themselves. How eager do employees appear to be in their willingness to set realistic but high goals?

I can't speak for all the employees, but I think they are in favor of setting goals as a way of understanding their job better. It gives them a chance to say, "I don't really like the job I'm in. I'd rather be in the store than in inventory control." It is a formal system in which they can make these things known to the management. So I think they'll be eager to participate in it.

Do you have any evidence of employees going beyond the call of duty in their jobs?

Yes, there are many examples. For instance, one of the biggest problems is getting products through customs. We had one employee who was trying to get something out of the Sheremetevo Airport. The customs authorities argued that they wanted a 30 percent duty. This employee thought that was too much. So he spent four hours going through the hierarchy of the customs organization and ended up paying no duty at all. That is what I call going beyond the call of duty. He could have just paid the duty. But he felt so angry that they wanted a 30 percent duty and argued for it, that he ended up going away without having to pay it. In recognition of his efforts I gave him a bonus of 20 percent of his monthly salary.

Another example of extra effort is from our electronic assembly operation in Obninsk located about sixty miles south of Moscow. It employs around eighty to eighty-five people. When we started this activity in 1988 we were told that there were problems in that plant with quality, the work ethic, and the fact that the people didn't like monotonous jobs. All three of those things are a concern in manufacturing an electronic component. You definitely want high quality because you don't want the final product being returned on account of your components. As far as the work ethic and productivity are concerned, the electronic assembly had to be within a certain range of output. Finally, putting components into a printed circuit board is a monotonous job. We did have high-tech automatic insertion equipment, but there were still some components that had to be inserted by hand. It turns out that the quality has been the best of any operation Polaroid has set up worldwide. Performance has been outstanding. We have received excellent feedback from workers who have made suggestions to improve the workplace. In effect, workers' interest in the job has been 180 degrees from all the concerns we had.

What do you attribute that to?

Again, only eighty people were selected by the management team from the partner's enterprise of 5,000 employees. So again we have selected those people who we hope will do the best job. They get rewarded for doing a good job, and they have the proper tools. That's an important point. A lot of people say workmanship is shoddy. For example, patching the streets or cementing the sidewalks or putting windows in an apartment house. But workers often don't have the right tools to do the job. They've got a metal hammer where a wooden mallet should be used, or a screwdriver where a trowel should be used. It's not that they don't want to do a good job, but that they don't have the right tools. If they experience this day in, day out, they lose motivation. You just can't do quality work. However, given the right tools and the right management and a positive atmosphere, it is just human nature that they will respond better. So our operation in Obninsk exemplifies what you can do when you give people the right tools and the right environment to work in.

How can you sustain such a level of enthusiasm? Do you think, perhaps, the novelty will wear off at some point for employees?

To say it won't wear off would be naive. However, a small operation is easier to control. When Dr. Land had 1,000 employees at Polaroid he knew everyone by name. But a lot has been lost with Polaroid's growth. That is true of any corporation. When a company is small, the distance from the top to the bottom of the hierarchy is small. So the individual employee doesn't feel the degree of ownership in a large corporation as in a small one. Another concern is to motivate the person who puts the lugs on a wheel. The thing we are learning is that the Soviet worker is motivated in the same way as the Western worker. The secret is management. You need to pay attention to the individual worker, to ensure that they are rewarded, that they understand the job, that they get trained in the job properly, have the right tools, and work in a safe area. That's how we intend to continue growing in the joint venture.

What other things do you do to make people feel appreciated?

You ask people how they can do this job better. The area that is new to Polaroid is that this is the first time we have had one-on-one daily contact with the consumer in our retail outlet. In that area in particular we were all learning because we are accustomed to selling our products through third parties. In dealing with the customers we wanted friendly clerks. The Soviet Union is noted for the scowl on the clerk's face. As a customer you're an imposition on them because you're making them work when they don't have to work. The Western companies that are in the Soviet Union don't want that image, even though you could sell just as many cameras with a scowl on your face. We want our workers to be happy. We want them to be able to use the cameras to the best of their abilities. We also want our sales people to give feedback to management on what we need to do better in the retail store. We do the same thing in manufacturing in which we try to create a work environment where they can be more efficient. Basically we ask people how to get more quality out of the eight or ten hours they work each day. In the end the financial part plays a big role in the Soviet Union, but the qualitative part is that we want our people to want to be able to participate in designing their jobs.

Do you also stage celebrations in the work place as a way of fostering a positive work environment?

Yes. But I'd say that's not new. The Soviets know how to celebrate! When someone's birthday comes up it's a big celebration. A woman gets flowers. A man gets a little vodka or cognac after work. Then on major holidays we celebrate in a restaurant. In the Soviet Union there is more group participation in celebrations, which is more a part of their culture.

Do you also provide your employees with valuable goods, access to medical facilities and things like that?

One of the areas in which we have a big advantage is that our product is a consumer product. Consumer products are difficult to get in the Soviet Union. Therefore we allocate some of our sales to enterprises that can reciprocate with goods that our employees want. For instance, if our employees want to buy bicycles, we would sell cameras in exchange for them. So it's easy for us to help our employees that way.

The other option is to buy Western goods for employees. We haven't done it yet, but it is a possibility. Until June 1991 it was illegal to pay an employee directly in hard currency. So some enterprises allocate a hard currency fund. Employees select goods from a catalog and the enterprise buys them from the fund.

Another way of providing Western goods is for the enterprise to have a hard currency credit card. Employees can use the credit card in hard currency food stores and beriozkas [specialty stores] to buy Western goods.

Give us a description, please, of the kinds of functions people are performing. What is the organizational structure?

Svetozor is a joint venture. It is comprised of an administrative headquarters and two operational activities of manufacturing and selling cameras and film. Within the joint venture we are controlling the quality of the process of manufacturing and selling the product. When we decided to start the printed circuit board operation, it was a larger activity of 100–150 people. In a larger operation it is more difficult to provide all the social benefits that employees expect. So we decided to put the activity into the partner's facility. Svetozor would buy the printed circuit board as a contractee. Polaroid provided the Western equipment that was needed. We designed the jobs for the operations people and trained them, but the operations people are paid by the partner, not by Svetozor.

You mentioned that a large portion of your concern and attention are devoted to training. How do you go about training?

There is operational training and administrative training. In both cases we brought Soviet employees to our Western operations in Scotland, Holland, and the United States. The training in Scotland focused on the technical aspects of assembling the camera. We even taught the management to assemble the cameras. Training in Polaroid culture and goals, materials management, shipping, and financial management were done in our Holland operation. We had the Soviets visit printed circuit board operations in the United States. Polaroid itself doesn't have a printed circuit board facility. The training was fairly formal and well outlined. Most of the formal training was done in the United States. It consisted of classroom training and instruction in how to maintain the test equipment for the cameras. In addition, our technical people go to the Soviet Union once a quarter to review and counsel on particular problems. It's a continuous process. But because of our earlier concerns about the work ethic, we spent a lot of time training people to ensure the success of the joint venture.

Do you recall examples of surprises for the Soviets when they were undergoing training in the West?

The Soviets were especially impressed by the cleanliness of the facilities and the health and safety conditions of the work environment.

How easy was it for the Soviet managers to incorporate the Polaroid management philosophy?

It's continuous. You can say words and people shake their heads, yes. But you find back in the work place that they don't really understand the words. Even the concept of the market economy. People say they understand it, but their actions prove that they don't. It's the same with the Polaroid philosophy of making the customer happy, helping the customer take good pictures, treating the customer like you would want to be treated. This, in my opinion, is not totally absorbed by the Soviets. We shut down the administrative offices and the store, in typical Soviet custom, from 1 P.M. to 2 P.M. for lunch. When a customer comes at that time there's no one to wait on them. It's the same thing with respect to the phones. It doesn't bother the general director if the phone goes unanswered during lunch. Those things were evidence to me that their approach to a customer's needs are not what a Western manufacturer believes is their obligation. The Soviets feel that the customer wants the product. Therefore, there is no need worry about making them happy. We need to change that attitude. It's a matter of continuous education and dialog about what's important to Polaroid and to the partners.

Do you plan to have continuing on-site American management in your venture?

We started off with three. The general director is a Russian. The first deputy is an American. We also felt that during the first two to four formative years it is important to have an American in charge of quality control. The new thinking in the United States is that quality control belongs in the work place under the control of the employees. It is important to have a Westerner who knows the new thinking as well as the standard technical quality control. It is important to have someone who can make that transition. The Soviets have expertise in statistical quality control.

The other area where we feel we need American management is materials management and financial operations. Because of the great differences in the two financial practices, we wanted a Westerner to oversee the financial aspects. This was not to correct what the Soviets do, because the joint venture has to be maintained within the Soviet financial system as well. Rather, like most Western companies, we use financial reports as management tools. The Soviets are not used to preparing documents as management tools. Instead, they prepare reports of what's happened.

Your venture has been in operation only a short time but you have shown us that you have already tackled a number of very difficult issues. As a result, your joint venture has enjoyed great success. We wish you much more.

Note

1. In August 1991 the exchange rates for changing dollars into rubles were as follows:
- Tourist Rate: $1 = 5.6 rubles. This was the rate of exchange at Soviet banks.
- Commercial Exchange Rate: $1 = 1.8 rubles. This was the rate at stores and restaurants that accept hard currency, and in cooperative/joint ventures.
- Official Exchange Rate: $1.60 = 1 ruble. This was the rate used to calculate foreign debt to the Soviet Union (except for Finland).
- Black Market Rate: $1 = 20 to 25 rubles.

Source: *Moscow* Magazine, August 1991.

By December 1991 the tourist rate and the black market rate were virtually equivalent at 10 rubles to the dollar. Since that time, the value of the ruble has continued to fall.

20

"Doing It All For You"
at Moscow McDonald's

An Interview with Glen Steeves,
Restaurant Manager, Moscow McDonald's,
by Oleg S. Vikhanskii

Oleg S. Vikhanskii: We are talking with Glen Steeves, a McDonald's employee from Canada, who is currently the operations manager of the Moscow McDonald's restaurant. What are your job functions?

Glen Steeves: I am the operations supervisor of the Moscow McDonald's joint venture. I am responsible for the opening of this restaurant along with several other individuals and I'll be responsible for supervising the other restaurants that we will be opening in Moscow in the next few years. At the same time I am also responsible for developing the personnel side of the joint venture and monitoring the training of the people here. I also work at the food processing plant in a consulting role on purchasing issues regarding different products that we use in the restaurant as we start to source more and more products here in the Soviet Union, and to determine whether they can be used in the restaurant.

How did the joint venture get its start?

Basically it started with a chance meeting at the 1976 Olympics in Montreal between George Cohan, the president and CEO of McDonald's of Canada, and the Soviet delegation. McDonald's had

This interview was conducted by Professor Oleg Vikhanskii, Director of the School of Management, Moscow State University, on March 9, 1991.

loaned some of our buses to the Soviet delegation. While George was touring the Olympic grounds with his wife and children, he saw the buses. He decided to go over and meet the people. One thing led to another. He took them to a nearby McDonald's restaurant across from the Olympic grounds. At the time it was the biggest and busiest McDonald's in the world. His comment to them was that he just wanted to make them feel at home because the lines were very long at the time.

From that point, George persevered and negotiated for fourteen years until we opened this restaurant. Originally they had signed a deal to open a restaurant during the Moscow Olympics in 1980, but that fell through for a variety of reasons. Finally, in 1988 we signed the deal. We opened this restaurant on January 31, 1990. We continue to be the largest and busiest McDonald's restaurant in the world. We average between 45,000 and 50,000 meals served a day. We had projected in a feasibility study that we would average 10,000 to 15,000 customers a day. On opening day we served 30,000 people. That was our slowest day. We have never been that slow since.

George has told stories that negotiations were difficult at first. One day McDonald's would think they had an agreement. The next day they would go back to the bargaining table to sign the papers and there would be a whole new team of negotiators, and they would have to start all over again. However, the policies of *perestroika* and *glasnost'* that were implemented when Mikhail Gorbachev came to power facilitated the opening of restaurants here. We now have a joint venture agreement for twenty new restaurants in the city of Moscow. That is how we will start as a base. We will build up a management team infrastructure to expand throughout the Soviet Union.

Most people don't realize that this is the largest restaurant that McDonald's has ever opened. It seats 700 people. There is a great market in the Soviet Union since the population approaches 300 million. In the United States the population is about 250 million and there are over 7,000 McDonald's restaurants there. We have only one in the Soviet Union, so the market opportunity is enormous. We served nine million customers last year in our first year of operation.

What are you doing with your ruble profits?

We're reinvesting our profits here in the local economy. We have a processing center in a region of Moscow called Solntsevo. At that plant we produce all the food products we use at the restaurant. That's unique to the McDonald's system. Nowhere else in the world are we our own supplier. We have had purchasing people from our German company as well as our Canadian company involved in sourcing the products in the Soviet Union over the last three years. It has been a difficult task, and they have done a tremendous job. One of the benefits of bringing McDonald's to the Soviet Union was in the food supply industry. We've been working in the fields with farmers to grow potato crops, lettuce, cucumbers, and raise beef. Our experts from around the world have come here and actually worked side by side with Soviet farmers and distributors and the manufacturing industry to provide us with the same quality products that we use all around the world.

How is the management organized?

Here in Moscow we have three facilities. The head office is at the Minsk Hotel. The food processing plant has its own office and purchasing department. In the restaurant we have the operations people who are responsible for the operation of the restaurant for the twelve hours that we are open every day. We have developed a Soviet management team. In January 1990 we started with twenty-eight people. We currently have forty salaried people on staff, an additional twenty trainees, as well as forty swing managers who work while they are attending university. They provide support for the full-time management team.

How did you go about recruiting people for the restaurant?

In December 1989 we put one ad in a Moscow newspaper. From that single ad we received in excess of 30,000 applications. At that time we anticipated that we would have 600 jobs. On opening day we realized we needed more people. By May we increased our staff to 1,200. The whole joint venture employs approximately 1,600 people. That number will continue to grow as we open more restaurants.

We reviewed all the applications we received from that one advertisement. We had to look for a number of things that we would not consider in North America. First, we had to ensure that people had a telephone so that we could contact them. This was an important consideration because telephones are not readily available to the majority of the population. Then we had to make sure that employees could get to the restaurant. We received applications from people who lived outside Moscow whose travel time to the restaurant was two hours. We restricted our choice of applicants to those whose travel time was less than one-half hour. We were also looking for people who had the schedules we required to operate the restaurant efficiently. We needed people who could start at eight in the morning and work until twelve at night. We also needed another fifty people to work from 12 midnight to 12 noon. They worked in staggered shifts of eight hours, but the people had to be available during those time periods.

We went through all the applications and interviewed nearly 5,000 people for 600 jobs. We did that over a three-week period. We had a support team of six people from our personnel department in Toronto and our Soviet management team consisted of twenty-eight people at that time. We set up the interview process by having two of our Soviet assistant managers interview every person in a two-step process. Both assistant managers had to agree that the person was a prospective McDonald's employee. If they didn't agree, the person was not passed on for a second interview. If they did agree, then the person was interviewed by one of our Soviet store managers together with one of the Canadian managers. Both of those people had to agree that the person was a potential McDonald's employee. If they got through that interview, they were hired.

Next we had an orientation program to explain what McDonald's is all about, the policies and procedures, and to tell the employees what opportunities were available for them in the company. This took place in December 1989. After we finished that process, we started cleaning up and organizing the restaurant once construction had been completed. That took us until the end of 1989, at which time the Canadians went home for the holidays from December 23 to January 3.

What kind of training program did you provide?

On January 9, 1990 we started training the first 600 crew people. The training went on for seventeen days. Employees were trained by the Soviet managers who themselves had received training in Canada. The four Moscow store managers were trained in Canada for nine months, and the assistant managers for four months. Each crew person received almost sixty hours of training. We organized parties for the parents of the crew people to give the employees experience at the front counter without having the pressure of regular customers. It was fun for them to show their parents what McDonald's was all about and what they could do. It also provided them an opportunity to acquire some additional training in a real-life situation without having to face real customers. We also had parties where we served the media. On January 31, 1990, we opened. We set a record for McDonald's by serving 30,000 customers that day. From there business has continued to grow.

What opportunities for advancement does McDonald's offer its employees in Moscow?

The greatest success story for us on the operations side of the restaurant is the number of people we have been able to develop into management personnel from the crew people we had originally hired in December 1989. We have already promoted more than thirty people to the salaried management team at different levels. We also have an ongoing training program for them. We're developing all our management team from the crew ranks. Many people who started as crew people with us have moved into management. That is a strength of McDonald's system throughout the world. We promote people from within. It is one of the key motivating factors for people working for us. They have the opportunity to advance to management. We provide them with the training they need to make them McDonald's experts. We like to say that we "inject ketchup in their veins." We "Mc-Donaldize" them.

Are your people employed full time or part time?

In North America 80 percent of McDonald's employees are students who work part time. In Moscow I started with that premise. Initially 40 percent of our people were full-time workers. However, by March 1990 I reversed that policy so that now 80 percent of our people work full time, that is, forty-one hours a week in the restaurant, and only 20 percent are part time. The overwhelming majority of our people are aged eighteen to thirty-five. We have only seventy-five people who are sixteen to eighteen years of age. There is different legislation that applies to students which makes it difficult for students to work and attend school at the same time.

It is easier and more effective for us over the long term to employ full-time people simply because of the nature of our business. In North America the peak period is between lunch hour and the dinner hour. Here our peak period starts the minute we open the doors at ten in the morning to the time we close at ten at night. It doesn't end, it's always the same pace. At the same time, a full-time work force provides us an opportunity to develop people into future management members and eventually to set up restaurants in the other republics of the Soviet Union.

Do you use the same systems and procedures as in other McDonald's restaurants around the world?

Absolutely. The training systems and all the procedures used here are exactly the same as what we use in Canada, Japan, England, or Spain. The procedures are the same as the ones we use everywhere around the world.

But Russians' behavior is different from Americans', isn't it?

I disagree with that. I remember the orientation sessions. People ranged from eighteen to fifty-five years old. Until they started talking, I thought I was back in Canada: they looked the same, they interacted the same, they were smiling, and they had a good time. Our employees take to McDonald's with a passion. They're very proud of what they're doing. What's more, they're very proud of the exciting opportunities.

Have we had to do anything different here because of different attitudes and behavior? No. We applied the same principles here in Moscow as we would in Canada. We have the same training program, and we evaluate employees the same way. We use the same motivational techniques to make it interesting it for them. For example, we have crew meetings every three months. This creates a sense of family, a sense of belonging to a specific company. Last summer, for example, we rented the large liners on the Moscow River and took them for a cruise. We had a big party with dinner, dancing, and entertainment, and George Cohan came and talked with the crew members.

One difference that we have to address in each country is the labor laws. Fundamentally they are the same here as elsewhere, but there are several things that we have to address with regard to the employment of students. People in the sixteen- to eighteen-year-old age bracket can only work limited hours, and they have to be allowed time off for exams. But that's exactly the same thing that we do in Canada.

Can you mention some differences in Russians' attitudes and behaviors?

We do a great deal of job screening as well as intensive interviewing. We believe we get the best people. Moreover, the training process, motivational system, and reward system certainly prevent attitude and behavior problems from arising in the restaurant. Employees' performance is reviewed every three months in terms of what they do well and how they can improve their performance.

Every month we have some sort of activity going on that makes working here different and special. For instance, we have large parties and dances on a regular basis. We also had a Halloween dance, even though it is not typically practiced in Moscow. The Canadians and the Russian crew members decorated the restaurant, and we all wore costumes and danced. It was just as we would have done in Canada. As George Cohan likes to say, it was a form of cultural exchange between Canadians and Russians.

I have nothing but great respect for the employees. What they do is tremendous. They are working in the busiest restaurant in the world in which there is no end to the line of customers. One of the things that customers mention is not only the quality of the food, but also the quality of the service. On opening day one of our Soviet partners turned to George Cohan and asked, "Where did you get those people?" George Cohan answered, "We got them right here."

Is your restaurant successful?

We've been enormously successful, probably beyond our wildest dreams. We projected that this restaurant would serve an average of 10,000 customers a day, and we actually serve 40,000 to 50,000. For example, last weekend on International Women's Day people were lined up for two hours.

Have you any problems with the crew people or management?

Not at all. We have tremendous success finding people and providing them with opportunities. Ten field people have already advanced by moving from the restaurant to our purchasing department. The person who started as the first director (general manager) of the restaurant has already been promoted to deputy director (deputy general manager) of our joint venture. One of the other managers is now a director of the restaurant.

Employees receive a great deal of training here. We have a training department where Russians are already involved in teaching classes to the lower levels of management. The Soviets are doing a great job and are running the restaurant. We have seven Western managers left here working in an ongoing training capacity with Soviet managers. When we opened we had more than forty-five Western managers. We went down to ten last summer.

What other problems are there in managing the restaurant?
Certainly the bureaucracy here is difficult to work with, as in any country. To open the restaurant we had to deal with different legislators. For example, we had to get a permit to make the building into a restaurant. It's different from what you have in Canada, Japan, or Germany. Still, you have to respect that. But we're dealing with it. We already have our own construction department because we are planning six more locations.

Another difficulty is purchasing. We want to source more and more of our products in Moscow. All our food products are currently sourced here, with a couple of exceptions. Most of our paper products are also sourced here. We are now working with a supplier to produce cups. At the beginning of the year we had to import our take-out bags and eating trays, but by February 1991 we had our tray made in the Soviet Union, and by April we had the bags made here. By June 1991 we'll have our cups and sandwich wrappers made in the USSR. All of our meat and potatoes are grown in the Soviet Union. We make our own ketchup and Big Mac sauce, and so on. We have the same sandwich here as in Canada, the United States, and Europe. We are very proud of what has happened. What was critical for our success was that we built our own food processing center in Solntsevo in which we invested $15 million U.S. dollars.

What is the main reason for your success?
People. Absolutely, people. It always starts with people. We are very fortunate to have the people we have. We are very excited about our opportunities here. As they say in North America, we are very bullish about the country. We think we're going to be very successful, otherwise we wouldn't have invested as much money as we have already. Although changes are taking place in the Soviet Union, we are optimistic about the future, and we're still moving ahead. We need people, we need infrastructure, and we need to expand. We'll start adding more restaurants in Moscow as well as all over the Soviet Union.

Thank you very much.
My pleasure.

Index